Chaat are the sweet, salty, spicy, crunchy, creamy, hot, and cold snacks—street food, really—found in Indian markets, train stations, and home kitchens. They can be as simple as fresh, tart pineapple tossed with pomegranate seeds and spices; as comforting as Himalayan-style chicken soup; and as vibrant as sweet-sour-salty puffed rice bhel puri. Complemented by Maneet's touching stories about growing up in India and cultural notes that speak to traditions, celebrations, and history, the recipes in *Chaat* represent the regionality, seasonality, and rich diversity of India's food and people.

MANEET CHAUHAN
AND JODY EDDY

Chaat

THE BEST RECIPES FROM THE KITCHENS, MARKETS, AND RAILWAYS OF INDIA

Published in the United States by Clarkson Potter/Publishers, an imprint of Random House, a division of Penguin Random House LLC, New York.
clarksonpotter.com

CLARKSON POTTER is a trademark and POTTER with colophon is a registered trademark of Penguin Random House LLC.

Library of Congress Cataloging-in-Publication Data has been applied for.

ISBN 978-1-9848-2388-5
eBook ISBN 978-1-9848-2389-2

Printed in South Korea

Book and cover design by Marysarah Quinn
Cover photography by Linda Xiao
Map illustration by Meighan Cavanaugh

10 9 8 7 6 5 4 3 2

FIRST EDITION

Chaat

CLARKSON POTTER/PUBLISHERS
NEW YORK

This book is dedicated to all the vendors throughout India who fuel our journeys and make them more delicious.

Contents

The North

The West

The South

The East

श्री पंचेश्वर महादेव मन्दिर
अनीता कॉलोनी बजाज नगर जयपुर-15
स्वच्छ भारत अभियान
गाँधी नगर स्टेशन
2018
कचरा पात्र में डालें।
छोले टिक्की, दही पपड़ी
सेवपुरी, भेलपुरी, पानीपुरी

जबलपुर
12121
12122
हजरत निजामुद्दीन

Introduction

The train wheels screech to a stop at the Jaipur Station. My mother, Hardeep, clasps my hand tightly, pulling me through the densely packed crowd of passengers also disembarking from the train. The sweltering air is thick with the bracing aroma of lemon and chiles. My anticipation grows as the sound of hundreds of chattering people fills my ears with a cloud of white noise until one piercing voice cuts through the chaos—the shrill cry of the bhel puri vendor, at last! My hungry eyes dart around, trying to locate the origin of the voice through a sea of vibrant saris and luggage porters clad in red linen shirts deftly balancing stacks of suitcases on their heads. There he is, behind a makeshift stand of metal tins overflowing with tomatoes, onions, cilantro, puffed rice, and limes. This man, a flavor alchemist, will transform these humble ingredients into an explosively delicious sweet, spicy, tangy, crunchy, creamy, and spicy snack called a chaat, the very chaat I dreamt about and pestered my mother about during the entire eight-hour train ride from New Delhi.

TOP: *Agol gappa vendor in Luknow.*
BOTTOM LEFT: *A bhel puri vendor.*
BOTTOM RIGHT: *Riding the rails in Delhi.*

Chaat are the iconic snacks of Indian cuisine. A literal translation of the Hindi word *chaat* is "to lick," and chaat have therefore come to describe almost anything that is so good you find yourself licking the palm leaf or banana leaf that it was served on. Each train station in India has a unique specialty, a quick bite that is not only tasty but also represents the culinary traditions of the region. I adore chaat itself, and as an adult looking back on these experiences of traveling throughout India by train, I realize I not only ate deliciously well, but also learned about the food history of my nation through these humble dishes rich in nuance, regionality, and character.

Bhel puri vendor, Jaipur.

My mother, a high school principal with an unwavering patience for my culinary desires, laughs and shakes her head as I drag her through the tightly packed throng of people, a human sea of motion, toward the bhel puri vendor. She knows me too well to deny me this singular pleasure. A crowd is gathered around him and I fear I will never get close enough to place my order. I bravely let go of my mother's hand and use my tiny fingers to push through the swell of people until I am eye to eye with a bowl of crunchy, airy puffed rice. I inhale deeply and my nose fills with the scent of raw onions and mint chutney. I catch the vendor's eyes through the telepathic strength of my longing just as I feel my mother's hand on my shoulder. I do not break my gaze with him to acknowledge her because I fear that if I do the next bowl of bhel puri will not have my name on it. The vendor grins and nods at me before he begins his magic show. He spoons puffed rice—rice that has been heated with hot air (like popcorn kernels) until it puffs up and has an airy texture—into a bowl made of pressed palms. With a flourish, he tops it with crunchy chickpea noodles called *sev*, raw onions, tomatoes, boiled potato cubes, and cilantro. He sprinkles it with a chile powder and pungent chaat masala and drizzles it with vibrant tamarind and fiery mint chutneys.

My mother hands him a few rupees, about five cents, and I offer a smile as I reach greedily for the bhel puri. My mouth waters in anticipation of this bewitching marriage of flavors and textures that is crunchy one moment and soft and tender the next, offering a flash of tanginess that succumbs to the heat of chile before it is tempered by the sweet tamarind and cooled by the mint. I can't focus on anything but getting a spoonful of bhel puri into my mouth until my mother leans down to my ear and whispers, "There is more to life than food, Maneet." I stop to contemplate her words for a moment, wooden spoonful of bhel puri hovering in front my mouth. I suspect she might be right and wonder what a day that did not pivot around food would be like. I decide to ponder her words later. For now, my bhel puri commands my undivided attention.

I grew up in the small town of Ranchi in eastern India (map, page 19), the capital of the state of Jharkhand, famed for its malpua, crispy spiced pancakes drenched in sugar syrup. Every summer, my family embarked upon a long train ride to the steamy town of Bangalore in southern India to visit my maternal grandparents. For our winter holiday, the train took us north to my paternal grandparents' home in Ludhiana, in the state of Punjab.

No matter whether we went north or south, our train journeys required two to three days of jangling over the rough steel tracks of the Indian rail network, a vestige of the British colonial era. The journey was typically a long, cramped, sweaty endeavor, but I never complained. This is because I knew every station delivered an endless picnic of chaat, inexpensive delicacies that my parents purchased from vendors clamoring for our rupees. Between stations, which for me translated as chaat stops, my sister would devour books while I daydreamed about food as well as the stories my father told me about his own experiences riding the rails in Russia, where he was occasionally sent for his job as an engineer. While the Russian dishes he described were different from the chaat of India, the romance for rail travel and culinary adventure was the same.

I first realized that food had power when I visited my older sister at university, arriving with containers stuffed with food that I had prepared at home before hopping on the train to reach her campus. I was only around fifteen at the time, but I realized at that young age that the person who brings the meal is the one who receives the love, and I craved seeing that first flicker of wonder and joy flashing in a person's eyes. I might have realized food's ability to conjure love from others in my teenage years, but my actual obsession with the flavors, textures, colors, and aromas of food was sparked during those formative train rides when I was just a girl.

At the stops we made during our train trips throughout India, snacks and chaat were always waiting for me, calling to me long before the train pulled into the station. On my mental map of India, the pins for each station conjure the taste memory of each chaat I devoured as a kid, each bite illuminating a chapter of the grand culinary history of my nation. I can't wait for the day when my husband, Vivek, and I will bring our own children, Shagun and Karma, on a train journey through India. I hope it will inspire the same love that I have for my country and its cuisine.

At the Visakhapatnam railway station on the Bay of Bengal, there was ampapad, a chewy mango fruit leather, and at the humid Madras station in the deep south, there was cooling thayir sadam, lemon and rice curd. In Kolhapur, a city of temples in Maharashtra State, we'd drink freshly pressed sugarcane juice, and in Mysore, delicate dosas stuffed with paneer awaited me among the palaces. At Karjat, vada pav, a spiced Indian fritter, came wrapped in Hindi newspaper squares, and in the gardens of Hubli, there was Hubli rice, a tangy yogurt rice spiked with chile peppers and onions and always served with a side of mango pickles. At the Solapur stop, where sugar factories abound, we stopped for barfi, an intensely sweet treat of flavored evaporated milk and ghee, and at Lonavala in the foothills outside Mumbai, chikki, a cashew nut brittle, awaited.

Chicken biryani was the pride of Hyderabad, where pearls and diamonds were once traded, and in Mangalore on the southwest coast, where bronze statues tower over the city, it was the egg biryani with a side of raita, a tangy yogurt sauce, that represented its citizens best. Dal vada, yellow lentil fritters, beckoned in the cotton-growing region of Calicut (where calico gets its name) and there were green pea and potato samosas in the southern Tamil Nadu capital of Chennai. Everyone else wanted to see the Taj Mahal in Agra except for me. I was there for the petha, golden squares of candied pumpkin. There was idiuppam or spicy rice noodles in the pilgrimage city of Rameshwaram, and in India's capital of New Delhi where ancient Mughal forts jostle for space with towering skyscrapers, the vendors were justifiably proud of their aloo chaat, sweet-and-sour potatoes gussied up with tangy yogurt, tamarind, mint chutney, and sev. Chai thickened with camel's milk awaited us at the colonial hill station of Surendranagar, and let's not forget the chaiwala, the ubiquitous vendors at every train stop throughout India who ladle the universally beloved masala tea into tiny white plastic cups, or more traditionally, terra-cotta cups that are tossed away once the chai is gone. Since the cups are comprised of nothing but dried clay, they are the ultimate in sustainable serving ware.

Feasting aboard the trains of India left an indelible mark upon me, and these early culinary experiences substantially influenced my decision to devote my life to food. I love preparing the chaat of my childhood for friends and family and sharing the stories of my clickety-clack journeys over vast Indian landscapes in train cars perfumed with turmeric, chile, ghee, tamarind, mint, and, yes, a little sweat.

The train routes of India may have been conceived by the British, but it was Indians who laid down the tracks and who gave life to each station. For the Indian people, these snacks are not merely deeply satisfying; they are elemental vestiges of their lives that can conjure their boundless love for their homeland with a single bite.

The varied cuisine of India is woefully misrepresented in the United States. I first discovered this after I graduated at the top of my class from a three-year culinary and hotel management program in Manipal, India. I moved to America to attend the Culinary Institute of America (CIA), in Hyde Park, New York, because one of my instructors in India told me it was the best culinary school I could attend in the world. According to my parents, if I wasn't going to be an engineer, a doctor, or an accountant, the three most-wished-for career paths for Indian children, I would have to be the best at whatever I chose to do. So of course I chose to go to the CIA.

After I arrived I was excited to check out the Indian restaurants near the school. I quickly discovered how woefully misrepresented Indian cuisine is in the US. Essentially, even today, most restaurants throughout the country serve versions of the top ten dishes offered at Indian wedding banquets. I was maybe four bites into a deplorable chicken tikka masala when I vowed to myself that I would become an Indian-cuisine crusader, changing people's perception of Indian cuisine as fussy and complicated, calling for an endless list of hard-to-source ingredients. Of course, there are complicated Indian recipes just as there are in any cuisine, but there are also quick dishes. Considering how addictive and simple to prepare street food and chaats are; how dizzying their diversity; how healthy, inexpensive, and fun to eat they are, there's no better vehicle for dispelling the notion that Indian cuisine consists only of a vindaloo with a bowl of gummy rice on the side. Chaat are a mighty snack that tells India's culinary story more adeptly than any other food.

Every chaat tells a story about the resourcefulness of the Indian people, the history of our nation, and in my opinion, because of their nuanced flavors, healthful ingredients, vibrant colors, heady aromas, and variety of textures, they are the very best cuisine that Indian cuisine has to offer. While chaats are the primary focus of this book, there are recipes for other types of snacks, meals, desserts, and drinks inspired by those that one might find at an Indian train station or on the streets of an Indian city, all adapted, refined, and updated to be home-cook friendly. *Technically,* these aren't chaat (see page 17) because they do not combine a variety of elements that come together to form a chaat, but they are iconic train station or regional delicacies and worthy of experiencing at home.

I invite you to join me on this epic journey that takes us beyond the familiar menu staples of the neighborhood Indian restaurant and delve into a world that is far more colorful, lively, and fun. I always say that chaat are such a joy to eat that these flavorful and unique dishes that will magnetically bring people to your table. But prepare yourself (as I've learned from hosting my own chaat parties): They might never want to leave!

A BRIEF HISTORY OF TRAINS IN INDIA

You can't talk about chaat without first understanding the importance of railways in India. India's train system transformed not only the way Indians traveled but also the way we understood the food culture of our nation. For the first time, a citizen could inexpensively move through the country relatively quickly (well, compared to walking, traveling by caravan, or simply not going at all!) while feasting upon the regional specialties showcased at each station stop. The train journeys were often long, sweltering affairs, but they deepened our understanding of our national cuisine and the pride we justifiably feel for it; and they inspired a new sense of respect and admiration among the people of my nation's twenty-nine states.

Construction of India's rail system began in 1845 with funding from the British East India Company in order to transport India's natural resources from one corner of the country to another. By 1851, the Solani Aqueduct Railway, the first operational train line was launched, followed a year later by the first passenger train. By 1880, there were nine thousand miles of track, connecting the three main hubs of Calcutta, Madras, and Bombay (now called Mumbai) and the hundreds of stations that lay between them.

India began independently manufacturing its own locomotives in 1895 in order to minimize expenses and tailor each train to its specific needs. Initially, each state's rail system operated autonomously because communication between states was limited, and bureaucracy was the rule of the day. During World War I and up until World War II, the railway system was used almost exclusively by the British to trans-

LEFT: *Old Dehli Railway Station.*
CENTER: *Train pulling in to Old Delhi.*
RIIGHT: *A station stop near Agra.*
FAR RIGHT: *A rickshaw ride in Chandni Chowk.*

port soldiers, ammunition, and supplies. Very few Indian citizens used trains as an everyday means of transport during this era.

In those years, the few Indians who wished to use the trains (except for a select group of wealthy upper-class citizens), were refused passage and we suffered greatly. During World War II, many of the trains were diverted to the Middle East, where the British staged supplies for battles in Europe and North Africa. No longer were we able to trade goods efficiently, access distant markets, or visit far-flung friends and relatives. With India's independence from Great Britain in 1947, the forty-two distinct railway systems that comprised thirty-two main lines were merged into a single entity that was renamed Indian Railways. Later modernization included the replacement of steam train cars with electrified tracks and the recent adoption of green fuel such as solar power by Indian Railways on certain routes.

Today, India has the fourth largest railway system in the world, behind the United States, China, and Russia, comprising nearly forty thousand miles of tracks and transporting twenty million people daily between 7,500 stations (the variety of chaat to experience could makes your head spin!). Because Indian trains are a relatively inexpensive way to travel, they have served as a key democratizing force in Indian society. The average per capita income in India is $1,600 US annually. This means that even though domestic flights are less expensive than they once were, they are still out of reach for most Indians, making train travel the transportation of choice, just as it has been for decades. Cars are also a luxury for many Indians,

and even if they have one, gas is expensive. And because of India's perpetual logjam of honking and snarled traffic, train travel is also one of the most efficient and reliable ways to get around the country. India measures just over 1,800 miles from west to east and just under 2,000 miles from north to south. It's a vast nation and train travel easily, efficiently (usually!), and inexpensively (mostly!) connects faraway places that would otherwise be challenging for many Indians to access. Trains are usually much more dependable than road travel. In recent years, toll roads have emerged that parallel many rural roads, but their rates make them out of reach for the majority of the population. I once took a toll road from Agra to Delhi, about a three-hour trip, and was joined on the whole length of the toll road by fewer than a dozen other cars.

While many of India's trains are standard throughout the nation in terms of classed cars, seating options, and aesthetics, there are unique train lines born of history or geography. There's the Darjeeling Himalayan Railway, also known as the "toy train," which for six hours winds its way from New Jalpaiguri to Darjeeling through fifty-one miles of Himalayan peaks that soar 7,400 feet above sea level. The whimsical train is straight out of a six-year-old boy's fantasy with its colorful cars evoking more Harry Potter's Hogwarts than Indian Railways—I know that my son, Karma, is going to lose his mind when he sees it!

With a climb of over 8,100 feet, the Nilgiri Mountain Railway presents an even more arduous journey. It's the steepest railway in India and the only one to use a rack and pinion system, an array of toothed gears that adapt rotational motion into linear motion in order to complete the job of moving the train up the precipitous tracks from Mettupalayam to the Nilgiri Hills.

My coauthor and coconspirator, Jody Eddy, and I rode a few of these unique trains during our research for this book, but mostly, we traveled with the masses on board the standard trains in third class, the dust from the wind blasting through the open windows and collecting between our teeth. These are the transportation and commerce lifelines of the Indian people. We stopped at some of my favorite train stations to experience the chaat that have been on offer for over 150 years. Each bite was a nostalgic trip back in time for me, the benchmarks of the Indian railway system, as fundamental to Indian identity as religion, politics, and cricket.

TOP: *Dahi sev puri.*
MIDDLE: *A chaat vendor in Amritsar.*
BOTTOM: *Chicken malai chaat.*

WHAT IS CHAAT ANYWAY?

Chaat are typically snacks or small meals that are tangy and sweet, fiery and crunchy, savory and sour all in one topsy-turvy bite. Some iconic chaat include Bhel Puri (page 111), Puchkas (page 249), and Aloo Chaat (page 27). In much the same way that Indians have mastered other aspects of their cuisine, chaat embody the perfect balance of texture, aroma, and color. Chaat often include a main element, such as idli or puffed rice (as in bhel puri), that is served with a variety of other ingredients such as chutneys, yogurt, and chaat masala, resulting in layered flavors, textures, colors, and aromas. So, for example, idli (page 163) is a recipe that on its own is not a chaat, but when it's combined with the other elements such as tamarind chutney and raita, is transformed into a chaat. Chaat can be pungent one moment and refreshing the next, followed by a flash of heat tempered by a jolt of sweetness that lingers just long enough to cool everything down and make you crave another spoonful. A chaat might be crunchy, silky, and toothsome within a single bite. It might taste like mint one moment, chile the next, and then roasted potatoes just before it all gives way to the lingering flavor of tamarind.

Some chaat are finished in a bite or two, some are served with a fork, and some could constitute an entire meal. When chaat are brought indoors and served in a modern home or restaurant, they become the shareable plates that are so popular today and can easily comprise a lunch or a dinner. A table filled with chaat also allows diners to experience a wide variety of dishes before moving onto the next. And the next. And the next.

Chaat are also typically made of fresh, healthy ingredients. There is the occasional indulgent one dripping with ghee or sticky with sugar syrup, but most chaat include ingredients like spices, herbs, vegetables, fruit, and legumes that Indians brilliantly transform into dishes that don't weigh you down and conjure cravings long after the last lentil fritter has been eaten and the final spiced starfruit slice has been swallowed. Chaat often appeal to vegetarians because many are free of animal proteins. Indians have mastered vegetarianism over the course of centuries, and India is one of the few nations in the world where vegetarian options are celebrated rather than perceived as an afterthought.

Chaat are also relatively inexpensive, usually comprising only a few easily sourced ingredients that are luxurious only once prepared and combined in a masterful way. Much like train travel, chaat in India is a great equalizer, accessible to virtually anyone.

Chaat are fun to prepare with children or a group of friends because most items can be made ahead of time, placed in separate bowls, and assembled as desired. It's almost as much fun to create a chaat as it is to eat it. (Almost!) Chaat easily impress cheeky guests and tend to please finicky eaters. Children love them because they are a joy to eat, and their approachable flavors are appealing to young palates. Chaats are also great for a convivial family night and, depending upon the chaat selection, can be a sensuous option for date night. But solo diners should not shy away from chaat, because they are still a fun dinner when only one person is seated at the table.

Jody and I wrote this book because we strongly believe that chaat is a relatively underappreciated cuisine in most parts of the world outside of India. I opened my Nashville-based restaurant Chaatable in 2018 (see the Chaatwich, below) in order to introduce visitors and locals alike to the magic of chaat, and the reception has been overwhelmingly positive. We hope this book will inspire even more people to introduce the concept into their cooking repertoire.

I've been eating chaat since I was able to swallow food, but Jody was new to the chaat game when we made our first visit to India over a decade ago. During that first trip (which inspired in Jody a lifelong obsession with Indian travel and cuisine), we kept a running tally of the chaat we consumed throughout our journey. We counted over six hundred dishes by the time we were on the plane home! For me, the trip was an opportunity to experience one of the aspects of India I love most. For Jody, it was an eye-opening, awe-inspiring culinary adventure that left an indelible mark, and is the reason we are writing this book together. It's time that all of those who are unaware of the endless virtues of chaat have the same revelation that Jody did so many years ago.

LEFT: *Peanut Brittle.*
MIDDLE: *Chaatwich (served at Chaatable).*
RIGHT: *Puchkas.*

LADAKH
Srinagar
JAMMU &
KASHMIR
HIMACHAL
PRADESH
Amritsar
PUNJAB
UTTARAKHAND
HARYANA
New Delhi
ARUNACHAL
PRADESH
UTTAR
PRADESH
Agra
SIKKIM
Jaipur
Lucknow
ASSAM
Guwahati
NAGALAND
RAJASTHAN
BIHAR
MEGHALAYA
MANIPUR
JHARKHAND
TRIPURA
WEST
BENGAL
MIZORAM
Ahmedabad
MADHYA
PRADESH
Ranchi
GUJARAT
Kolkata
CHHATTISGARH
ODISHA
Puri
MAHARASHTRA
Mumbai
Pune
TELANGANA
Hyderabad
GOA
ANDHRA
PRADESH
KARNATAKA
Chennai
Mangalore
KERALA
TAMIL NADU
Ernakulam

TOP: *Naan throwers.*
MIDDLE: *A railway vendor in Mumbai.*
BOTTOM: *Kala Chana Chaat. Biryani in Agra.*

The North

New Delhi

Amritsar

Srinagar

Agra and Lucknow

ARUNACHAL PRADESH
SIKKIM
ASSAM
Guwahati

New Delhi

Aloo Chaat
Tamarind Chutney
Green Chutney
Cilantro-Mint Chutney
Ghee
Ram Ladoo
Aloo Tikki Chole Chaat
Shakarkandi Chaat

A paan vendor in Chandni Chowk Market.

The Old Junction railway station in New Delhi, built by the British-Indian government in 1903, is one of India's busiest train stations, seeing nearly 200,000 passengers on more than 250 trains each day. My parents moved to Delhi only in 2004, but I passed through the Old Junction station countless times as a girl since it serves as a hub for so many rail lines throughout the country. The seemingly endless chaat options there begin with the vendors who jostle for space within Old Junction, meaning, to my great relief, that I can begin chowing down the moment I step off the train. The first Old Junction train route connected Delhi to Calcutta, but today, visitors from every corner of India pass through here. The building is constructed of the same distinctive red bricks used to build the landmark Mughal Red Fort that looms over this warren of spindly cobblestone streets and crumbling facades.

Today, when I disembark in Delhi, I usually tell my extremely prompt and fretful parents that my arrival time is several hours later than it actually is because it affords me time to get lost in the maze of Chandni Chowk to eat all the chaat I can find before heading home. Chandni Chowk is a market twenty feet from the station, and a visit to this sprawling warren of streets crammed with chaat vendors before boarding the train is an absolute must. The chaat are the stuff of my dreams, just as they have been the creative fuel for authors, musicians, artists, and food lovers since the market was first established by the fifth Mughal emperor, Shah Jahan, in the mid-seventeenth century. There are more than three centuries of history represented in every chaat you encounter. Mughlai cuisine has deep roots in the chaat recipes of Delhi. The royal cuisine of the Indo-Persian empire, which was influenced by Turkish, Iranian, Central Asian, and Pakistani culinary traditions, thrived from the early seventeenth century to the early eighteenth century. Historians still debate what led to the empire's decline, but some speculate it was due to extreme excess. If the rich flavors of the chaat and other recipes they left behind are any indication, I suspect they're right—I wouldn't want to be friends with the person who visits Chandni Chowk without the intention of leaving exhausted, overstimulated, and completely stuffed.

The market presents an irresistible invitation to surrender and get lost in this place that assaults the senses on every level—even in my daydreams I can taste freshly the fried jalebis that glisten with sweet sugar syrup or the cooling shaved radish and mint chutney that gets added to fluffy lentil fritters called ram ladoo (see page 34). In between bites, a dusty wind infused with cloves, chiles, cumin, and fenugreek lingers in the air from the nearby spice market, so heavily perfumed with scents that vendors wear cloth masks over their mouths and noses in an attempt to ward off sneezing fits (it doesn't help).

I usually have to be dragged away from Chandni Chowk, still clinging to a half-eaten mutton kebab from Karim's, a legendary restaurant first established as a hotel in 1913 by Mohammed Aziz, a chef who learned his trade in the royal court of the Mughal emperors. The kebabs of the Mughal court in Delhi were so famous they were even mentioned by Marco Polo (although I doubt he loved them as much as I do).

Karim's has been operated by the same family for four generations and is lauded for its naan throwers, who put on a show for visitors. It is said that kebabs originated in medieval times when Turkish soldiers shaped these marinated meat delicacies onto their swords before cooking them over campfires. Although the swords might be a thing of the past, Karim's still embodies a bygone era when food served as the great democratizer: The same dishes, cooked over the red-blue flames and hiss of the grill, were relished by emperors and commoners alike. I love

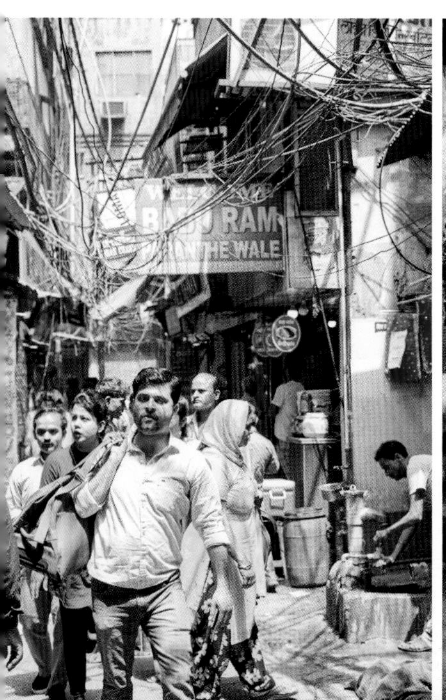

watching people as they devour the decadent Mughal street food, so enchanted that they fail to notice the golden streams of red-chile-flecked ghee dripping down their fingers.

Karim's is still a relative newcomer compared to other famed chaat shops in Chandni Chowk. The Old Famous Jalebi Wala, famed for its hand-piped funnel cakes, sticky with sugar syrup, was founded by Nemi Chand Jain in 1884. Older still is Gaya Prasad Paranthewala Shop, a sixth-generation classic that has been serving parathas stuffed with everything from green chiles and paneer to eggplant and even bananas since 1872. It's located on Paranthe Wali Gala, a narrow corridor no wider than a rickshaw that means "lane of paratha makers," a reference to a time when over a dozen paratha shops operated here. Today only two remain.

I hop on the train, well-fed and beyond satiated, usually on my way to my parents' train stop in New Delhi, several stations away. Once I arrive at their seventh-floor apartment, where the balcony overflows with my dad's potted hibiscus, nasturtium, and orange trees, I have to pretend that I'm starving because my mom always has a full meal waiting for me—including a stack of her parathas (she is known far and wide for them, along with her silky white hair and the way she makes every visitor who passes through her front door feel as if they never want to leave) and she typically makes me a stack of them, stuffed with raw red carrots and dripping with an obscene amount of ghee. I sit down and eat them with gusto—it would break her heart if she knew what I had spent the day doing.

The bustling streets of Chandni Chowk.

THEN

Aloo Chaat

There's almost always an aloo (potato) chaat vendor at the Old Junction train station near Chandni Chowk. I usually hear the sizzle of frying potatoes and catch their earthy aroma before I spot him. This chaat recipe is found throughout most of northern India and also makes an appearance in some eastern and western regions, where the ingredients vary based upon what vegetables are in season; that said, tomatoes, red onions, radishes, and cucumbers are all frequent dance partners.

I recommend peeling the potatoes once they're cool enough to handle but still warm enough so the skins will slip off easily, and then frying them up just after peeling to avoid gumminess. I like to use Kashmiri red chile powder in this recipe, but any fiery red chile powder will do. This chaat doesn't keep well and should be eaten before the sev (fried chickpea noodles) get a chance to become soggy.

SERVES 4

PREPARATION TIME: 30 minutes

3 tablespoons ghee, store-bought or homemade (page 33)

2 large russet potatoes, boiled whole, peeled while warm, and cut into ½-inch cubes

½ teaspoon Kashmiri or other red chile powder

½ teaspoon ground toasted cumin

½ teaspoon chaat masala, plus more to taste

1 small red onion, finely chopped

¼ cup whole-milk yogurt

Kosher salt

2 tablespoons Green Chutney (page 30)

2 tablespoons tamarind chutney, store-bought or homemade (page 29)

¼ cup sev, plus more if desired

Pomegranate seeds, for serving

Cilantro leaves, for serving

In a sauté pan, heat the ghee over medium heat until hot but not smoking. Add the potatoes and fry until golden brown and just starting to crisp up, 6 to 8 minutes, turning frequently to ensure even coloring. Transfer the potatoes to a large bowl and add the chile powder, cumin, chaat masala, and onion. Stir gently until the potatoes are evenly coated with the spices.

In a small bowl, whisk together the yogurt, 1 teaspoon water, and salt to taste. Gently stir the green chutney and tamarind chutney into the potatoes, season with salt, and transfer to a serving platter.

Sprinkle with sev, drizzle with the seasoned yogurt, and garnish with pomegranate seeds and cilantro. If desired, season with additional chaat masala and add more sev.

OPPOSITE: *Street vendor in Delhi making aloo chaat.*

Tamarind Chutney

Tamarind pulp is used in countless recipes (such as the Tamarind Rice, page 165) to add a distinctive tanginess to rice, curry, and even cocktails (see Tamarind Gin and Tonic, page 209). In chaat recipes, tamarind chutney is a required ingredient because it adds the signature pungency that so many chaat require to achieve their perfect alchemy of flavors. This chutney has a slightly mouth-puckering outcome, similar to what you might experience when tasting an unripe plum. The jaggery, dates, and raisins add sweetness, the ginger gives it brightness, and the chaat masala offers that deep umami flavor that you also find in ingredients like tomatoes and shiitake mushrooms. It might seem fussy to prepare a fresh batch at home, but the vibrant from-scratch flavors easily beat store-bought varieties. The wonders of tamarind fruit, from a leguminous tree that thrives throughout the tropical regions of Africa and Asia, cannot be overstated. It's also integral to traditional Indian medicine, where it's used for everything from treating fever and ulcers to healing wounds, lowering blood sugar, losing weight, and reversing fatty liver disease. Industrious Indian homemakers even use it to polish up their copper pans and bowls!

MAKES about 1½ cups
PREPARATION TIME: 30 minutes

1 tablespoon vegetable oil
1 teaspoon cumin seeds
1 teaspoon coriander seeds
1 teaspoon fennel seeds
1 teaspoon red chile flakes
1 tablespoon finely chopped fresh ginger
¼ cup golden raisins
¼ cup pitted dates, coarsely chopped
1 (16-ounce) block seedless tamarind pulp, coarsely chopped
1 cup jaggery or dark brown sugar
1 teaspoon chaat masala
½ teaspoon black salt (kala namak)
1 teaspoon ground ginger
Kosher salt

In a sauté pan, heat the oil over medium heat until it glistens, about 2 minutes. Add the cumin, coriander, fennel, and chile flakes and sauté until aromatic, about 2 minutes. Add the fresh ginger, raisins, dates, tamarind, and jaggery, increase the heat to medium-high, and bring to a boil. Reduce the heat to medium and cook until the sauce is thick and coats the back of a spoon, about 10 minutes, stirring with a wooden spoon occasionally to prevent scorching and to encourage the flavors to mingle.

Remove the pan from the heat and stir in the chaat masala, black salt, and ground ginger. Transfer the chutney to a food processor or blender and blend on high speed until smooth. Taste and season with salt. The chutney will keep in a covered container in the refrigerator for up to 2 weeks.

OPPOSITE: *The repertoire of a New Delhi chaat vendor always includes tamarind chutney.*

Green Chutney

MAKES about 1 cup
PREPARATION TIME: 10 minutes

This classic chutney is a workhorse staple in the Indian pantry and is used countless times throughout this book. It will keep refrigerated in a covered container for up to one week. After that, the vivid green color will begin to lose its vibrancy, but thankfully it won't lose its flavor as quickly and should keep for an additional week. Peel fresh ginger using the edge of a spoon, and wear gloves when seeding the chiles. I use long, slender Indian green chiles, but serrano chiles work in a pinch. My mom used to tell me that sometimes she thought my mind was a chutney because there were always so many thoughts whizzing around inside all at once. I took this as a compliment, because chutney makes virtually any Indian recipe taste better. I also love to slather it on burger buns, use it to perk up sandwiches, add it to roasted vegetables to give them a better backstory, drop a dollop onto soups and stews to light them up, and spoon it over scrambled eggs to dress them up a bit.

2 tablespoons chana dal

½ teaspoon ground cumin, roasted

½ teaspoon sugar

½ teaspoon kosher salt, plus more to taste

1 teaspoon chaat masala

Pinch of hing (asafetida)

1 tablespoon fresh lemon juice, plus more to taste

½ cup tightly packed fresh mint leaves

1 cup tightly packed fresh cilantro leaves

3 garlic cloves

3 serrano chiles, seeded

3-inch knob fresh ginger, peeled with a spoon and coarsely chopped

Heat a cast-iron pan over high heat until nearly smoking. Add the dal and toast, swirling the pan the entire time, until it takes on a light golden brown color. Immediately transfer the dal to a bowl or onto a plate to prevent it from overtoasting.

In a food processor, combine the toasted dal and the rest of the ingredients and blend until quite smooth (it will still be a little chunky). Add water, 1 tablespoon at a time, to achieve a thick consistency that holds together on a spoon and is not runny. Taste and season with additional salt and lemon juice according to taste.

Cilantro-Mint Chutney

This green chutney recipe has the perfect combination of freshness from the mint and cilantro plus heat from the chiles and vibrancy from the lime juice. Be sure to wear gloves when seeding the green chiles, because if you touch your eyes later on, you will regret it once the burn sets in. The chutney can be refrigerated for up to 2 weeks in an airtight container—note that after 1 week it will begin to lose its vibrancy and at 2 weeks its flavor diminishes.

MAKES a generous 1 cup chutney
PREPARATION TIME: 10 minutes

1 cup tightly packed fresh cilantro leaves

1 cup tightly packed fresh mint leaves

Pulp from 1 small mango (about ¼ cup)

5 serrano chiles, seeded

¼ cup fresh lime juice, plus more to taste

Kosher salt

In a food processor or blender, combine the cilantro, mint, mango, chiles, lime juice, and salt to taste and blend at high speed until smooth. Add water as needed to achieve a thick and slightly chunky consistency. Adjust the seasoning with lime juice and salt as needed.

CHUTNEYS

There are almost as many Indian chutney recipes as there are people in India. Coconut Chutney (page 159) is popular in the south, where it is paired with dosas (recipes pages 186 and 189) and idli (see Idli Chaat, page 163). In the north, chutneys tend to be heavier and more savory. The green (page 30), mint and tamarind chutneys (page 29) in this chapter are universal. Most Indians wouldn't dream of eating some of the nation's most iconic recipes, such as Lucknowi Seekh Kebabs (page 80) without Green Chutney, or having Aloo Chaat (page 27) without a drizzle of Tamarind Chutney. Chutneys are typically concocted as a blend of vegetables, fruits, and spices that were originally devised as a means of preserving meat and fish on long journeys. While chutneys originated in India around 2,500 years ago, the concept quickly took root in kitchens throughout the world when the Romans, and later the British, brought their favorite chutney recipes back from India. In Italy, mostarda (the honey, mustard, and oil-based condiment) most likely originated from Indian chutneys, and in England, spiced fruit compotes made from ingredients like dates, figs, and raisins were inspired by Indian chutneys. The origin of the word chutney is *chatni* in Hindi and in the Northern Urdu language; it means "to lick"—and I'd gladly lick any chutney bowl clean.

It's tempting to stock up on store-bought chutneys, but be forewarned that many of these are packed with sugar and preservatives. Homemade chutneys can be prepared in large batches and added to virtually any savory dish. Many chutney recipes, such as Tamarind Chutney, can be water-bath-canned in the same way that jam or jelly is, while certain recipes such as Coconut Chutney, can be frozen for several months. I would not suggest freezing the green chutney recipes in this book, however, because they run the risk of becoming watery. In India, you can find small packets of chutney—like ketchup or mustard packets in the U.S.—to doctor up a chaat or meal. My mom used to pack an assortment of chutney packets for our family during long train journeys—because she knew no vendor meal would be complete without a ribbon of chutney to brighten up its flavor.

WHAT GHEE IS AND HOW TO MAKE IT

There's a time and place for regular butter, and then there are those recipes that call for the flavor of butter but with a bolder twist. That's where ghee comes in. It's regular butter that has been rendered through heating to remove the milk solids and water, leaving behind nothing but velvety, golden fat that has a deep, earthy note that floods every corner of the mouth with flavor and lingers long after it's gone. In India, it's hard to imagine many of the most iconic dishes without ghee. It's a staple in every Indian pantry, beloved for its ability to add a nutty flavor to a dish and to withstand high temperatures.

Because the water and milk solids have been removed, ghee has a higher smoke point than butter—you can heat it to around 400°F without risk of burning. This makes it perfect for Indian recipes that require sautéing or frying at high heat over a long period of time.

Ghee is less useful in baking, since its flavor is earthier and more robust than melted butter and can easily overwhelm breads and pastries. Its heartiness is perfect for warm desserts like Gajar ka Halwa (page 44) because it stands up to the richness of the semolina pudding and enhances its flavor without overtaking it. Though similar to Western clarified butter, ghee adds an extra flourish to Middle Eastern and South Asian dishes, since it's cooked for a longer period of time, resulting in a nutty flavor and deep golden color.

Ghee

MAKES approximately 1½ cups
PREPARATION TIME: 1 hour

1 pound (4 sticks) unsalted butter

In a saucepan, melt the butter over medium-high heat until a layer of milk solids and water separate out from the butterfat and rise, creating a white cap on the surface, 8 to 11 minutes. Increase the heat to high, bring the butter to a boil, and boil until the white cap becomes frothy. Reduce the heat to low and continue cooking until the cap at the surface begins to break apart, 7 to 10 minutes. Continue to gently simmer until the milk solids on the surface sink to the bottom of the pot and bubbles cease to form, 6 to 8 minutes more. Using a silicone spatula, scrape any residue that forms on the sides of the pan into the ghee, where it will sink to the bottom of the pan.

Continue to cook until the ghee takes on a nutty aroma and turns golden brown. This should take about 30 minutes, stirring every few minutes to encourage uniform cooking.

Line a sieve or colander with cheesecloth and set over a heatproof container. Gently and slowly pour the ghee through the cheesecloth into the container. Be very careful during this step to prevent the ghee from splashing and burning your hands. Discard the cheesecloth and set the ghee aside to cool to room temperature in the uncovered container.

Once the ghee cools to room temperature, cover the container and refrigerate until you need to use it. (The ghee will harden in the refrigerator but can be liquefied over medium heat before using.) It will keep refrigerated for up to 6 months.

OPPOSITE: *A Jalebi vendor in Chandni Chowk fries his decadent fermented batter sweetened with sugar syrup in a simmering pan of ghee.*

Ram Ladoo

(FLUFFY LENTIL FRITTERS WITH GREEN CHILE CHUTNEY AND GRATED RADISH)

MAKES about 24 fritters

PREPARATION TIME: 3 hours 30 minutes (includes 3 hours to soak the mung dal)

A roundup of Delhi chaat would not be complete without a recipe for ram ladoo, fluffy round fritters made with two kinds of dal (chana dal and mung dal) that are crispy on the outside and airy on the inside. Their bright yellow color, which comes from the dal and the turmeric, evokes the Delhi sun on a kurta-drenching summer day (a Kurta is a long, lightweight shirt). The first time I tasted this irresistible chaat was from a vendor waiting outside the Delhi's National Rail Museum, which is devoted exclusively to the celebration of India's railway system. Jody and I spent the morning exploring the museum, which was founded in 1977 and covers a whopping ten acres of precious city land. Once we had our fill of train history—which included examples of train coaches, steam and diesel engines, and even a ride on a toy train (page 16) that we felt pretty silly on alongside the other passengers, who were most likely all under the age of eight—we discovered the ram ladoo vendor. He placed three yellow fritters into a palm leaf bowl, then topped them with shaved daikon radish and a drizzle of spicy green chutney. Somehow, I had never enjoyed ram ladoo before and loved that Jody and I were experiencing it for the first time together. It was a revelation for both of us.

This recipe instructs that the fritters be served hot, but the vendors of New Delhi, who stack them up in irresistible rows in their tiny stands, serve them cold, and there's really nothing better on a sweltering Delhi day. Ladoos are typically sweet spherical snacks sold all over India, but I might prefer this savory version. It's believed that the first ladoos were used as medicine by the ancient Indian physician Sushruta, who prescribed ones made with sesame seeds to his patients. His nearly 2,500-year-old medical text is of the first and most important ever written and forms the foundation of Ayurvedic cuisine, with instruction on how to use seven hundred plants medicinally. I'm not sure if Sushruta considered ram ladoos a cure-all, but when topped with a handful of refreshing grated radish and some fiery green chile chutney, they've certainly proved to be an elixir for me over the years. Note that the dals need to be soaked for 3 hours before making the fritters.

- **1 cup mung dal**
- **1 cup chana dal**
- **1 tablespoon grated fresh ginger**
- **2 teaspoons ground turmeric**
- **1 teaspoon hing (asafetida)**
- **Vegetable oil, for deep-frying (about 6 cups)**
- **Kosher salt**

- **Grated daikon radish, for serving**
- **Cilantro-Mint Chutney (page 31), for serving**

In a sieve, combine the mung dal and chana dal and rinse well under running water. Transfer to a large bowl and add water to cover by double the height of the dals. Soak for 3 hours.

Drain the dals and transfer to a food processor. Pulse until they form a thick paste, then process until light and fluffy. Add the ginger, turmeric, and hing and process until incorporated. The

OPPOSITE: *Scenes from Chandni Chowk near the Old Junction Train Station in Delhi.*

mixture should have the consistency of a fluffy batter, with a light, aerated texture.

Line a plate with a double layer of paper towels. Pour enough oil into a deep, heavy-bottomed pot to reach about 2 inches from the rim. Heat over medium-high heat until the oil reaches 325°F on an instant-read thermometer. Working in batches of 3 or 4 (do not overcrowd the pan), use a slotted spoon to drop 1-inch balls of batter into the oil. The fritters should immediately rise to the surface. Fry until they are just starting to turn golden brown and are cooked through, about 4 minutes, using a slotted spoon to turn the fritters to ensure even cooking and coloring. Transfer the fritters to the paper towels and season with salt. Allow the oil to return to frying temperature between batches.

Serve the fritters topped with a generous handful of grated daikon and a drizzle of chutney. It's preferable to serve the fritters hot, but they are also appetizing at room temperature.

Aloo Tikki Chole Chaat

(PEA-STUFFED POTATO FRITTERS WITH CHICKPEAS AND CHANA MASALA)

MAKES about 12 aloo tikkis (serves 6)

PREPARATION TIME: 1 hour

Aloo tikki are stuffed and fried potato patties that form a critical part of this popular chaat from Chandni Chowk (see page 23). My kids love the patties on their own, but I prefer to transform them into a chaat by serving them atop a spoonful of *chole*, which means chickpea in Hindi, and then drizzling them with both green and tamarind chutneys and thinned-out yogurt. When all of these crunchy, sweet, spicy, and tangy ingredients are combined, something akin to chaat heaven is achieved. My favorite aloo tikki chole chaat vendor serves this delicacy at the same tiny, portable chaat stand that his father, grandfather, and great-grandfather did before him. The last time I found him in Chandni Chowk (he's always in the same spot, standing between a paan vendor, page 24, and a cobbler), he told me that his grandfather used to serve this chaat within the Old Junction station until stiff competition from vendors selling the same chaat inspired him to carry his stand across the road to Chandni Chowk. He explained that the paan vendor and cobbler have also been in the same spot for at least three generations, and that they grew up together, playing as children in the dizzying maze of streets that comprise this ancient neighborhood before inheriting their small but sustainable businesses from their fathers.

Don't overstuff the aloo tikki or else the spiced pea filling will ooze out during frying. Anardana, which are dried pomegranate seeds, add an appealing tanginess to all sorts of Indian recipes, including biryanis and curries. They're higher in antioxidants than green tea or red wine.

CHOLE

1 tablespoon vegetable oil

1 teaspoon cumin seeds

1 medium red onion, finely chopped

2 teaspoons store-bought ginger-garlic paste

½ teaspoon ground turmeric

1 teaspoon Kashmiri or other red chile powder

1½ teaspoons ground coriander

1 tablespoon anardana powder

2 teaspoons chana masala

Pinch of hing (asafetida)

1 cup tomato puree

1 cup cooked chickpeas

Kosher salt

ALOO TIKKI STUFFING

1 cup thawed frozen green peas, mashed

1 tablespoon finely chopped fresh ginger

1 teaspoon chaat masala

1 teaspoon cumin seeds, toasted and ground

Kashmiri or other red chile powder

Kosher salt

Make the chole: In a sauté pan, heat the oil over medium heat. Add the cumin seeds and sauté until fragrant, stirring occasionally, about 1 minute. Add the onion and sauté until translucent, about 4 minutes more. Stir in the ginger-garlic paste and sauté until the raw aroma disappears, about 3 minutes. Add the turmeric, chile powder, coriander, anardana, chana masala, and hing and sauté until aromatic, about 1 minute. Reduce the heat to low, add the tomato puree, and cook until the oil starts to cling to the edge of the tomato mixture, 3 to 4 minutes. Add the chickpeas and 1 cup water, cover, and bring to a boil over medium-high heat. Reduce the heat to low and simmer until tender, about 8 more minutes. Season with salt.

Make the aloo tikki stuffing: In a medium bowl, combine the peas, ginger, chaat masala, ground cumin, and chile powder and stir gently to combine. Season with salt and set aside.

Make the aloo tikki: In a large bowl, mash the potatoes until smooth—take care to not overmash or the potatoes will become too sticky. Add the onion, serrano, garlic, black pepper, cilantro, and milk and stir gently to combine. Season with salt. Shape the mixture into 1½-inch balls and then gently flatten each ball to a ½-inch-thick disk.

Place about 2 teaspoons of aloo tikki stuffing in the center of each disk. Nimbly fold the edges around the stuffing, closing securely until the stuffing is completely covered by the potato. Using your hand, gently flatten out into a 1-inch-thick patty (the tikki).

Line a plate with a double layer of paper towels and arrange another plate (no towels) next to it. Fill a bowl with about 3 inches of rice flour (enough to coat all of the tikkis). Pour 1 inch oil into a heavy-bottomed saucepan and heat over medium-high heat to 350°F on an instant-read thermometer.

Dredge each tikki through the rice flour, shaking each one to remove excess flour before transferring it to the unlined plate. Once the oil is ready, reduce the heat to medium-low. Working in batches of 4 or 5 tikkis (do not overcrowd the pan), use a slotted metal spoon to drop them into the oil. Fry until golden brown and slightly crispy on both sides, turning over in the oil using the spoon to ensure even coloring, 5 to 6 minutes total. Transfer the fried tikkis to the paper towels and season with salt. Allow the oil to return to frying temperature between batches.

Assemble the chaat: In a small bowl, whisk together the yogurt with 1 tablespoon water to thin it, and add salt to taste. Divide the chole among six small bowls or plates and top each with 2 tikkis. Drizzle with yogurt, cilantro-mint chutney, and tamarind chutney. Sprinkle with sev, onion, and cilantro. Finish with a squeeze of lemon juice and a pinch of chaat masala.

ALOO TIKKI

4 russet potatoes, peeled and boiled whole until tender

1 small red onion, finely chopped

1 serrano chile, seeded and coarsely chopped

1 garlic clove, minced

½ teaspoon freshly ground black pepper

Leaves from 2 sprigs cilantro, finely chopped

1 tablespoon whole milk

Kosher salt

Rice flour, for dredging

Vegetable oil, for shallow-frying

CHAAT

1 cup whole-milk yogurt

Kosher salt

Cilantro-Mint Chutney (page 31)

Tamarind Chutney, store-bought or homemade (page 29)

1 cup sev

1 medium red onion, finely chopped

Coarsely chopped fresh cilantro leaves

Lemon wedges

Chaat masala

Shakarkandi Chaat

(SWEET POTATO AND STAR FRUIT CHAAT)

This is one of the first chaat vendors that I seek out when I step off the train at Old Junction in Old Delhi. There's almost always one waiting for me with his simple folding stand holding a large metal bowl filled with roasted sweet potatoes, their skins charred from being cooked over a wood fire, alongside a smaller bowl overflowing with vivid green star fruit. You need to try this chaat to believe that crunchy star fruit and creamy roasted sweet potatoes were made for one another. Chaat masala and a squeeze of lemon add depth and vibrancy and coax these two ingredients together to form one of Delhi's simplest yet most unique chaat recipes. It's traditionally served in a tiny palm-frond bowl with a toothpick as a utensil. Simple to prepare, healthy, colorful, and fun to eat, I like nothing better than surprising friends who are new to the chaat game with this brilliant (and brilliantly easy) recipe.

SERVES 6

PREPARATION TIME: 10 minutes

3 large sweet potatoes

Vegetable oil, as needed

Kosher salt

2 star fruit, thinly sliced crosswise

2 teaspoons chaat masala, or more to taste

1 tablespoon finely chopped cilantro

½ teaspoon red chile powder

Juice of 1 lemon, or more to taste

Preheat the oven to 425°F.

Rub each sweet potato with oil and prick all over with a fork, then sprinkle them all over with salt. Wrap each potato individually in foil and roast until tender, 45 to 55 minutes.

Once the potatoes are cool enough to handle, peel them and cut into 1-inch cubes. In a large bowl, toss the sweet potatoes with the star fruit, chaat masala, cilantro, chile powder, and lemon juice until everything is well coated. Serve while the potatoes are still warm, preferably with toothpicks.

Amritsar

- Dal Makhani
- Gajar ka Halwa
- Chapatis
- Sarson ka Saag
- Amritsari Fish
- Punjabi Lassi

Every winter, my family set off on an epic northbound forty-eight-hour, nine-hundred-mile journey from our home in Ranchi near West Bengal to the train station in Amritsar in the state of Punjab in northern India to visit my paternal grandparents for two weeks in the nearby city of Ludhiana. I was of course excited to see my grandparents, but that part of me that is always dreaming about my next culinary adventure—even, and especially, when I was a little girl—was fixated on gajar ka halwa, a warm spiced carrot pudding, which I knew would be the first familiar sight to greet me in the train station.

As our train pulled into Amritsar Junction, with its signature white columns crowned with ornate gilded minarets, the bracingly chilly winter morning would dissipate as soon as I had a bowl of gajar ka halwa cupped in my hands to warm them. The chaos of the station disappeared as I scooped bite after bite of the luscious carrot pudding into my mouth.

When I became an adult, my curiosity for food extended beyond just flavor to the cultural and historical significance of a dish. I learned that gajar ka halwa was introduced to Punjab by the Mughals in the sixteenth century, around the same time when Amritsar was founded in 1577 by the fourth Sikh guru Ram Das.

The state of Punjab is a significant place for my family that transcends even the all-important carrot pudding. Punjab is the birthplace and beating heart of my religion, Sikhism, and if we decided to disembark from the train to do a little sightseeing before we reached my grandparents' house, the first place we visited was Harmandir Sahib, also known as the Golden Temple, the most important pilgrimage site for Sikhs. I've visited this temple countless times over the years, but the site of its regal golden facade glistening in the sun beneath a bright blue sky and reflected in the massive pool of water surrounding it never ceases to catch my breath. The colorful turbans the men wear are a visual reminder of the religious tolerance and philanthropic generosity my religion has always represented for me.

Sikh temples are known as *gurudwaras*, and one of the reasons I'm proud to be a Sikh is because in every gurudwara throughout the world, volunteers gather to cook and serve three meals per day to anyone who needs or wants one. Millions of hungry people are fed daily regardless of their religious affiliation. It's a glorious thing to witness: hundreds of people seated in long rows on the floor of the gurudwara awaiting their meal that has been cooked by anyone who arrives that day to volunteer in the *langar*, or community kitchen.

In Sikhism—at just over five hundred years old it is one of the world's newest religions and the planet's fifth largest with over twenty million devotees—we believe that everyone is equal to one another, regardless of their religion, and that it is our duty to serve each other without consideration of background, denomination, race, or class.

But there is more to my connection to Punjab than carrot pudding and my religion; there is the story of my family, which I wasn't told about until I was old enough to absorb this painful part of our history (although I'm not sure anyone would ever be old enough to hear it). My grandparents were living in what is now Pakistan before the Partition that occurred after India gained its independence from the British in 1947. Along with four and a half million other Sikhs and Hindus, they were ordered to leave for India, while the six million Muslims living in India were forced to flee to Pakistan. It was a chaotic and confusing time for my family, just as it was for everyone caught up in the chaos. My grandfather was traveling with my grandmother and young aunt, whom they dressed as a boy because they feared what might happen should her gender be discovered.

When they reached the border, my grandfather, who was carrying a gun to defend his family if necessary, whispered to my grandmother and aunt that should the situation become dangerous, he would shoot them and then himself to avoid the inevitable. Fortunately, they made it across the border to India without incident. When my parents told me this story, I was overcome with grief. But my sorrow was soon replaced by an admiration for the tenacity and bravery of my family. Their journey became fixed in my mind, and whenever I struggle, I return to it as a source of motivation, an abiding belief that I can overcome any obstacle that I encounter.

One of the other ways in which Punjab shaped me and inspired me to become a chef came from the stories my grandparents would tell during our visits of the incessant hunger and perpetual search to find food that they faced following the Partition. Whenever I disembark at Amritsar Junction today to visit my family, I reflect back upon the stories my family told me of constantly being hungry, I think of the gurudwaras, and I see the indelible influence they had over my decision to become a chef. As a child, I wished for nothing more than that first bite of gajar ka halwa. As I grew into my adulthood, my wish became to feed the people I love and to ensure they will never be hungry again. As a chef, I can do just that.

Dal Makhani

(KIDNEY BEANS AND LENTILS WITH BUTTER)

SERVES 8

PREPARATION TIME: 3 hours, plus 8 hours to soak the beans

Makhani is a Hindi word that means with butter, and dal makhani has no patience for those who are shy when it comes to the amount of butter added to bring the lentils and beans (the dal) to a creamy and blissful finish—you must approach this dish with abandon, or not at all. This is how Punjabis do it, and their passion for dal makhani has caught on in virtually every corner of India. *Dal*, which means "pulse" in Hindi, is a beloved staple throughout the country, its variations as dizzying as the diversity of dals flourishing in the fields (see page 265).

4 ounces dried kidney beans, soaked in water overnight

8 ounces black urad dal

1½ tablespoons garam masala

½ tablespoon Kashmiri or other red chile powder

3 tablespoons store-bought ginger-garlic paste

½ cup tomato paste

1 pound (4 sticks) unsalted butter, cut into 1-inch cubes

Kosher salt

Chapatis (page 46), warmed, for serving

Drain the soaked beans. In a medium saucepan, combine the kidney beans and enough water to cover them by 3 inches. Bring the water to a boil over high heat, then reduce the heat to medium-low, cover the pan, and cook gently until the beans are just tender, about 20 minutes. Drain and reserve the beans.

In a large heavy-bottomed pot, combine the dal, garam masala, chile powder, and 8 cups water. Bring to a boil over medium-high heat. Reduce the heat to medium and simmer until the dal has absorbed the water and is soft and mushy. Stir occasionally while the dal cooks to encourage it to soften and break down, adding more water if necessary to prevent scorching.

Add the kidney beans and ginger-garlic paste and cook over low heat until tender, about 1 hour, stirring occasionally. Add more water if necessary to maintain a slightly thick consistency that does not turn pasty. Add the tomato paste and continue to cook until nearly all of the liquid is absorbed, about 1 more hour, stirring occasionally.

Now it's time to add the butter (don't be shy). Stir in about one-third of the butter cubes, mixing until they have completely melted and been absorbed by the dal. Do the same with the next two batches until your dal makhani beckons with its come-hither, buttery state. Season to taste with salt. Serve hot with a side of warm chapatis to mop up all of the rich goodness. Dal makhani will keep refrigerated in a covered container for up to 1 week.

Gajar ka Halwa

(CARROT PUDDING WITH SAFFRON AND PISTACHIOS)

SERVES 6
PREPARATION TIME: 1 hour

This velvety carrot pudding thickened with sweetened condensed milk and paneer, an Indian cow's milk cheese similar to farmer cheese, is subtly spiced with cardamom and garnished with pistachios. It's wintertime comfort food in Punjab, where frigid temperatures are no match for this warm dessert, traditionally made from red Punjabi carrots only available in the winter (photo, page 40).

In spite of its simplicity, this sweet feels celebratory and is often served at Indian temple festivals and during the winter holiday of Diwali, the festival of lights. *Diyas*, traditional clay oil lamps, light the homes of millions of Indian families during Diwali, and although it's a Hindu festival, it's enjoyed by people from all denominations.

5 cups whole milk

2 pounds carrots, peeled and grated

4 green cardamom pods

A few saffron threads

2 tablespoons sugar

4 tablespoons ghee, store-bought or homemade (page 33)

½ cup paneer, preferably homemade (page 256)

1 (14-ounce) can condensed milk

2 tablespoons coarsely chopped toasted cashews

2 tablespoons coarsely chopped toasted pistachios

2 tablespoons golden raisins

In a large saucepan, heat the whole milk over medium-high heat, stirring occasionally with a wooden spoon, until warmed through, about 4 minutes. To prevent scorching, do not let the milk come to a boil.

Add the carrots, cardamom, saffron, and sugar and reduce the heat to medium. Cook until most of the milk has evaporated, the carrots are tender, and the pudding is beginning to thicken, stirring occasionally to prevent the carrots from burning and the milk from boiling over. This should take about 15 minutes.

Add the ghee and the paneer and cook for another 10 minutes to melt the ghee and dissolve the paneer until it is fully incorporated, stirring occasionally. Add the condensed milk and reduce the heat to low. Cook until the pudding is thick enough to stand a spoon in, another 25 to 30 minutes.

Remove the pan from the heat and gently stir in the cashews, pistachios, and raisins. Serve while the pudding is still hot, as it's at its most comforting at this stage. I doubt if you will have any leftovers (this is a seconds and thirds kind of chaat), but if you do, it will keep in your refrigerator in a covered container for a day or two. Reheat the pudding in a saucepan over medium heat with a tablespoon or two of milk to help it regain its creamy consistency before serving.

Chapatis

MAKES 10 to 12 chapatis
PREPARATION TIME: 30 minutes

It sometimes seems like chapatis make the world go round in India. We love bread (see Indian Breads, page 48) and words such as naan, papadam, paratha, and chapati make our mouths water long before these aromatic flatbreads hit the table. Chapati is a flatbread made with whole wheat flour that gives it a slightly chewy-nubby texture and a warm brown color. The best way to eat chapati is either slathered in ghee (see What Ghee Is, page 32) if they're consumed alone or as a utensil to dip into dishes like Dal Makhani (page 43). We eat them for breakfast, lunch, and dinner, and they also frequently accompany chaat since they can stand in for a utensil, making chapatis the ultimate sustainable spoon or fork. Indians use a flat griddle called a *tava,* which is similar to the *comal* of Mexico and Central America. Tavas are made of iron, stainless steel, or aluminum. They are relatively inexpensive and available at most kitchen supply stores. If you don't have a tava, a cast-iron or stainless steel pan can be substituted. Be sure to serve chapatis hot off the griddle. No Indian worth their ghee would ever eat a lukewarm chapati.

3 cups Indian whole wheat flour (see Note)

1 teaspoon table salt

1 tablespoon vegetable oil, plus more for the bowl

¾ cup lukewarm water, plus more if needed

Ghee, store-bought or homemade (page 33), for serving

On a clean work surface, make a mound with 2 cups of the flour. Sprinkle the salt on top and then create a well in the center. Pour the oil and water into the well and begin to bring everything together using your hands. The liquid should be completely incorporated into the dry ingredients until a loose dough has formed. Knead the dough until it forms a smooth ball that bounces back just slightly when you poke your finger into it. This should take about 5 minutes. Place the dough into a bowl slicked with oil and then cover the bowl with a damp cloth. Let it sit at room temperature until it has puffed up slightly and its surface feels a bit dry when you touch it, about 30 minutes.

Place the remaining 1 cup flour in a bowl. Divide the dough into 10 to 12 equal portions and roll each portion between your palms into a ball. Dredge each one through the flour, gently shaking it to remove any excess. Working with one at a time (and keeping the other balls covered with a damp towel), set a ball on a lightly floured work surface and use a rolling pin to roll it into a 6-inch round that is ⅛ inch thick. Transfer to a lightly floured sheet pan and cover with a damp towel while rolling out the rest of the chapatis.

Place a cast-iron or nonstick griddle over medium-high heat until it's hot, 4 to 5 minutes. Test it by flicking a few drops of water onto it. If it sizzles, it's good to go.

If you have a gas stovetop: Place the first chapati on the hot griddle and cook for 4 minutes. Remove the griddle from the flame and, using tongs, flip your chapati over and place the second side directly over the flame. This should cause it to puff up for a moment, which is what gives a chapati its light texture once it settles again. After it settles, continue to cook it over the flame for another 30 seconds before transferring it to a plate (if the chapati begins to burn or take on too much color, reduce the heat).

If you have an electric stovetop: Keep your chapati on the griddle for 2 minutes. Wad up a paper towel and press gently and very carefully around the entire circumference of the chapati after it has cooked for 2 minutes. Once the edges of the chapati just begin to dry out, it's ready to be flipped over. Use tongs to flip it over and use the paper towel to press the second side again in the same way as you did the first. Cook the second side for about 2 minutes—the step with the paper towel should cause the chapati to puff up on the griddle without the need for an open flame.

To serve, spoon about 1 tablespoon of butter or ghee over the chapati. I know this seems like an excessive amount of ghee (and it is!), but this is my mom's recipe and she always serves chapatis this way. If you're health conscious, you don't need to go full throttle on ghee like we do in the Chauhan household, but I promise you, sometimes it's just what's needed to jump-start your day.

NOTE: *Indian whole wheat flour is called* atta *and is available at Indian markets. It's the foundation for several Indian flatbreads, including naan, puri, and roti, and is typically made from durum wheat. Unlike most whole wheat flour in America and Europe, atta is milled using a stone wheel, which results in a very fine powder. The pressure of the stone grinding also heats the atta slightly as it is ground, resulting in a slightly toasty flavor, a trademark of Indian wheat flatbreads. While American whole wheat flour will work in a pinch, for a truly authentic Indian experience, making a trip to an Indian market to pick up a bag of atta is well worth the trek.*

Kachori

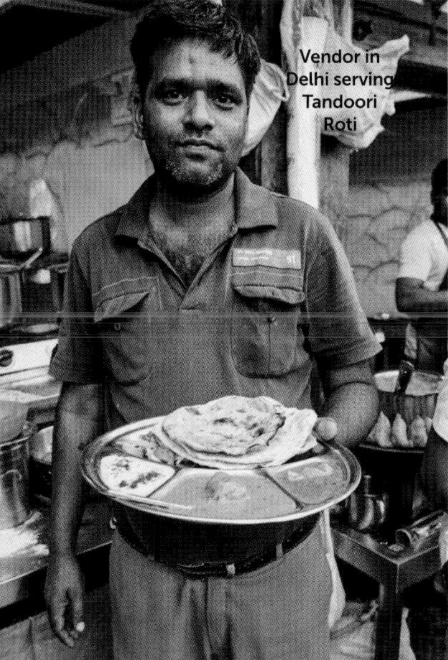

Vendor in Delhi serving Tandoori Roti

Puri

INDIAN BREADS

Like rice and chai, Indian bread is a staple at virtually every meal. There are countless recipes for bread throughout the country, with each state boasting its own unique varieties. For me, the benchmark of a seasoned Indian cook is whether or not they're able to execute traditional Indian breads like whole wheat chapatis and dosas, a fermented flatbread similar in texture and thickness to a crepe. Novices usually produce versions of these flatbreads that end up looking like Texas or Australia when they *should* be perfectly round (I'll forgive them because that's how I started, too). For traditional Indian flatbreads, it's not only the shape that's critical, it's also about efficiency and the speed at which they are made. We love bread in India and never, ever stop at just one piece of naan, papadam, or *appam*. Bread makers need to prepare themselves properly for serving as quickly and as hot as possible, one piece after another. We're like goldfish when it comes to bread. We just can't stop ourselves until we're cut off from the source. That's something the bread maker should remember, too! There comes a time during every baking session when you have to say, "Enough is enough!" Here are a few of my favorite Indian breads:

- **Appam:** a thin crepe made from a batter of fermented rice flour and coconut milk
- **Baati:** a hard, unleavened bread made from ghee and wheat flour that is popular in the desert areas of Rajasthan (see Dal Baati Churma Chaat, page 99)
- **Bhatura:** a deep-fried bread popular in northern India that often accompanies chickpea or potato curries; it's made with yogurt, all-purpose flour, and ghee (see What Ghee Is, page 32)
- **Chapati:** similar to roti, an unleavened bread served in virtually every part of India, made with whole wheat flour and oil (see Chapati, page 46)
- **Chole Bhatura**
- **Dosa:** a fermented crepe made with a black lentil and rice flour batter; it is typically filled with ingredients such as spices, paneer, or vegetables before being lightly rolled or folded. It's a staple bread in southern India (see Neer Dosa, page 186, and Tuppa Dosa, page 189)
- **Idli:** a steamed bread from southern India made with a fermented black lentil and rice flour batter (see Idli Chaat, page 163)
- **Kachori:** a deep-fried unleavened bread stuffed with lentils popular in northern India (see Raj Kachori Chaat, page 103)
- **Kulcha:** a leavened bread from northern India made with wheat flour (see pantry, page 265)
- **Litti**
- **Naan:** a leavened flatbread found throughout India, made from whole wheat or all-purpose flour, water, and yeast, and traditionally baked in an oven called a tandoor

- **Papadam:** a crispy flatbread made from dal that is either fried or cooked over an open-flame; they are popular throughout India
- **Paratha:** a stuffed flatbread from northern India made from whole wheat flour that is typically fried in oil or baked on a griddle called a *tava* (see Mughlai Paratha, page 240)
- **Puri:** a whole-wheat, deep-fried unleavened bread
- **Roti**
- **Sheer Mal**

Chole Bhatura

Litti

Khamear Naan

Potato Kachori

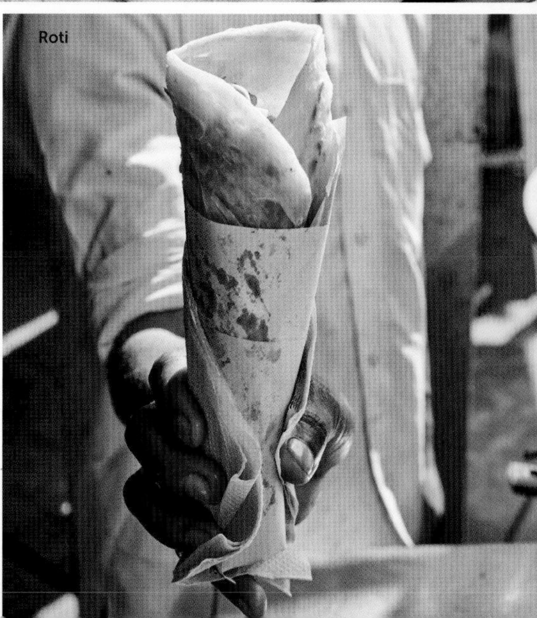
Roti

Sarson ka Saag

(SPICY GREENS)

SERVES 4

PREPARATION TIME: 1 hour

Like so many other recipes in Punjab where butter is king, this recipe calls for a copious amount of it. Butter does not rule the table in other regions of India as it does in the north, but every once in a while, it's a joy to use butter with reckless abandon like any true Punjabi would. Saag is an Indian dish of leafy greens that give the dish its green color and earthy flavor. In many parts of India, saag's base is composed solely of spinach leaves, but the traditional Punjabi way of serving it is with equal amounts of spinach, mustard, and fenugreek greens (or any greens grown on the farm), which gives it a deeper, more robust flavor. Saag is often enjoyed with the Indian fresh cheese paneer, but in Punjab, it's usually enjoyed without paneer and is instead topped while still very hot with a generous amount of butter that melts ever so perfectly into the greens, mellowing them out while at the same time giving them a silken texture. Utensils are usually replaced by makki ki roti, an Indian flatbread similar to Chapati (page 46) that is made with corn flour instead of wheat flour (and is therefore gluten-free).

2 green serrano chiles

8 ounces mustard greens, stems removed, leaves rinsed well under cold running water and coarsely chopped

8 ounces spinach, stems removed, leaves rinsed well under cold running water and coarsely chopped

8 ounces fenugreek greens, stems removed, leaves rinsed well under cold running water and coarsely chopped (if you can't find fresh fenugreek leaves, substitute with an equal amount of spinach leaves or collard greens)

3 tablespoons grated fresh ginger

Kosher salt

4 tablespoons unsalted butter

2 tablespoons corn flour (makki ka atta)

3 tablespoons ghee, store-bought or homemade (page 33), plus more for serving

1 large yellow onion, coarsely chopped

In a large pot, combine 1 cup water, the chiles, mustard greens, spinach, fenugreek greens, and ginger and bring to a simmer over medium-high heat. Cook, adding water if necessary to prevent scorching and stirring occasionally with a wooden spoon, until the chiles and greens are tender and the ginger is aromatic, 7 to 9 minutes. Set a sieve or colander over a large bowl and drain, reserving the greens and cooking liquid separately.

Transfer the greens to a blender and pulse until you have a coarse paste. Add a little of the cooking liquid if necessary to achieve this consistency. Season to taste with salt.

In the pot used to cook the greens, melt the butter over medium heat. Add the flour and cook, stirring constantly with a wooden spoon, until the flour begins to turn golden brown and take on a nutty aroma, 5 to 7 minutes. Watch closely during this step to avoid burning the flour. Add the reserved cooking liquid and stir until the mixture is just beginning to thicken and the flour mixture is well incorporated, 3 to 4 minutes. Return the greens to the pot and stir well. Cook over low heat, stirring occasionally, until the greens are broken down and the saag is a uniform dark-green, about 10 minutes. Remove from the heat and set aside.

In a large nonstick skillet, melt the ghee over medium heat. Add the onion and sauté until golden brown, about 5 minutes. Add the ginger-garlic paste, coriander, cumin, and garam masala and sauté until the oil separates from the solids, about 10 minutes. Once this happens, add the saag and continue to stir until everything is combined and the air is filled with a spicy aroma. Season to taste with salt.

Spoon the saag into four bowls and top each with a generous dollop of ghee or butter. Serve with a side of hot chapatis or makki ki roti.

1 tablespoon store-bought ginger-garlic paste

1 teaspoon ground coriander

1 teaspoon ground cumin

1 teaspoon garam masala

Chapatis (page 46) or makki ki roti, for serving

Amritsari Fish

SERVES 4

PREPARATION TIME: 1 hour (includes 30 minutes to marinate the fish)

These fish nuggets are one of my favorite snacks at the Amritsar train station. The aroma of chiles and lime and the crackling sound the fish makes as it fries and crisps on the griddle prove irresistible to anyone within smelling or listening distance. This is one of those recipes that was invented in one place in India but is so tasty it's now available in virtually every corner of the country. The recipe calls for tilapia fillets, but any firm whitefish such as cod or halibut will do. It also works well with salmon or any other species that can remain intact during frying. The coating also partners nicely with oysters or shrimp. The most important thing is to serve it piping hot, but I can assure you that this won't be a challenge, since these beauties will be gobbled up the second they hit the plate.

1 pound tilapia fillets, skinned, rinsed, and patted dry

Kosher salt

1 tablespoon Kashmiri or other red chile powder

1 teaspoon hing (asafetida)

1 teaspoon ground turmeric

1 teaspoon ground fenugreek (kasoori methi)

½ teaspoon ajwain seeds

3 tablespoons store-bought ginger-garlic paste

1 tablespoon fresh lime juice, plus lime wedges for serving

½ cup chickpea flour (besan)

¼ cup rice flour

2 large eggs

Vegetable oil, for shallow-frying

Chaat masala

Cut each fillet into bite-sized pieces and season with salt. In a large bowl, combine the chile powder, hing, turmeric, fenugreek, ajwain, ginger-garlic paste, lime juice, chickpea flour, and rice flour and stir until incorporated. Add the fish and gently turn the pieces over in the spice mixture to ensure they are well coated. Refrigerate for 30 to 60 minutes to marinate.

Remove the fish from the bowl, gently shaking each piece to remove any excess coating, and set aside on a plate. Add the eggs to the bowl and whisk to make a batter. Line a plate with a double layer of paper towels.

Pour ½ inch oil into a nonstick skillet. Heat the oil over medium-high heat until a pinch of flour sizzles when flicked into it. Dredge each piece of fish in the batter just before frying. Working in batches of about 6 portions of fish (to avoid crowding the pan; the pieces should not touch one another), lower the fish into the oil with a fish spatula and fry until the coating just begins to turn golden brown, about 2 minutes. Gently flip the fish over and fry until golden brown on the second side, another 2 to 3 minutes. Use the fish spatula or a slotted spoon to transfer the fish to the paper towels and sprinkle with salt and chaat masala. Allow the oil to return to frying temperature between batches. Serve the fish hot with lime wedges.

OPPOSITE: *The seafood vendors of India.*

11356
कल्याण
11356

Punjabi Lassi

(SWEET-SPICED SAFFRON YOGURT DRINK)

MAKES 2 lassis

PREPARATION TIME: 10 minutes

Punjab means "the land of five rivers," a reference to the waters that nourish the bountiful agricultural land this region is celebrated for. The cows that gorge themselves on the nutrient-dense grass produce rich and flavorful milk that I think is best when transformed into lassis, a sweet or savory drink with a yogurt base that is blended until it is light and velvety. In India, lassis are traditionally served in terra-cotta cups called kulhars that keep the lassi cool even on the most sweltering Punjabi day. Once the lassi is finished, the kulhar is usually discarded by dropping it on the ground, where it smashes into pieces. This might be disconcerting for a tourist who admires the craftsmanship of the elegantly shaped cup, but for an Indian, it's the ultimate symbol of sustainability, since the terra-cotta is made of nothing but earth and water baked beneath the Indian sun. Lassis are served at many train stations throughout India, but I like mine best from the station in Punjab. It tastes like home to me.

Lassis come in a variety of sweet and savory flavors limited only by resources and the imagination. My favorite lassi story is the one my mom told me a few years ago. When I was just a few years old, we were visiting my father's maternal side of the family in the Punjabi village of Sherpur, where the air is perfumed with the honeyed aroma of Kinnow, a hybrid citrus derived from mandarin oranges. My mother awoke at sunrise to the sound of a washing machine in full swing. In the next room she found her grandmother-in-law sitting next to the machine. My mom told the old woman how impressed she was that she awoke so early to take care of the day's washing. My great-grandmother responded, "I'm not washing clothes, I'm making lassis. There's nothing better than a washing machine to get the job done right." When I asked my mom if she thought we should install a washing machine to prepare lassis at our restaurant in Nashville, I received her standard eye roll that means, "Oh, Maneet, you always go too far." Rest assured, even if you don't want to attempt to use your washing machine to churn your lassi, this recipe will have you on your way to Punjabi lassi heaven in no time. Be sure to check out Lassi Flavors (opposite) for more lassi inspiration.

2 cups whole-milk yogurt (do not use Greek yogurt)

1 cup whole milk

¾ cup packed light brown sugar

½ teaspoon ground cardamom

2 tablespoons heavy cream

Ice, as needed

Finely chopped toasted pistachios, for serving

Saffron threads, for serving

In a blender, combine the yogurt and milk and blend on high speed until smooth, about 1 minute. Add the brown sugar and cardamom and continue to blend until the sugar has dissolved and a light foamy layer forms on the surface, about 90 seconds more. Add the cream and pulse until it's incorporated. Fill 2 tall glasses with ice and divide the lassi between them. Sprinkle with pistachios and a few strands of saffron and serve.

LASSI FLAVORS

The sky's the limit when it comes to flavoring a lassi. Here are some ideas—just add the ingredients to the blender when you would have added the cardamom in the recipe opposite, and then proceed as instructed.

- ½ cup coarsely chopped toasted walnuts or almonds
- ½ cup mango, blood orange, pineapple, or watermelon juice
- 1 teaspoon rose water
- ½ cup strawberries, blackberries, or peeled peaches
- ¼ cup Chai (page 220)
- ¼ cup papaya + 1 tablespoon honey
- ¼ cup coarsely chopped chocolate + 1 tablespoon coarsely chopped toasted hazelnuts
- Finely chopped leaves of 1 mint sprig + ½ teaspoon ground cinnamon
- 2 tablespoons brewed espresso

OPPOSITE: *Lassis in Chandni Chowk.*
ABOVE: *A Punjabi milk bar.*

PUNJAB'S MILK BARS

Vendors in Punjab have been serving chilled glasses of Punjabi-style flavored milk for decades. The milk is blended with a variety of fresh, local, and seasonal ingredients such as pistachios, almonds, strawberries, papaya, and pineapple, and I can attest that there is nothing better on a scorching-hot day than a glass of icy milk sweetened with fresh fruit and garnished with toasted nuts and a few threads of luxurious saffron. A few Indian milk bars, such as Verka and Khangura, have become famous and are must-visit destinations immediately upon stepping off the train. The milk bars are casual walk-up stands where patrons hang out drinking their flavored milk in small glasses that are returned to the vendor after they've finished. They are one more reason why I will continue to make the long journey from my home in the United States to India, where the noise and chaos, snarled traffic, and throngs of people energize my spirit and comfort my heart. I've internalized the colors, aromas, flavors, and sounds of India and carry them with me wherever I go.

Srinagar

Srinagar, the largest city in the Kashmiri Valley and the northernmost city in India, has a population of over one million people and sits 5,200 feet above sea level in the Himalayas. The mountains surround Srinagar like a snow-white crown, casting a twilight-blue shadow over the walnut, fig, and apricot trees that flourish in this state renowned for its natural beauty and cool temperatures due to its elevation. Kashmiri dishes like rista (meatballs in a rich red chile sauce) and lamb yakhni (lamb slow-cooked in a spiced yogurt sauce) perfume the city's ancient streets, which have seen their share of strife throughout the decades.

Most of the conversations about Kashmir that I remember from my childhood revolved around the precarious peace in the region. Kashmir perpetually hovered on the brink of war due to the territorial conflict between India and Pakistan. I was nervous to visit until the desire to taste the food of the region overtook my fear of being swept up in conflict. Roses were the first thing I smelled when I disembarked at the train station in Jammu, followed by faint notes of cinnamon and clove. I followed my nose to the kahwa tea vendor and was handed a terra-cotta cup filled with Kashmir's legendary tea. I closed my eyes and took my first sip of this delicate tea that I had only heard about but had never tasted. My anxiety about being in Kashmir diminished with each sip of this brilliant beverage that has come to represent for me the elegance and mystery of the region.

Kahwa has a permanent place on my restaurant's menu in Nashville. Whenever I have the opportunity to serve it to guests, I share with them the story of Kashmir. I don't talk to them about the conflict, but instead I tell them about the resiliency of its people, the unique nature of its cuisine, the glint of sunlight reflected on the surface of Dal Lake, and the soaring mountaintops that rise above a place of uncommon beauty and grace. When I inhale the aroma of kahwa, I am transported back to the Srinagar station that I visited so many years ago. I remember thinking then, just as I do now, that if only those embroiled in the conflict could sit together in the shade of one of Kashmir's famed walnut trees to share a cup of kahwa, its beguiling nature might entice them to find common ground and remember their shared history.

Because Kashmir is a predominantly Muslim region of the country, beef is not prohibited as it is in Hindu areas, resulting in beef-forward street food such as seek tujj, a barbecued beef kebab. Perhaps one of the most important flavors in the Kashmiri canon is saffron, which is collected from the purple crocus. Each flower produces three saffron stamens that are painstakingly hand-harvested by farmers for two to three weeks in early winter. While Iran might produce 90 percent of the world's saffron, Kashmiri saffron is known to be sweeter, with a more nuanced aroma than its Iranian counterpart.

Sadly, the beauty of Kashmir—both its cuisine and surroundings—is often eclipsed by the ongoing conflict in the region that began with the partition of 1947, when India was divided into two independent states, Pakistan and India. Kashmir and its predominantly Muslim population was granted relative autonomy even though it remains a part of India. Travel to Kashmir has the potential to be dangerous, and I advise anyone traveling there to check first for regional travel advisories. Due to the ongoing conflict, the closest railway station to Srinagar is in the Kashmiri city of Jammu, 165 miles to the south. After you leave the station, the final leg of the journey is easily completed by bus or hired driver (an inexpensive luxury in India). A direct train line that will connect Jammu to Srinagar as well as to Leh, an even more remote Himalayan outpost in Kashmir, is currently being constructed. After years of discussion and planning, serious progress was finally made in 2002, and the line is expected to be completed in 2020 (but don't take my word for it; everything in India takes longer than originally planned).

When I arrive at the Jammu station, I first seek out the kahwa tea vendor and then load up on dried fruit and nuts to fortify myself during the mountainous drive to Srinagar. Even without the convenience of a rail line to transport me directly to Srinagar, the extra effort required to get there is worth it, because I know the *shikaras* (wooden gondolas) of Dal Lake, the ornate Islamic gardens where almond, cherry, and plum trees flourish, and the graciousness of the Kashmiri people await me.

My first stop in Srinagar is Dal Lake. Referred to as "Srinagar's jewel," it is the second largest lake in Kashmir, positioned in the shadow of the Himalayan mountain range. It's famed for its opulent houseboats built during the British colonial era and for its shikaras—the elegant, hand-carved boats unique to this region—that deftly skim the surface of the water, ferrying passengers from one side of the lake to the other, as well as taking fortunate houseboat owners, a combination of expats and locals, to their front doors. And for culinary obsessives like me, a shikara is not just an opportunity to enjoy a peaceful boat ride across one of

India's most beautiful lakes, but is also access to saffron, one of the world's most precious and expensive spices. During the saffron harvest, saffron vendors row their shikaras right up to your own, carrying beaten-up tins, as big as cigar boxes, filled with Kashmiri saffron. Saffron flourishes in Kashmir due to the cool, dry climate and rich soil, which produces a saffron with a headier aroma and deeper red color. The saffron for sale on Dal Lake is an issue for me because even though most people would be satisfied with a single box of red gold, I tend to unload each vendor's entire supply, often a few dozen boxes per boat. Fortunately, I've never had an issue at customs, which is an auspicious thing because the Kashmiri saffron that I pick up in India finds its way into virtually every component of my menus back home in Nashville—even into craft beer. It's a tribute to the saffron we source from a region of the world that has seen its share of conflict for decades but has managed to thrive in spite of it. The unique flavor profile of Kashmiri cuisine and the history of heartbreak and triumph in the face of adversity stitched into each recipe reflect the resiliency and strength of the Kashmiri people, who have endured so much heartache over the years, transcending their hardships one saffron-laced recipe at a time.

Kashmiri Kahwa Tea

MAKES 2 cups
PREPARATION TIME: 10 minutes

Kahwa tea is available at many train stations in Kashmir and is sold by vendors on virtually every street corner. It's the perfect introduction to the region because its luxurious ingredients and complex flavor reflect the nuance and sophistication of Kashmir's culinary lexicon. No one knows exactly when the ritualistic preparation of kahwa tea began, but its enticing blend of spices, nuts, and potent Kashmiri green tea has been warming Kashmiris for centuries. The tea grown in Kashmir found its way to the region from China through Tibet. Black and white tea is popular in Kashmir, but green tea is the traditional variety used in kahwa. It's believed that traders who followed the spice route and stopped for requisite tea breaks along the way spread the tradition of kahwa tea from Kashmir to Pakistan, Afghanistan, and throughout Central Asia. The word *kahwa* is derived from the Arabic word *qahwa,* which means "aromatic beverage," a fitting moniker for a tea where the sugar and milk of traditional Indian masala chai is omitted in favor of regal aromatics like rose petals and saffron. Feel free to experiment with this recipe by adding ingredients such as dates, dried apricots, apples, raisins, pistachios, and walnuts. These ingredients add flavor to the tea, and once the liquid is gone, they are typically spooned up and eaten for the kahwa finale. Traditionally, a brass or copper tea kettle called a samovar, also found throughout the Middle East and Russia, is used to brew the tea over a charcoal fire before it's poured into tiny tea cups called khosas. Of course, a saucepan set over any heat source gets the job done (nearly) as well.

12 saffron threads, plus more for garnish

4-inch cinnamon stick

2 whole cloves

1 teaspoon crumbled dried rose petals

2 green cardamom pods, crushed

1 tablespoon loose-leaf green tea

1 tablespoon honey

Slivered almonds, for garnish

In a saucepan, bring 3 cups water to a boil. Reduce the heat to medium-low, add the saffron, cinnamon, cloves, rose petals, and cardamom and simmer gently until the spices are softened and aromatic, about 4 minutes. Remove the saucepan from the heat, add the tea, and stir in the honey. Steep for 4 more minutes, then strain the tea into 2 cups. Sprinkle with almonds and a few saffron threads and serve very hot.

Nadir Monji

(SPICY, CRISPY-FRIED LOTUS ROOT)

This is a spicy snack of crispy-fried lotus root that most often is served lashed with tamarind and green chile chutneys and a cup of kahwa tea. It's a common street food throughout Kashmir, where it's served in a newspaper cone—making it a popular train snack, too, since it's easily portable and the lotus root holds up well on long train trips. Kids love this snack not only because it's crunchy (and a bit greasy!) but also because sliced lotus root has a fun shape resembling a wagon wheel. At my home, nadir monji is a go-to playdate recipe that my daughter, Shagun, always requests on her birthday. I can't wait for the day when we can experience it together the way it should be enjoyed: at the train station in Jammu, washed down with a glass of vibrant Kashmiri apple juice.

SERVES 4

PREPARATION TIME: 15 minutes

1 cup rice flour

2 teaspoons Kashmiri or other red chile powder

½ teaspoon ajwain seeds

1 teaspoon cumin seeds, toasted

Kosher salt

2 cups thinly sliced peeled lotus root (available at Asian and Indian markets)

Vegetable oil, for deep-frying

Tamarind Chutney, store-bought or homemade (page 29), for serving

Green Chutney (page 30), for serving

In a large bowl, stir together the rice flour, chile powder, ajwain, and cumin. Season with salt. Pat the lotus slices dry to remove excess moisture and line a plate with paper towels for draining.

Pour 5 inches oil into a deep heavy-bottomed pot and heat over medium-high heat to 350°F on an instant-read thermometer (or until a pinch of flour flicked on the surface sizzles), 7 to 9 minutes.

Dredge the lotus in the seasoned flour, shaking it in your palm to remove any excess. Working a few pieces at a time (do not overcrowd the pot), fry the lotus until golden brown on both sides, 3 to 4 minutes, using a slotted spoon to turn it as it fries to ensure even coloring. Use the slotted spoon to transfer the fried lotus to the paper towels. Season with more salt while still piping hot. Allow the oil to return to frying temperature between batches.

Serve immediately with tamarind and green chutneys.

Kashmiri Lamb Yakhni

(BRAISED LEG OF LAMB)

SERVES 6

PREPARATION TIME: 1 hour 15 minutes, plus 1 hour to salt the lamb

Slow-cooked yakhni is traditionally served at celebrations and on feast days in Kashmir, but the preparation is so simple and the flavors so deep and rich that it's a nice everyday dish, too, especially on cool fall or winter evenings when something comforting is required. Street and train vendors in Kashmir prepare huge batches of yakhni in the early morning, spooning single-portion servings into tin bowls that hungry passengers devour on their way to the train. It's one of those dishes that can be prepared ahead of time, kept warm, and served later, its flavor growing more complex and enticing the longer it's given to develop. Feel free to swap in beef or goat for the lamb cubes. The key is to simmer it slowly over low heat to enable the flavors to mingle and the meat to become exceptionally tender. The yogurt adds a tanginess and the ghee added richness.

Kosher salt

2½ pounds boneless lamb leg, trimmed of fat and sinew and cut into 1-inch cubes

1 cup mustard oil (see page 266)

¼ teaspoon hing (asafetida)

3 tablespoons ground fennel

2 tablespoons ground ginger

6 green cardamom pods

6 black cardamom pods

4-inch cinnamon stick

2 bay leaves

¼ cup cumin seeds, toasted

6 whole cloves

4 cups whole-milk yogurt

1 tablespoon red chile paste (see page 266)

8 tablespoons ghee, store-bought or homemade (page 33)

Finely chopped cilantro, for garnish

Basmati Rice (page 262), for serving

Generously salt the lamb and set aside in a covered bowl for 1 hour.

In a large heavy-bottomed pot, heat ½ cup of the mustard oil over high heat until the oil is nearly smoking, 8 to 10 minutes. Add the hing and then immediately add the lamb and sear until it develops a golden brown crust all over, about 5 minutes.

Add enough water to cover the lamb by 1 inch and use a wooden spoon to scrape up any browned bits sticking to the bottom of the pot. Stir the fennel, ginger, cardamom pods, cinnamon, and bay leaves into the liquid in the pot, reduce the heat to medium-low, half-cover the pot with a lid, and simmer until the lamb is cooked through and tender, about 45 minutes. Stir occasionally to prevent scorching. Remove from the heat and discard the bay leaves.

In a sauté pan, heat the remaining ½ cup oil over high heat. Add the cumin and cloves and cook until aromatic, about 1 minute, stirring to prevent scorching. Add the yogurt and chile paste and whisk constantly until the yogurt starts to simmer. Do not let it boil. Stir the ghee into the yogurt mixture and then pour it over the lamb. Set the pot over low heat and cook, stirring occasionally, for 5 minutes to warm it through. Remove from the heat and garnish with cilantro. Serve with rice.

A wazwan feast

WAZWAN

No visit to Kashmir is complete without at least one *wazwan* feast, prepared by a revered figure in the community called a *waza*. It's more than a meal: It illuminates the cultural identity of Kashmir and the unique character of its people, with the meal eaten with your hands rather than with cutlery (your fingers will inevitably be stained red and yellow by the end of the meal from the saffron and turmeric that lace many of the dishes). Even when you know what to expect from the Kashmiri extravaganza of wazwan, the first experience (and every one thereafter) is an eye-popping, gut-splitting, joyous celebration of excess that arrives to the table in as many as thirty-six distinct dishes, with chicken or lamb, a symbol of abundance and revelry, featured in nearly every one.

I actually experienced my first wazwan extravaganza in Jaipur, not Kashmir. It was prepared at the home of my husband Vivek's Kashmiri friends, who wouldn't tell us what they were making except to say, "Don't worry. It's going to blow your minds." I usually meet a boast like that with suspicion, since it takes a lot to "blow my mind" from a culinary perspective. But as we waited in the dining room, a mosaic of intensely fragrant spices such as Kashmiri red chiles, cardamom, cloves, and cinnamon that I couldn't quite pick apart piqued my interest and I began to suspect that they might be right. It was appropriate that we experienced our first Kashmiri wazwan feast in the Indian state of Rajasthan, the land of the maharajas, since we indulged like royalty that night. Vivek and I stumbled into bed hours later, stuffed, slightly delirious, and ridiculously happy. I dreamt that evening of the trip to Kashmir I had yet to take and immediately started planning it the next morning. I felt stressed a few months later on the train ride to Jammu, my gateway to Kashmir. How was I ever going to fit a wazwan feast into each day of my visit, in between all the train and street food I planned on inhaling?

Fortunately, even if you don't have the two hours or more required to thoroughly enjoy a wazwan experience, whether at a home or restaurant, during your time in Kashmir, many of the dishes, such as rista (page 70), yakhni (page 64), and tabakh maaz (page 68), are served by vendors in portable, individual portions in and nearby the train stations of Kashmir.

Tabakh Maaz

(TWICE-COOKED CARAMELIZED LAMB RIBS)

SERVES 4

PREPARATION TIME: 1 hour 30 minutes, plus 1 hour to salt the lamb

Tabakh maaz is a lamb rib recipe typically included in the sumptuous Kashmiri wazwan celebration (see page 67). Leave the fat cap on the ribs for more flavor and to hold the ribs together while they cook. The ribs are braised slowly in a seasoned broth thickened with whole milk until the meat is falling from the bone. Then the ribs are seared in ghee until golden brown on both sides, resulting in a deeply caramelized flavor.

Kosher salt

1½ pounds lamb ribs (about 20 ribs), cut between the ribs into 4 segments

5 green cardamom pods

3 black cardamom pods

2 bay leaves

2 cinnamon sticks

1 tablespoon cumin seeds

1 tablespoon fennel seeds

½ tablespoon ground ginger

1 teaspoon ground turmeric

Pinch of hing (asafetida)

3 garlic cloves, peeled

1½ cups whole milk

3 tablespoons ghee, store-bought or homemade (page 33)

Basmati Rice, for serving (page 262)

Salt the ribs and set aside at room temperature for 1 hour.

In a large heavy-bottomed pot, combine the ribs and enough water to cover them by 1 inch. Bring to a boil over high heat, skimming the surface often to remove any foam that gathers there. After about 10 minutes, add the green and black cardamom, bay leaves, cinnamon, cumin, fennel, ginger, turmeric, hing, and garlic. Season with salt and then bring back to a boil. Reduce the heat to medium-low and stir in the milk. Cover and cook until the lamb is falling from the bone, about 1 hour. Adjust the heat as needed to prevent the liquid from boiling and curdling the milk. Transfer the ribs to a plate and discard the cooking liquid.

In a sauté pan, heat the ghee over medium heat until melted, about 3 minutes. Add the ribs and fry until golden brown on both sides, about 3 minutes per side. Season with more salt and serve hot with rice.

Rista

(SPICED LAMB MEATBALLS WITH SPICY RED SAUCE AND RICE)

SERVES 4

PREPARATION TIME: 45 minutes

Another staple of the Kashmiri wazwan celebration, rista is the Kashmiri version of spaghetti and meatballs—but the meatballs, bathed in a fiery red chile sauce, are made of spiced lamb and fried onions, and instead of spaghetti, they are served over cumin-laced rice. Like many of the staples from the wazwan feast, rista is sometimes served at Kashmiri street stalls where a small tin bowl is filled with rice and topped with a meatball and a spoonful of red sauce. Rista is a crowd-pleaser, delighting children and adults alike, and is a festive dish to serve at dinner parties with a side of naan (see Indian breads, page 48). Ground beef can be substituted for the lamb if you prefer, and the meatballs and sauce can be made up to a day ahead and refrigerated in a covered container.

MEATBALLS

3 tablespoons vegetable oil

1 large white onion, coarsely chopped

¼ cup store-bought ginger-garlic paste

8 serrano chiles, coarsely chopped

1 pound ground lamb

Leaves of ½ bunch cilantro, coarsely chopped

1 teaspoon kosher salt

SAUCE

1 teaspoon cumin seeds

1 black cardamom pod

4 green cardamom pods

Pinch of freshly grated nutmeg

6 black peppercorns

¼ cup store-bought ginger-garlic paste

2 tablespoons vegetable oil

2 medium yellow onions, coarsely chopped

1 teaspoon Kashmiri or other red chile powder

Make the meatballs: In a sauté pan, heat 1 tablespoon of the oil over medium-high heat. Add the white onion and cook until deeply caramelized and slightly crispy, 8 to 10 minutes. If the onion starts to scorch, reduce the heat to medium.

In a small bowl, use the back of a spoon to mash together the ginger-garlic paste and the green chiles until incorporated (the chiles will remain chunky). Transfer the mixture to a large bowl and mix in the lamb, fried onions, and cilantro until well blended. Stir in the salt. Roll the mixture into 1-inch balls (you will end up with about 12 meatballs).

Line a plate with paper towels. In a sauté pan, heat the remaining 2 tablespoons oil over high heat, about 4 minutes. Add the meatballs and fry them until golden brown on all sides and cooked through, 7 to 8 minutes. Transfer to the paper towels and set aside.

Make the sauce: Using a spice grinder, blend the cumin, black cardamom and green cardamom, nutmeg, and peppercorns into a coarse powder. Transfer to a small bowl and mash in the ginger-garlic paste.

In a sauté pan, heat the oil over medium-high heat. Add the yellow onions and cook until translucent, 5 to 7 minutes. Add the red chile powder, turmeric, cilantro, bay leaves, tomatoes, and tomato paste and cook until the spices are aromatic, stirring occasionally to prevent scorching, about 7 minutes. Season with salt, add 1 cup water, and cook, stirring until a gravy is formed, 12 to 14 minutes. Reduce the heat to medium-low and simmer gently until the sauce is thick enough to coat the back of a wooden spoon, about 5 minutes.

Add the meatballs to the sauce in a single layer, cover the pan, and cook for 5 minutes to warm the meatballs through. Roll the meatballs around once or twice to ensure they are evenly coated by the sauce.

Serve with rice.

½ teaspoon ground turmeric

Leaves of ½ bunch cilantro, coarsely chopped

2 bay leaves

2 large tomatoes, coarsely chopped

1 tablespoon tomato paste

Kosher salt

Basmati Rice (page 262), for serving

Kong Phirin

(CREAMY SAFFRON-SEMOLINA PUDDING)

SERVES 4
PREPARATION TIME: 20 minutes

This creamy semolina pudding perfumed with saffron and garnished with almonds is enjoyed throughout Kashmir as a way to conclude a meal with something that is not too sweet but just decadent enough to feel a bit indulgent. I tried it for the first time just outside of the Jammu station, where a vendor was serving it in small terra-cotta cups. I quickly spooned it into my mouth because my driver who was going to take me the rest of the way to Srinagar had arrived—it was so good, that I bought two more portions (for about ten cents each), one for me and one for the driver. I learned that day that offering your driver saffron pudding before commencing a journey is the best way to get him to agree to your radio station and air conditioning preferences!

Khong phirin is an easy dish to prepare. The only trick is to avoid boiling the milk as it cooks to prevent curdling. Semolina flour, referred to as suji or rava in India, gives the pudding an ivory color and smooth yet slightly toothsome texture. Back home in Nashville, this is a comfort food dessert that my young son, Karma, requests virtually every day. I find it nearly impossible to resist the longing in his enormous brown eyes and usually whip up a batch at least once a week. I'm not sure who likes it more, Karma or his dad, Vivek, whom I can pretty much talk into completing any task with the promise of pudding.

4 cups whole milk

2/3 cup semolina

12 saffron threads, plus more for garnish

6 tablespoons sugar

1/2 teaspoon ground cardamom

Pinch of kosher salt

Slivered almonds, toasted, for garnish

In a heavy-bottomed medium saucepan, bring the milk to a vigorous simmer (take care not to let it boil) over medium-high heat, stirring occasionally with a wooden spoon to prevent the milk from scorching or boiling over. Reduce the heat to low and, stirring constantly with a wooden spoon, slowly add the semolina. Cook, stirring, until the mixture is thick enough to coat the back of the spoon, 7 to 9 minutes. Add the saffron and increase the heat to medium. Stirring constantly, continue to cook until the mixture is as thick as a thin pancake batter.

Add the sugar and cardamom and stir until the sugar is dissolved, 3 to 4 minutes. Season with the salt. Remove the saucepan from the heat and transfer the pudding to four 4-ounce serving bowls. Garnish with saffron and almonds. At this point, it can be served warm for a soft, comforting pudding or refrigerated until set and served cold. The pudding will keep covered with plastic wrap in the refrigerator for up to 2 days.

TOP: *Kong Phirin (the version at Karim's is saffron-free).* **BOTTOM LEFT:** *Train passengers come in all ages.* **BOTTOM RIGHT:** *Kong Phirin.*

KARIM'S
SINCE

Agra and Lucknow

Tokri Chaat
Lucknowi Seekh Kebabs
Moth ki Chaat
Bread Pakoras
Kala Chana Chaat
Agra ka Petha

Agra was a frequent train stop when I was a child traveling with my family from my hometown of Ranchi to my grandparent's house in Punjab. The train always arrived just as the sun was rising. While my parents and sister were sleeping soundly in their snug train bunks, I was awake watching carefully for the blue and white sign labeled "Agra." I shook my father the moment I caught sight of it until he emerged from his sound slumber. Grabbing his steady hand securely in my own, I'd drag the poor man through the throngs of train passengers to the open door of the train, the ground rushing past us until the train finally screeched to a stop at the station. My dutiful dad followed me reluctantly through the sea of humanity, even though he didn't actually want to get off at this stop. But he never protested, because I suspect he knew he couldn't win. The train usually stops in each station for only 5 to 6 minutes, so it's a race to the chaat finish.

I was here for the *petha*, a ridiculously sweet Indian snack, iconic of Agra, made from sugar and white pumpkin. The train vendors who sold it stacked their cardboard petha boxes in neat towers, each rectangular container filled with a dozen or so sugared, bite-sized squares that were far too enticing for my sweet tooth to resist. We had only a moment to exchange our rupees for as many boxes as my tiny hands could carry before the train took off again. It was an anxiety-fueled purchase, because we were both worried the train would leave without us; but it always ended in a wave of relief the second I settled back into my cozy train bunk, clinging tightly to my Agra treasure just as the train wheels began to moan beneath me. It was only in that moment, since departing from Ranchi, that I let the train rock me to sleep for the first time since beginning our journey, curled contentedly around my small but precious stack of petha boxes.

During my college years it dawned on me that petha is not the singular priority for the majority of Agra tourists. Most of them are there to see that *other* Agra wonder known as the Taj Mahal. Arguably India's most famous attraction, this gleaming white confection of a building was commissioned by the Mughal Emperor Shah Jahan as a tomb for his most beloved wife, Mumtaz Mahal. My college friend's father worked in Agra, and thanks to her invitation to visit him, I finally stepped off the train at Agra Cantonment, Agra's largest train station, for longer than two minutes to see one of the most famous buildings in the world. Its majesty filled me with awe, but even as I stood before it with my mouth wide open in astonishment, I couldn't help but fantasize about the petha awaiting me at the station.

There are two cities in the state of Uttar Pradesh that I traveled to along my Ranchi-to-Punjab journey that deserve to be called out for their significance to both train buffs and food lovers: Agra, which is nestled beside the Yamuna River, and Uttar Pradesh's capital, Lucknow. They share many culinary traditions born of common historical events, including the influence of the Mughal Empire from the sixteenth to the eighteenth centuries.

Lucknow, India's eleventh most populous city, with nearly three million residents, is renowned for its artists, who contribute to a rich cultural heritage reflected in the nuance and depth of this city's culinary character. This is the heart of Awadhi cuisine, a tapestry of Middle Eastern and Central Asian influences reflected in the heavily spiced curries, roasted lamb, and creamy red chile-based gravies that are beloved throughout this region. Lucknow was established by Middle Eastern emperors known as Newabs in the eighteenth century as the capital of their empire. Their culinary legacy is most prominently illustrated by Lucknowi kebabs, which are cooked over an open fire and are always the food focus of my visit.

Lucknow's largest train station, Charbagh, first started receiving trains in 1867. It's as famed for the white Mughal-inspired minarets that grace its redbrick facade

FAR LEFT: *Mutton burra kebab.*
MIDDLE: *A chaat vendor in Agra.*
RIGHT: *Shiekh kebab*
FAR RIGHT: *Puchkas.*

as it is for the kebab vendors lined up outside the station, whose skewers of minced meat sizzle over open flames that they keep burning from sunrise to well after sunset. The first time I tried a kebab as a child, I heard the crackling fires before the aroma of grease, chile pepper, and cumin hit my nose, guiding me to the line of kebab vendors enmeshed in the primal dance of meat cooking over an open flame. The vendor loosened the kebab until it released from the skewer, transferred it to a newspaper square, and placed it in my small hand. I was about to take a bite when my father stopped me and instructed me to blow on it to cool it down lest I burn my mouth. After what felt like eternity, he said, "Okay, give it a try."

It was that bite of a kebab at the train station in Lucknow that changed the direction of my life. Its complex flavor profile was a revelation. I wasn't sure exactly what I was tasting, but I wanted nothing more than to figure it out. I pondered it all the way to my paternal grandmother Surinder Chauhan's house in Punjab, fascinated by its bewitching texture, aroma, and flavor. My grandmother was a strong, dynamic woman who somehow managed to know exactly what was going on in the lives of all our relatives, no matter how distant from her home. Her inquisitive nature appealed to my own, her indomitable spirit sparking a flame within me. My grandmother empowered me to think for myself and have confidence in the strength and wisdom of my own convictions. When I arrived at her house after tasting my first Lucknowi kebab, the first thing I said to her was that I wanted to be a chef, a rare profession for an Indian woman at the time. Instead of discouraging me, she immediately responded, "Then you must do it. You can be anything you want to be."

Tokri Chaat

(POTATO BASKETS STUFFED WITH VEGETABLE PATTIES)

SERVES 6

PREPARATION TIME: 1 hour 30 minutes, plus overnight to soak the peas

Tokri chaat is a popular snack in northern India, where it's served by the vendors who spill out of the train stations in Agra and Lucknow. It consists of a festive potato basket that is filled with peas and vegetable patties that are drizzled with yogurt and garnished with pomegranate seeds. To prepare the potato baskets, you will need 2 wire mesh tea strainers (the kind you place over a teacup to hold loose tea leaves), one whose base is at least ½ inch smaller than the other so that they fit snugly inside each other for frying.

PEAS

2 cups small dried white peas (safed vatana), soaked in water overnight

2 teaspoons garam masala

2 teaspoons amchur powder

Pinch of hing (asafetida)

Kosher salt

Fresh lemon juice

POTATO BASKETS

3 russet potatoes, peeled

2 tablespoons all-purpose flour

1½ tablespoons cornstarch

2 teaspoons chaat masala

Vegetable oil

Kosher salt

TIKKIS

1 large red beet, peeled and grated

1 cup finely chopped spinach

1 russet potato, boiled whole until tender, peeled, and mashed

1 cup fresh green peas (use frozen if necessary)

Cook the peas: Drain the peas and place them in a medium saucepan with water to cover by 2 inches. Bring to a boil over high heat, then reduce the heat to medium and simmer gently until the peas are tender, about 20 minutes. Drain and transfer to a medium bowl. Add the garam masala, amchur powder, and hing and gently combine until the peas are well coated. Season with salt and lemon juice.

Meanwhile, make the potato baskets: Set up a large bowl of ice and water. Grate the potatoes on the small holes of a box grater and soak them in the ice water for 20 minutes.

Drain the potatoes, wrap them in a clean, dry kitchen cloth, and squeeze to remove the excess water. Transfer to a bowl and stir in the flour, cornstarch, chaat masala, and 1 tablespoon vegetable oil until the potatoes are well coated. Season with salt and toss to combine.

Line a plate with paper towels. Pour 5 inches vegetable oil into a medium-size, deep heavy-bottomed pan and heat over high heat to 350°F on an instant-read thermometer (or when a drop of water flicked into the oil sizzles).

While the oil heats, press about 2 tablespoons of the potatoes around the outside of the smaller strainer until it is about ¼ inch thick. Place the larger strainer over the potatoes and press the two strainers together. Hold the handles of the two strainers together and using an oven mitt carefully lower the potato basket into the oil. Fry until the basket is golden brown inside and out, about 4 minutes (take extra care to avoid burning yourself). Remove the strainers and gently remove the outer strainer from the inner one to reveal the potato basket. Using a paring knife, loosen the edges of the basket from the smaller strainer and once it is loose, turn it out onto the paper towels and season with salt. Repeat this process with the remaining potatoes, allowing the oil to return to temperature after each frying session.

Make the tikkis: In a large bowl, combine the beet, spinach, mashed potato, peas, ginger, cilantro, and garam masala and toss to combine. Season with salt. Shape the tikkis into 1½-inch patties and freeze them on a sheet pan for 10 minutes.

Line a plate with paper towels. Pour ¾ inch oil into a sauté pan and set the pan over medium-high heat until small bubbles begin to form, 4 to 5 minutes.

While the oil heats, in a small bowl, whisk together 1 tablespoon of the cornstarch and ⅓ cup room temperature water to form a slurry and set aside for 2 minutes.

Dredge the tikkis in the cornstarch slurry, shaking to remove excess liquid. Fry the tikkis in the hot oil until they are cooked through and golden brown on both sides, about 2 minutes per side, using a metal spatula to flip them over halfway through cooking. Transfer the tikkis to the paper towels to drain, and season with salt. The tikkis can be refrigerated in a covered container for up to 1 day.

Prepare the yogurt: In a medium bowl, whisk together the yogurt, sugar, lemon juice, chaat masala, chile powder, and salt until well combined.

Assemble the chaat: Set a potato basket at the center of a small plate and place a fried tikki inside. Spoon enough peas on top to cover the tikki, and drizzle with yogurt and tamarind chutney. Serve sprinkled with pomegranate seeds, cilantro, chile powder, and cumin and serve immediately.

1-inch piece fresh ginger, peeled with a spoon and finely chopped

½ cup finely chopped fresh cilantro leaves

1 teaspoon garam masala

Kosher salt

Vegetable oil, for shallow-frying

2 tablespoons cornstarch

YOGURT

1 cup whole-milk yogurt

2 teaspoons sugar

1 teaspoon fresh lemon juice

½ teaspoon chaat masala

¼ teaspoon Kashmiri or other red chile powder

½ teaspoon table salt

CHAAT

Tamarind Chutney, store-bought or homemade (page 29)

Pomegranate seeds

Coarsely chopped fresh cilantro leaves

Kashmiri or other red chile powder

Ground toasted cumin

Lucknowi Seekh Kebabs

(SPICED LAMB KEBABS)

MAKES about 12 kebabs

PREPARATION TIME: 1 hour 15 minutes (includes 1 hour to chill the kebab meat)

Kebabs are the kings of street food around the train station in Lucknow, where Awadhi cuisine, with its Middle Eastern influences from the Mughal era, permeates the lamb kebab mixture, resulting in a complex alchemy of flavor (yes, there is a long list of spices involved, but they're so worth it!). Be sure to knead the ground lamb with the spices and other ingredients for a substantial period of time in order to properly meld the mixture so the meat is well seasoned throughout. If you prefer, you can substitute ground beef or pork (or a combination) for the lamb. Kebabs are traditionally grilled over an open flame, but I've offered an oven baking and frying method to make the process doable for all seasons. Of course, if you'd like to grill them, by all means please do—but be warned, their aroma is sure to entice the neighbors, just as it entices passengers who gather round the kebab vendor at the Lucknow train station, their eyes eager with kebab anticipation. Note that after blending the meat mixture, it needs to chill for 1 hour in the refrigerator prior to making and cooking the kebabs. You'll need twelve 16-to-22-inch metal kebab skewers for this.

1 pound ground lamb

1 large red onion, finely chopped

1 large egg

3 tablespoons finely chopped fresh cilantro

2 tablespoons finely chopped fresh mint

2 tablespoons store-bought ginger-garlic paste

2 tablespoons cashew butter, almond butter, or peanut butter

1 tablespoon papaya pulp (optional; see Note)

1 tablespoon whole-milk yogurt

1-inch piece fresh ginger, peeled with a spoon and finely chopped

2 teaspoons garam masala

2 teaspoons ajwain seeds

2 teaspoons amchur powder

2 tablespoons chaat masala

3 tablespoons cumin seeds, toasted

2 teaspoons coriander seeds

1 teaspoon freshly ground black pepper

½ teaspoon freshly grated nutmeg

In a large bowl, combine the lamb, onion, egg, cilantro, mint, ginger-garlic paste, cashew butter, papaya pulp (if using), yogurt, ginger, garam masala, ajwain, amchur, chaat masala, cumin, coriander seeds, black pepper, and nutmeg. Season with salt. Knead for about 5 minutes to ensure everything is well incorporated. Cover the bowl and refrigerate for 1 hour.

Preheat the oven to 450°F.

Remove about ½ cup of the kebab meat and shape it over a metal skewer in a hot dog shape that's about 1 inch thick and 6 inches long. Repeat the process with the remaining meat and skewers. (At this stage, the kebabs can be covered and refrigerated for up to 1 day.)

Arrange the skewers on a sheet pan and bake until cooked through, about 20 minutes, rotating the kebabs twice during the cooking process.

In a large sauté pan, heat the ghee over high heat and fry the kebabs in batches while spooning the ghee over them and occasionally rotating them throughout the process. Once each kebab is golden brown, season with salt. Repeat with the remaining kebabs. Serve very hot with lemon wedges and green chutney.

NOTE: *The papaya pulp serves as a meat tenderizer, breaking down the meat and softening it as it chills and cooks. It can be omitted if you have difficulty sourcing it or you can make your own by mashing fresh papaya flesh into a pulp using a fork.*

Kosher salt

4 tablespoons ghee, store-bought or homemade (page 33)

Lemon wedges, for serving

Green Chutney (page 30), for serving

Moth ki Chaat

(SPROUTED MOTH BEAN CHAAT)

This healthy chaat recipe features moth beans, called *matki* in Hindi, that are sprouted overnight for a slightly fermented flavor and loads of nutritional benefits such as antioxidants and the ability to more easily absorb essential nutrients such as calcium, zinc, and magnesium. Moth beans are small brown beans about the size of black-eyed peas that can be found at Indian markets. Any small bean of equal size can be substituted. This is a popular chaat in Agra, Lucknow, and throughout most of northern India.

SERVES 6

PREPARATION TIME: 30 minutes, plus a few days to sprout the moth beans

1 cup moth beans (or any small beans, such as black-eyed peas or pink beans)

1 large russet potato

1 large tomato, cored and coarsely chopped

1 medium red onion, finely chopped

1 cucumber, coarsely chopped

3 serrano chiles, seeded and finely chopped

½ cup lightly packed coarsely chopped fresh cilantro, plus more for garnish

2 teaspoons chaat masala

½ teaspoon Kashmiri or other red chile powder

Fresh lemon juice

Kosher salt

Rinse the beans under cool running water to remove any debris. Place the beans in a medium bowl and cover them with enough water to fill the bowl to the top. Soak them at room temperature until tender throughout, about 12 hours.

Drain the beans and place them at the center of a clean cotton kitchen towel that is slightly dampened. Wrap the towel around the beans to form a pouch and tie a knot at the top. Set the pouch aside in a warm place for 24 hours. Check the beans, and if they haven't sprouted yet, have patience—they will sprout eventually. Conditions such as room temperature factor into how long this process takes.

Bring a medium saucepan of water to a boil and add the unpeeled potato. Boil the potato until a paring knife easily slips into the center, about 15 minutes. Drain the potato and set aside to cool slightly. Once it is cool enough to handle, peel the potato and cut it into 1-inch cubes.

Once the beans have sprouted, toss them together in a large bowl with the potato cubes, tomato, onion, cucumber, serranos, cilantro, chaat masala, and chile powder. Season to taste with lemon juice and salt and garnish with cilantro. Eat straight from the bowl or spoon into smaller bowls for single servings.

Bread Pakoras

(FRIED BREAD AND MASHED-POTATO-STUFFED SANDWICHES)

MAKES 8 pakoras
PREPARATION TIME: 30 minutes

Meet your new favorite breakfast sandwich. Of course they can be enjoyed any time of day, but my family prefers them to jump-start our mornings or as late-night snacks, when the crunchy, chickpea-battered bread stuffed with mashed potatoes seems like a truly decadent treat. This is one of my favorite indulgences, and my motto with them is that if you're going to eat a bread pakora, you have to surrender to the indulgence! Bread pakoras are yet another snack that you can find throughout the train station in Agra, where the sizzle of the frying pakoras fills the air. This is a great snack to prepare when you have leftover mashed potatoes from the night before. I find them the perfect companion for a cup of hot chai from the chaiwala or from my own tea kettle when I'm making bread pakoras at home.

2 tablespoons finely chopped fresh cilantro leaves

2 teaspoons fresh lemon juice

1 teaspoon finely chopped green chile

1 teaspoon ajwain seeds

½ teaspoon ground turmeric

½ teaspoon baking soda

1 cup chickpea flour (besan)

Kosher salt

1½ cups salted mashed potatoes

8 slices white or whole wheat bread

Vegetable oil, for deep-frying

Cilantro-Mint Chutney (page 31), for serving

In a large bowl, whisk together 1½ cups water, the cilantro, lemon juice, green chile, ajwain, turmeric, and baking soda. Stir in the chickpea flour and mix until the batter is well combined. It should be the consistency of pancake batter, so add more water 1 tablespoon at a time if it's too thick. Season with salt.

Spread one-quarter of the mashed potatoes over one of the bread slices and top with another to form a sandwich. Repeat with the remaining potatoes and bread slices. Cut each sandwich in half diagonally.

Line a plate with paper towels. Pour 2 inches oil into a deep heavy-bottomed saucepan and heat over high heat to 350°F on an instant-read thermometer. Dip one of the sandwiches in the batter, making sure both sides of the bread are well coated, pull it out, and let the excess batter drip back into the bowl. Use a slotted spoon to carefully lower the pakora into the oil, taking care to do so gently to avoid splattering. Fry the pakora until it turns golden brown, about 2 minutes, then carefully turn it over and fry the other side until golden brown, 2 to 3 minutes more. Use the slotted spoon to remove the pakora from the oil and transfer it to the paper towels to drain. Season with salt on both sides. Repeat the process with the rest of the sandwiches and serve the fried pakoras while hot and with the chutney.

CHAAT AND BEER

I love pairing wine with virtually anything; pairing wine with a hectic day, pairing wine with an afternoon of tending to a screaming child, pairing wine with doing my taxes. But when it comes to what beverage I prefer to pair with chaat, it's beer. At my Nashville-based restaurant, Chaatable, we have beer on tap from Mantra Artisan Ales, the brewery I co-founded with my husband, Vivek, in the nearby town of Murfreesboro. Our inspiration for the brewery was born of our belief that beer is the perfect beverage to drink with Indian cuisine and of our desire to have a beer that mirrored the flavor profiles of the cuisine.

We brew seasonal and one-off beers, but we also have mainstays such as our Saffron IPA (brewed with Kashmiri saffron and cardamom), Battleground (a pilsner brewed with coriander seeds and orange peel), and Japa Milk Chai Stout, which reflects the spice blend used in chai tea. I think beer is the ideal beverage pairing for Indian cuisine. I would recommend them for your next chaat party. Light, hop-forward IPAs and lagers work well, but sours and Belgian-style beer work well, too. Set up a tub filled with ice, fill it with your favorite styles, and shimmy it up to the chaat table. Nothing could be simpler or more celebratory.

Kala Chana Chaat

(BLACK CHICKPEA SALAD)

This quick and easy chaat recipe features kala chana, which are black chickpeas (yellow chickpeas will work in a pinch—and to make this super fast, you can use rinsed canned chickpeas). The mango adds a sweet note while the mint freshens it up. This chaat, which I'd equate to Indian comfort food with its stew-like texture and approachable flavors, is almost always available at the Agra train station. I love it on a winter's day when there's a chill in the air; but even if it's a steaming hot July afternoon in India, I'll make a beeline to the vendor the moment I spot him.

SERVES 4

PREPARATION TIME: 20 minutes, plus 1 hour to cook the chickpeas

- **1 cup dried kala chana (or canned yellow chickpeas)**
- **1 small red onion, finely chopped**
- **1 small tomato, coarsely chopped**
- **1 green chile, seeded and finely chopped**
- **1 teaspoon chaat masala**
- **½ teaspoon cumin seeds, toasted**
- **¼ teaspoon Kashmiri or other red chile powder**
- **½ teaspoon amchur powder**
- **½ cup coarsely chopped fresh mango (about ½ medium)**
- **2 tablespoons finely chopped fresh cilantro leaves**
- **1 tablespoon finely chopped fresh mint leaves**
- **1 tablespoon fresh lemon juice**
- **Kosher salt**

In a saucepan, combine the kala chana and water to cover by 3 inches. Bring the water to a boil over high heat, reduce the heat to medium-low, and simmer, uncovered, until the kala chana is tender, 50 to 60 minutes. Drain well.

In a large bowl, stir together the cooked chickpeas, onion, tomato, green chile, chaat masala, cumin, chile powder, and amchur. Stir to combine, then add the mango, cilantro, mint, and lemon juice and stir gently to combine. Season with salt and serve immediately.

Agra ka Petha

(CANDIED PUMPKIN)

MAKES about forty-eight 1-inch squares

PREPARATION TIME: 3 hours (includes about 2½ hours to soak the pumpkin)

Petha is the sticky-sweet pumpkin snack I always looked forward to most at the train stop in Agra. This pumpkin "jelly" is a delicacy of this region, and there is no better place to pick up several boxes of it than at the station, where it is sold in a bewildering variety of flavors, including chocolate, strawberry, papaya, mango, pistachio, walnut, almond, and saffron. This recipe calls for rose water and cardamom, the petha flavor combination I adored as a child, but feel free to swap out these ingredients for others that are mentioned, or to experiment with your own favorite flavor combinations. Ash gourd, also known as winter melon or white pumpkin, is what is used in the petha of Agra, but if you have difficulty sourcing it, an orange sugar pumpkin can also be substituted. Alum (potassium aluminum sulfate) is required to stiffen the petha while it cools. It can be found in the pickling or baking section of most grocery stores or at Indian markets.

3 pounds white pumpkin, seeded, peeled, and cut into 1-inch chunks

2 teaspoons alum

1 tablespoon fresh lemon juice

4 cups granulated sugar

5 green cardamom pods

2 tablespoons rose water

Prick the pumpkin pieces all over with a fork. This is to allow the other ingredients to permeate the flesh and soften it more easily. Arrange the pumpkin in a large heavy-bottomed pot and add enough cold water to cover it by 1 inch. Add 1 teaspoon of the alum and the lemon juice and bring to a boil over high heat. Reduce the heat to medium and simmer for 10 minutes. Drain and rinse under cold running water until all residue has been washed away, about 3 minutes.

Place the pumpkin in a large bowl along with the remaining 1 teaspoon alum. Add enough water to cover the pumpkin, and set aside to soak for 2 hours. Rinse under cold running water to remove any residue, about 3 minutes.

In a heavy-bottomed pot, combine the sugar, cardamom, and 3 cups water and bring to a boil over high heat. Reduce the heat to medium-high, add the pumpkin, and simmer until the pumpkin has softened yet still retains its shape and is translucent, about 30 minutes, stirring occasionally and skimming any foam that might collect on the surface of the liquid. During this time, the liquid will transform into syrup that is as thick as warm honey. Stir in the rose water and remove the pot from the heat.

Use a slotted spoon to transfer the petha to a sheet pan to cool (discard the syrup and cardamom pods). Be sure the petha is arranged with space between the pieces to prevent them from sticking together. Serve once the petha has cooled completely, or store in a single layer in a covered container at room temperature for up to 1 week.

TOP LEFT: *Petha including saffron, orange, rose, and paan.*
LEFT: *White pumpkin petha.*
ABOVE: *A petha vendor on the train to Agra.*

DIESEL

The West

Jaipur
Mumbai
Goa
Pune and Ahmedabad

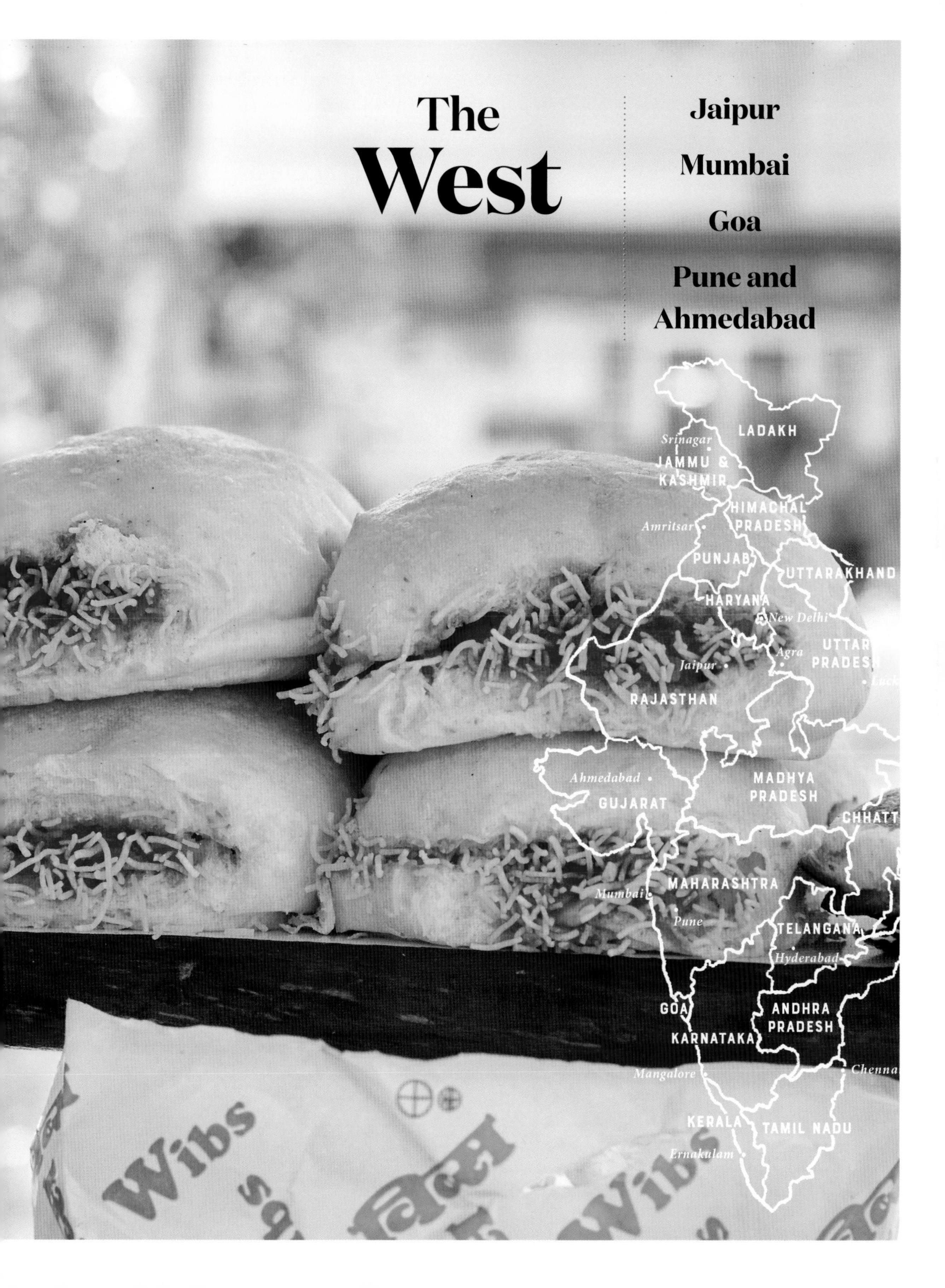

Jaipur

- Fresh Lime Sodas
- Sabudana Khichdi
- Dal Baati Churma Chaat
- Raj Kachori Chaat

Jaipur's Gandhi Nagar Railway Station

My husband, Vivek, is from Jaipur, and through its cuisine I have gained insight into his childhood and learned to understand what makes him tick. Vivek's aunt Chetna Singh holds many of the family's culinary secrets that have been passed down from one generation to the next in an oral history that tells the story of ancestors who cooked for royalty, hunted game for the maharajas, and embarked upon long journeys in camel caravans in a quest for rare spices. From the moment we arrive in Jaipur until we depart a week or two later, I'm at his aunt's side learning the secrets of royal cuisine—like how to add a silky sheen to a red chile sauce and where to forage for plants such as wild ferns and nettles that are fundamental to many recipes.

Jaipur is the heart of the Rajasthani state, an arid region in the west that has been the home for centuries to the maharajas, which means "great kings" in Sanskrit. The legacy of the maharajas in Jaipur is reflected in the regal dishes and culinary practices still cherished in this region. As a young girl, whenever my family announced we were taking a trip from Ranchi to Jaipur, I'd immediately begin to fantasize about the beeline we would make straight from the train station to the iconic sweet shop Rawat where legendary confections such as rabdi (a sweet condensed-milk baked custard), ghevar (a ring cake made of wheat flour that is soaked in sugar syrup after it's baked), and mawa kachori (a pastry stuffed with fruit and nuts) compete for space with over fifty other sugary delicacies on the sparkling shelves of this decades-old market. Raj kachori, a huge, crispy puff stuffed with potatoes, chickpeas, and spices, drizzled with yogurt, tamarind and green chutneys, and garnished with pomegranate seeds and sev, was my chaat of choice to get the festivities started in this city as renowned for its royal cuisine as it is for its iconic pink forts.

The principles of royal cuisine, made popular hundreds of years ago in this region and still prevalent today, are not what you might think. They do not concern luxury ingredients, but are instead guided by the belief that cooking for maharajas should be done in a deliberate way, with every consideration paid to obtaining the freshest, highest quality foods.

LEFT: *A shack vendor at a train station in Jaipur.*
MIDDLE: *Gandhi Nagar train station in Jaipur.*
RIGHT: *Papadum vendor.*

Game meat such as deer, wild boar, partridge, and pheasant, all of which are illegal to serve in India today due to food safety concerns, were a critical component of royal cuisine, as was the belief that the origin story of an ingredient as well as the history of the dish should be known and appreciated. I consider the *khansamas*, the professional cooks who prepared the dishes comprising a royal menu, to have been well ahead of their time: Their quest for food narratives and origin stories would have made them feel right at home in our contemporary culinary world, where authentic and artisanal ingredients are highly prized by today's most renowned chefs.

One of my favorite places to discover chaat is at the Gandhi Nagar railway station in the Bajal Nagar neighborhood of Jaipur. It's one of the only railway stations in India operated entirely by women. As an Indian woman who had to fight and claw her way through a male-dominated industry to find success, I am in awe of the forty women who run Gandhi Nagar. The station is almost entirely covered with murals celebrating the history and cultural heritage of Jaipur. There's a dairy bar in one corner of the station serving ice cold milk, lassis (page 54), and the immensely popular ice cream pop called kulfi. My favorite vendor at Bajal Nagar is the dal baati churma chaat vendor. It's here that I'm reminded that although royal cuisine is the most revered culinary tradition in Jaipur, it's the humble ingredients that comprise this simple chaat—chickpeas, green chiles, and ghee—that make my culinary world go round.

Fresh Lime Sodas

Refreshing lime soda is a beverage enjoyed in virtually every corner of India, but in the desert climate of Rajasthan after an afternoon of inhaling chaat (and a bit of sand), this vibrant drink is especially welcome. Add a shot or two of vodka or gin for a grown-up alternative. Substitute orange or lemon juice and slices for the lime, if desired.

MAKES 2 sodas
PREPARATION TIME: 5 minutes

¼ cup sugar

Ice

2 tablespoons fresh lime juice

Club soda

Lime slices, for garnish

Mint sprigs, for garnish

In a small saucepan, combine the sugar and ¼ cup water and bring to a boil over high heat. Reduce the heat to medium and gently simmer until a syrup is formed that is thick enough to coat the back of a wooden spoon, 7 to 9 minutes. Remove from the heat and let the syrup cool to room temperature.

Fill 2 Collins glasses with ice and divide the syrup and lime juice between the glasses. Add enough club soda to fill to the top of each glass. Stir to combine, and garnish with a lime slice and mint sprig.

Sabudana Khichdi

(TAPIOCA PILAF WITH CHILES, POTATOES, AND PEANUTS)

SERVES 4

PREPARATION TIME: 20 minutes, plus 4 to 6 hours to soak the sago

This popular tapioca pearl pilaf is served throughout many parts of India, including Jaipur, where it's often consumed to break Hindu fasting days such as Navrati, which is celebrated in the autumn, and Shivratri, which takes place in late winter. It's also commonly available just outside the Jaipur train station, especially in the cooler fall and winter months. The nubby texture of the tapioca pearls is balanced by crunchy peanuts and a drizzle of tangy yogurt. If you have trouble sourcing curry leaves (you can find them in Indian markets and some Asian and Middle Eastern markets, too), lime zest is a good substitute. Sabudana khichdi is popular any time of day, but it's been a breakfast favorite of mine since I was a kid. This might sound like blasphemy to sabudana purists, but I especially love it topped with a runny poached egg!

2 cups sago (large tapioca pearls)

4 tablespoons ghee, store-bought or homemade (page 33)

8 fresh curry leaves (optional)

2 green chiles, halved, seeded, and finely chopped

1-inch piece fresh ginger, peeled with a spoon and finely chopped

1 tablespoon cumin seeds

2 russet potatoes, peeled and coarsely chopped

½ cup roasted peanuts, finely chopped

Juice of 1 lime

Kosher salt

Finely chopped fresh cilantro

Place the sago in a colander and rinse under cold running water until the water runs clear (this is the most important step because it removes the excess starch in order to avoid the dreaded sticky sabudana). Transfer the sago to a bowl, add enough cold water to cover the sago by 3 inches, and soak at room temperature until tender, 4 to 6 hours. Rinse once more under cold running water to remove any additional starch.

In a medium sauté pan, heat the ghee over medium-high heat. Add the curry leaves (if using), green chiles, ginger, and cumin and sauté until aromatic, about 2 minutes. Reduce the heat to medium-low, add the potatoes, and sauté until tender, stirring occasionally, 8 to 10 minutes. Add a little water during the process if the spices or potatoes begin to scorch or burn. Add the sago and peanuts and sauté until the peanuts are tender, about 5 minutes longer. Remove the pan from the heat and stir in the lime juice. Season with salt. Garnish with cilantro and serve in individual serving bowls while still warm.

OPPOSITE: *Sabudana Khichdi.*
BOTTOM LEFT: *A railway vendor in Jaipur.*
BOTTOM RIGHT: *A passenger at the Gandhi Nagar Railway Station.*

Dal Baati Churma Chaat

(LENTILS WITH WHEAT ROLLS)

This was one of the dishes I most looked forward to on our rides to Jaipur Station. Baati are hard wheat rolls that are served with warm dal, so perfect on a winter's day, especially with the roll to soak up the savory juices from the lentils. Churma is a powder that is made of wheat and semolina flours, spices, ghee, and a variety of nuts. Traveling through the parched desert with views of camels strolling languidly through the honey-hued landscape, I imagined this chaat, made of wheat rolls, dal, and the powder with its signature nutty finish. Making it is a bit labor-intensive, but know that while all of the elements are enjoyable on their own, when they are brought together into a single bowl, they really find their voice. If you find the dal varieties (see page 265) overwhelming, just opt for one or two, such as mung dal and masoor dal. You can also substitute store-bought wheat rolls to make this recipe a little less demanding.

SERVES 4

PREPARATION TIME: 1 hour

CHURMA

1 cup whole wheat flour

¼ cup semolina

8 tablespoons ghee, store-bought or homemade (page 33), melted

Vegetable oil, for shallow-frying

Kosher salt

¼ cup sliced almonds

2 tablespoons finely chopped pistachios

2 tablespoons finely chopped cashews

¼ cup powdered sugar

1 teaspoon ground cardamom

DAL

¼ cup chana dal

¼ cup arhar dal

¼ mung dal

¼ cup black urad dal

¼ cup white urad dal

½ teaspoon ground turmeric

3 tablespoons ghee, store-bought or homemade (page 33)

Make the churma: Sift the whole wheat flour into a large bowl and stir in the semolina and half of the melted ghee. Add ½ cup water and knead until you have a stiff, dry dough, 4 to 5 minutes. Add additional water if the dough does not hold together. Divide the dough into 10 equal portions and roll each into a ball. Using the palm of your hand, gently compress each ball until it forms a disk that is about 1 inch thick.

Line a plate with paper towels. Pour ½ inch oil into a medium sauté pan and heat over high heat until the oil glistens, about 3 minutes. Once a pinch of flour sizzles when it meets the surface of the oil, use tongs or a metal spatula to transfer the churma to the oil, being careful not to overcrowd the pan. Fry until golden brown on one side, about 2 minutes. Flip and repeat on the other side. Transfer to the paper towels to drain, and season with salt. Repeat with the remaining churma. Let them cool to room temperature.

When cool, break the churma into bite-sized pieces and place in a food processor. Process until a fine powder forms, 3 to 4 minutes. Transfer the meal to a sieve and sift into a large bowl. Stir in the almonds, pistachios, cashews, sugar, cardamom, and the remaining 4 tablespoons of melted ghee. Set aside.

(RECIPE AND INGREDIENTS CONTINUE)

- 4 whole cloves
- 2 dried red chiles
- 2 green cardamom pods
- 2 black cardamom pods
- 1 teaspoon cumin seeds
- 1 cinnamon stick
- 1 bay leaf
- Pinch of hing (asafetida)
- 1 large red onion, finely chopped
- 2 green chiles, finely chopped
- 2 medium tomatoes, coarsely chopped
- 2 tablespoons store-bought ginger-garlic paste
- ½ teaspoon coriander seeds
- ½ teaspoon turmeric
- ½ teaspoon Kashmiri or other red chile powder
- ½ teaspoon garam masala
- Lemon juice
- Kosher salt

Make the dal: In a colander, combine the dals and rinse under cold running water for 3 to 4 minutes to remove debris. Transfer them to a large heavy-bottomed pot. Add 5 cups water and the turmeric and bring to a boil over high heat. Reduce the heat to medium and simmer the dal until tender and all of the water has been absorbed, about 25 minutes. Stir occasionally during the cooking process to prevent scorching.

Meanwhile, in a large sauté pan, melt the ghee over medium-high heat. Add the cloves, red chiles, green and black cardamom, cumin, cinnamon, bay leaf, and hing and sauté, stirring often, until aromatic and the spices begin to crackle, about 2 minutes. Add onion and green chiles and sauté until tender, about 3 minutes. Add the tomatoes and ginger-garlic paste and sauté until the tomatoes begin to fall apart, about 3 minutes longer. Add the coriander, turmeric, chile powder, garam masala, and ¼ cup water and sauté until the sauce begins to thicken, about 4 minutes. Add this to the dal and cook over medium heat, stirring occasionally, until incorporated, about 3 minutes. Discard the bay leaf and cinnamon stick. Season to taste with lemon juice and salt.

Make the baatis: Preheat the oven to 350°F.

In a large bowl, stir together the whole wheat flour, semolina, 4 tablespoons of the ghee, and the baking powder. Season with salt. Stir in the yogurt, turn out onto a clean work surface, and knead into a semi-stiff dough, about 4 minutes. If the dough is too stiff or will not come together properly, add water 1 tablespoon at a time until you have a stiff dough. Divide the dough into 12 portions and roll into balls.

Flatten the balls with your palm into disks about ½ inch thick and press an indentation in the center of each one using your thumb. Arrange on a sheet pan and bake until they are golden brown and cooked through, 30 to 35 minutes, using tongs to turn them over halfway through baking. Remove the pan from the oven.

Line a plate with paper towels. Add the remaining 8 tablespoons ghee to a medium bowl. Working with one baati at a time, place a kitchen towel in your hand and set a baati on the towel. Cover the baati and gently press it with the palm of your hand to crack the hot baati open slightly and add to the bowl of ghee. Soak the baatis until the ghee is absorbed, about 2 minutes, before transferring them to the paper towels to drain. Season the baatis with salt.

To assemble the chaat: Spoon a portion of the dal into a small bowl and drizzle with ghee. Sprinkle the dal with the churma and top with 2 baatis. Drizzle with additional ghee. Garnish with onion, cucumber, tomato, and dried rose petals. Sprinkle with lemon juice and serve.

BAATIS

1¼ cups whole wheat flour

½ cup semolina

12 tablespoons melted ghee, store-bought or homemade (page 33)

½ teaspoon baking powder

Kosher salt

½ cup whole-milk yogurt

FOR ASSEMBLY

Melted ghee, store-bought or homemade (page 33)

Finely chopped red onion

Finely chopped cucumber

Finely chopped tomato

Dried rose petals

Lemon juice

A TRAIN FIT FOR ROYALS

There is a train line in India that embodies the regal lifestyle of the maharajas, the royal class in India until national independence in 1947. This extravagant train, which was used exclusively by the maharajas, has been preserved for those who can afford to make the multiday journey (tickets are a few thousand dollars as opposed to tickets on a standard sleeper train, which are usually under fifty dollars). The Palace on Wheels takes a 250-mile loop from New Delhi to Jaipur to Agra, and is one of the most celebrated and luxurious trains. The cabins are ornately decorated with wall-to-wall carpeting, plush twin beds, regal tapestries, and even a turn-down service. Linen-covered tables, five-star meals comprising Rajasthani and continental dishes, and a sommelier await in the lavish restaurant. There's even a spa car that offers massages and Ayurvedic healing services. This is a train primarily enjoyed by tourists and train buffs who are seeking an experience that harkens back to the romance and opulence of luxury train travel. It's India's equivalent of the Orient Express.

LEFT: *A disembarking train passenger in Rajasthan.* **TOP:** *Sweets in Jaipur.* **RIGHT:** *A bhel puri vendor in Jaipur.*

Raj Kachori Chaat

(POTATO AND CHICKPEA-STUFFED WHEAT PUFFS)

I never visit India without seeking out at least one raj kachori during my trip. It's impossible not to experience a rush of delight and wonder when a vendor presents it. With its jewel-like colors of ruby red from the pomegranate seeds and emerald green from the chutney—which is drizzled over a humongous crispy puff stuffed with chickpeas and potatoes that are drenched in yogurt and garnished with crunchy sev—seeing it is a thrill every single time. The best place to find raj kachori is at the train stations and food markets in Jaipur. It's fitting that raj kachori's origins are in Rajasthan, since its regal colors, decadent size, and burst of sweet, salty, spicy, and tangy flavors teetering on the verge of the ridiculous all speak to a dish that could easily be the chaat of the maharajas, the chaat of kings. The secret to perfecting this recipe is not to hold back. The moment you think you're going too far, keep going—add more pomegranate seeds, more yogurt, more chutney! This is not a chaat with demure intentions. No, it's a celebratory chaat made for festive times.

SERVES 4

PREPARATION TIME: 1 hour (includes 30 minutes to rest the puris), plus 4 hours to soak the dal

CHAAT STUFFING

½ cup mung dal

1 russet potato

½ cup canned yellow chickpeas

PURI

1½ cups all-purpose flour

½ cup semolina

¼ teaspoon baking soda

½ teaspoon table salt

½ cup lukewarm water

2 tablespoons vegetable oil, plus more for deep-frying

CHAAT

1 cup whole-milk yogurt

Kosher salt

¼ cup Green Chutney (page 30)

¼ cup Tamarind Chutney, store-bought or homemade (page 29)

1 teaspoon Kashmiri or other red chile powder

1 teaspoon cumin seeds, toasted

1 teaspoon chaat masala

1 teaspoon amchur powder

Prepare the chaat stuffing: In a medium bowl, combine the mung dal and water to cover by 3 inches. Soak for at least 4 hours. Drain and transfer the mung dal to a saucepan. Add enough water to cover by 3 inches. Bring to a boil over high heat, reduce the heat to medium, and simmer until the dal is tender, about 30 minutes. Drain well.

Meanwhile, in a saucepan combine the potato with enough water to cover by 3 inches. Bring the water to a boil over high heat, reduce the heat to medium, and simmer until the potato is tender, about 15 minutes. Drain, and when the potato is cool enough to handle, peel and cut into ½-inch cubes. Note that if the potato is still warm when it's peeled, the skin should slip away, requiring nothing but your hands to remove it.

Set the dal, potato, and chickpeas aside while you make the puri.

Make the puri: In a large bowl, sift together the all-purpose flour, semolina, baking soda, and salt. Create a well in the center and add the warm water and oil. Pull everything together until it forms a shaggy ball and then knead into a stiff dough on a clean, lightly

(RECIPE AND INGREDIENTS CONTINUE)

floured work surface. Add additional water by the tablespoon if the dough struggles to come together. Knead until the surface of the dough is smooth and slightly shiny, about 4 minutes. Place the dough in a bowl, cover with a damp cloth, and set aside at room temperature until the dough is rested, about 30 minutes.

Sev

Boondi (see Note), optional

Pomegranate seeds

Finely chopped fresh cilantro leaves

Finely chopped red onion

Lightly flour a clean work surface and roll the dough out to ⅛ inch thick. Using a 4-inch round biscuit cutter, cut out 4 puri rounds. Discard the scraps.

Line a plate with paper towels. Pour 6 inches oil into a deep heavy-bottomed pot and heat the oil to 350°F on an instant-read thermometer. Carefully drop one puri into the oil. It will puff up into a ball after about 2 minutes. Using a slotted spoon, continuously push it down into the oil, while turning it over a few times, to ensure even cooking time and a uniform color. Once the puri just begins to turn golden brown, after about 3 minutes total, carefully transfer it to the paper towels to drain. Continue to fry all the puris, letting the oil return to 350°F before adding the next puri. Set them aside until they cool to room temperature. This enables the shells to become crispy.

NOTE: *Boondi is an Indian sweet comprised of chickpea flour that is sweetened and fried. It's available at Indian markets and can be omitted should it be difficult to source.*

Assemble the chaat: In a medium bowl, whisk together the yogurt, 2 tablespoons water, and salt to taste. Set aside.

Use your thumb to gently press about a 1½-inch hole into the top of a puri. Set the puri in a bowl and stuff with 1 tablespoon potato, 1 tablespoon chickpeas, and 2 tablespoons mung dal. Spoon a generous amount of yogurt on top and drizzle with green and tamarind chutneys. Sprinkle with chile powder, cumin, chaat masala, and amchur and season with salt. Garnish with sev, boondi (if using), pomegranate, cilantro, and onion. Repeat the process with the remaining puris. Serve immediately.

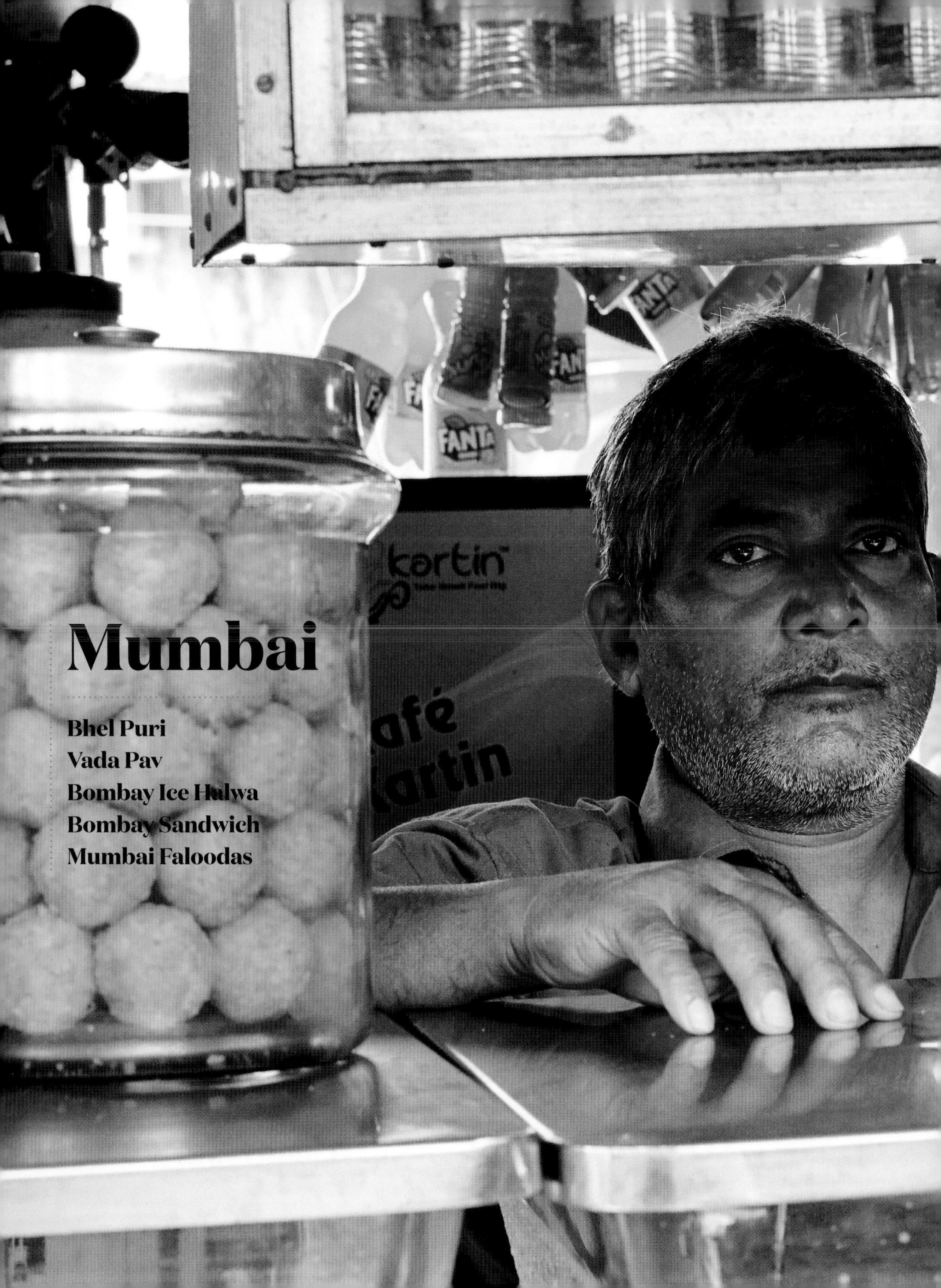

Mumbai

Bhel Puri
Vada Pav
Bombay Ice Halwa
Bombay Sandwich
Mumbai Faloodas

There's a book called *Maximum City: Bombay Lost and Found* by Suketu Mehta that I always think of when my train pulls into the Chhatrapati Shivaji Terminus station (formerly and sometimes still referred to as Victoria Terminus) in Mumbai. *Maximum City* captures the chaotic energy of a city that is perpetually on hyperdrive, running at maximum capacity at all times, never at rest and always pulsating with movement, color, and a bit of bedlam. I could spend a lifetime in the chaat scenes of this wondrously chaotic place. When I was traveling through Mumbai as a child, or later as a university student, the city's intensity overwhelmed me to such a degree that whenever I passed through it, I felt slightly paralyzed, sensing I was only scratching Mumbai's culinary surface, never quite burrowing deep enough to truly understand its food culture.

It was my sister Reeti's husband, Kushal, who finally flung the gastronomic door of Mumbai wide open for me. Kushal is from Mumbai, and because he lived with Reeti in Chicago where I was a chef at a local restaurant for nearly seven years, I spent a lot of quality time with them (mostly in their home kitchen) learning about Mumbai's recipes and culinary traditions, such as how to properly stack the ingredients in a Bombay sandwich and how to knead ice halwa dough. My stateside lessons enriched my visits to this beguiling city because I finally understood where I needed to go to find the best chaat and exactly what to order once I got there. Many of these ambrosial dishes were waiting to be discovered right in the train station, like bhel puri and the Bombay sandwich. But when I stepped off the train after my Chicago education, Mumbai was no longer any random maximum city, it was my maximum city. There are so many facets of Mumbai that I find utterly fascinating, many of which are linked to the railway stations. Mumbai is not only the hub of Bollywood, the Indian movie industry, but it is also the epicenter of finance and commerce. These unusual bedfellows shape the city, whose ultramodern buildings and cutting-edge fashion sense are infused with the quirky energy of a dance-soaked Bollywood film. To serve such a massive and sprawling city, not one but five major stations, and over one hundred local stations, are required, each specializing in different chaat and treats to discover.

Mumbai (formerly known as Bombay) was a critical player during the British colonial era and nowhere is this illustrated more clearly than at the Chhatrapati Shivaji Terminus railway station in the center of the city. Once called Victoria Terminus and today a UNESCO World Heritage Site, this station opened in 1887 and has served as one of India's busiest train stations ever since. Its vast, ornately designed interior reflects a bygone era of British architecture and colonial excess, and the station still bustles with the pulse of thousands of people who spill out of the trains each day.

Besides being a cultural and business hub, Mumbai is a critical Indian seaport and is surrounded by water on three sides. The passengers who pour out of the trains each morning include hundreds of street vendors who arrive at the station carrying baskets on their heads overflowing with fish from one of the myriad seaside markets supplying fresh seafood, like crab, clams, and shrimp, to India's most populous city, with more than twenty-three million people. Deliverymen known as dabbawalas (opposite) are the next wave of train passengers who fill the station in the late morning, on their way to deliver lunch boxes known as tiffins to thousands of Mumbai's office workers each day. Seeing them acrobatically carrying their wooden boxes stuffed with tiffins, teetering on the brink of collapse at all times, is a wondrous thing.

The chaat of Mumbai share the same energy that perpetually pulses through the city. There's something ingenious about the way the seemingly unrelated ingredients in a Bombay sandwich (made of beets, tomatoes, cucumbers, potatoes, and onions) come together with spicy green chutney and pungent chaat masala or the manner in which a falooda, with its tapioca noodles, basil seeds, and ice cream, melds in a topsy-turvy, slightly surreal way that mirrors the mesmerizing chaos of Mumbai. For the uninitiated, all of the random elements don't seem to fit until you step into the madness of it all and realize how adeptly the puzzle pieces lock together. It creates a bewildering pandemonium fueled by chaat as fascinating and nuanced as the people who populate this spellbinding city by the sea.

DHOBI GAAT

Fish and tiffins are my object of fascination at Chhatrapati, but at the Mahalaxmi Station, I'm all about the laundry. It's here at Dhobi Gaat, the largest open-air laundry service in the world, that seven hundred men known as *dhobis* use flogging stones to wash clothing in concrete basins for thousands of residences and businesses each day. Restaurants are one of the most important clients for the dhobis, who hang tablecloths, aprons, chef uniforms, and napkins in tidy rows to flutter as they dry in the briny Mumbai wind.

DABBAWALAS

One of the things I love best about the train stations of Mumbai is the sight of dozens of dabbawalas spilling out of train cars in the late morning wearing their white hats called topis and white linen pajamas called kurtas. Dabbawala translates as "one who carries a box," and in this case the box, called a tiffin, is composed of stackable metal containers filled with homemade dishes like butter chicken, dal makhani, and chapatis.

Mumbai's dabbawala system was devised in 1890 by Mahadeo Havaji Bachche to satisfy the hunger pangs of workers throughout the city. This was long before the era of fast food began, and workers needed to pack their own lunches. Back then, there were about one hundred dabbawalas who picked up lunches packed in tiffin boxes in the early morning from the office employees' families living throughout the countryside. The dabbawalas traveled by train into the city, where they delivered the hot meal to the designated recipient before picking up the empty tiffin at the end of the day to return it to the family. Today, most of the tiffin meals are prepared by central commissaries rather than by families of the office employees—but there are many facets of this fascinating system that remain the same today as they did over 125 years ago.

For example, to get around the fact that many of the dabbawalas are illiterate, a color-coded numbering system designates origin, train line, and destination for the prepared lunch. The numbers are scrawled across the lid of each tiffin, and in spite of the fact that the dabbawala labor force swelled from one hundred men at the turn of the twentieth century to an estimated five hundred thousand employees today who make around two hundred thousand deliveries daily, it's estimated that there is only one mistake per six million transactions! This was a number estimated by the current president of the dabbawala labor union, because he hoped to be granted Six Sigma status (a designation indicating that a business only has 3.4 mistakes per every one million transactions). Even though it was never officially granted, it has inspired leaders of Fortune 500 companies and even Prince Charles to closely explore what makes the dabbawala system such a success.

The formation of a union for the dabbawalas in 1930 ensured job security as well as a steady, dependable income. Each dabbawala is required to contribute his own topi, kurta, wooden crate to carry the tiffins, and two bicycles, one for their use and one as a backup in case the other one becomes damaged. In exchange, he receives on average 8,000 rupees (around $130 US) per month and job security for life. Considering that the average annual income for an Indian is around $1,600, this is a competitive wage. Earnings are divided equally among the members of each union, and employees, most of whom come from a single village near the city of Pune (see page 135), are required to work six days per week. Witnessing the expertly choreographed dance of these culinary artists at one of Mumbai's train stations as they descend upon the city each day is truly a marvel.

Bhel Puri

(PUFFED RICE AND VEGETABLE CHAAT)

Bhel puri, a chaat made of puffed rice, red onions, tomatoes, and cilantro, is one of India's most popular snacks and nearly every region throughout the nation has its own variation, infusing this colorful and nutritious snack with traditional ingredients. In Agra, you might find bhel (for short) made with toasted peanuts, while in Srinagar it's sometimes topped with a green pea sauce. For me, nowhere can rival the show that vendors put on when making bhel puri beneath the ornate arches of the Victoria Terminus. They first spoon all of the ingredients into a large bowl before stirring them up ceremoniously until everything is incorporated. They scoop the chaat into a disposable bowl or a giant cone made from a newspaper before sprinkling it with chaat masala and a squeeze of lime juice. While I love this version best, I have to say that the bhel you can buy along the boardwalk near the beaches is a very close rival—it's virtually a requirement to indulge in bhel during a beach day in Mumbai. Here I share the traditional bhel puri recipe of Mumbai, but feel free to have fun with bhel experimentation by adding peanuts, pomegranate seeds, or even toasted cashews. Mixing together different flavors is as addictive and fun as the chaat itself! While bhel puri is traditionally served in a large cone made from newspaper, you can also serve it in bowls or piled high on a plate.

SERVES 4

PREPARATION TIME: 10 minutes, plus 20 minutes to cook the potato

1 large potato, boiled, peeled, and finely chopped (about 1 cup)

1 medium red onion, finely chopped

1 large tomato, finely chopped

2 serrano chiles, finely chopped

½ cup loosely packed finely chopped fresh cilantro

½ small mango, finely chopped

2 tablespoons Cilantro-Mint Chutney (page 31)

2 tablespoons Tamarind Chutney, store-bought or homemade (page 29)

2 teaspoons cumin seeds, toasted

1 tablespoon chaat masala

1 teaspoon Kashmiri or other red chile powder

½ cup fresh lemon juice (about 2 lemons)

4 cups puffed rice

Kosher salt

Sev

In a large bowl, mix together the potato, onion, tomato, serranos, cilantro, mango, cilantro-mint chutney, tamarind chutney, cumin, chaat masala, chile powder, and lemon juice. Stir well and then add the puffed rice, stirring gently to combine. Season with salt.

Spoon into a cone or bowl and garnish generously with sev. Serve immediately or the puffed rice will become soggy.

Vada Pav

(POTATO FRITTER SANDWICH)

SERVES 4

PREPARATION TIME: 30 minutes

This sandwich is a vegetarian's dream. It's also a nice option for meat lovers looking for a sandwich stuffed with something just as enticing as a burger. Vada pav, one of Mumbai's most popular street foods, is a potato fritter the size of a baseball stuffed into a flaky white bun, smeared with coconut and spicy green chile chutneys, and then squished until it's small enough to fit into your mouth. They're so much fun to eat and are one of my favorite chaat to have on sticky, hot Mumbai afternoons. I loved them when I was a kid because the size of the vada felt insurmountable until I finally sorted out a way to shove it into my mouth, which simply means I squeezed it down enough and opened my mouth wide enough to fit it all inside! I'm looking forward to sharing the exhilarating vada pav experience with my own kids the next time we're in Mumbai.

VADA

3 russet potatoes

2 tablespoons vegetable oil, plus more for deep-frying

1 teaspoon brown mustard seeds

1 teaspoon cumin seeds

½ teaspoon hing (asafetida)

4 fresh curry leaves

1 teaspoon ground turmeric

½ teaspoon Kashmiri or other red chile powder

1-inch piece fresh ginger, peeled with a spoon and finely chopped

2 garlic cloves, minced

Kosher salt

½ cup lightly packed finely chopped fresh cilantro leaves

2 teaspoons chaat masala

Fresh lime juice

1 cup chickpea flour (besan)

1 teaspoon ground coriander

Make the vada: In a saucepan, combine the potatoes and enough water to cover by 3 inches. Bring to a boil over high heat, reduce the heat to medium, and simmer until tender, about 15 minutes. Drain, and once the potatoes are cool enough to handle, peel them using your hands (the skin should slip right off). Place the potatoes in a bowl and mash them with a fork until they are mashed but still slightly chunky.

In a sauté pan, heat 2 tablespoons of oil over medium-high heat until the oil glistens. Add the mustard seeds and cumin seeds and sauté until they begin to hiss, about 2 minutes. Add the hing, curry leaves, turmeric, chile powder, ginger, and garlic. Sauté, stirring often, until the garlic is tender, about 4 minutes. Remove the pan from the heat. Season with salt and then transfer to a large bowl.

Add the potatoes, cilantro, and chaat masala to the spice mixture in the bowl. Stir with a wooden spoon until everything is incorporated. Season with lime juice and salt to taste. Form the mixture into four 2-inch balls and arrange them on a plate in a single layer. Cover with a damp cloth and set aside at room temperature.

In a large bowl, whisk together the chickpea flour and enough water (begin with ¼ cup) to form a paste that resembles thick cake batter. It should not be runny. Stir in the coriander and season with salt.

Line a plate with paper towels. Pour 5 inches oil into a deep heavy-bottomed pot and heat to 350°F on an instant-read thermometer. Dredge the potato balls in the chickpea batter until they are well coated. Shake to remove any excess. Using a slotted spoon, gently lower a vada into the oil and fry until golden brown on all sides, 4 to 6 minutes. Turn with the spoon as it fries to ensure even cooking and browning. Transfer to the paper towels to drain and season with salt. Repeat with the remaining vada.

Assemble the chaat: In a sauté pan, melt the butter over medium heat. Split the buns and place them in the pan, interior-side down; fry until light golden brown, about 1 minute. Place one bun, open and interior sides facing up, on each of four plates. Slather both sides of the bun with green chutney, then spoon coconut chutney on top. Place a vada on the bottom bun and top with fried chiles (if using). Serve with additional chutneys on the side.

CHAAT

1 tablespoon unsalted butter

4 flaky white buns, such as potato or brioche buns

Green Chutney (page 30)

Coconut Chutney, store-bought or homemade (page 159)

Pan-fried serrano chiles (optional)

Bombay Ice Halwa

SERVES 6

PREPARATION TIME: 30 minutes, plus several hours to set the halwa

Ice halwa, also referred to as paper halwa and Mahim halwa, after the Mumbai neighborhood where it was invented, is a beloved delicacy throughout the city and a favorite sweet during Indian holidays like Diwali, the festival of lights celebrated during the autumn months. It's kind of like the Indian version of an Italian ice. The primary ingredients include milk, semolina, sugar, and ghee, a basic and lovely foundation for flavor experimentation—like adding dried dates or figs or topping with crunchy sea salt. The sweet shops in the Mahim district sell everything from rose and saffron halwa garnished with pistachios, almonds, and silver and gold leaf to candied orange halwa with ground cinnamon and cloves. Ice halwa is fairly easy to make, but the trick is in getting the texture right. In the first stage of cooking it seizes up into a ball—I assure you that this is normal. Additional ghee will loosen it up and coax it on its way to a smooth and glossy finish. Take your time, keep the heat low, don't take your eyes off it. With patience and tending to, it will finally reach the desired semifirm and velvety result. It typically takes between 2 and 4 hours of refrigeration for the halwa to set completely, but I've had batches that take up to 24 hours to set. This is a result of the humidity in the environment when the halwa is prepared.

Unsalted butter, at room temperature, for the parchment paper

2 cups whole milk

1 cup sugar

¼ cup semolina flour

5 to 6 tablespoons ghee, store-bought or homemade (page 33)

¼ cup cornstarch

1 teaspoon orange food coloring (or color of preference)

1 teaspoon ground cardamom

Finely chopped pistachios (or finely chopped nuts of preference), about ½ cup

Silver leaf or gold leaf (optional)

Line a sheet pan with parchment paper and coat it with a thin layer of butter. Coat a second sheet of parchment paper (the same size as the first) with butter and set everything aside.

In a large nonstick saucepan, whisk together the milk, sugar, semolina, 4 tablespoons of the ghee, and the cornstarch over medium heat. Heat, stirring nearly constantly to prevent scorching, until the mixture begins to thicken and develops a paste-like consistency, about 5 minutes. Do not let the mixture boil. After 5 minutes, the halwa will detach from the pan sides and form a soft ball. If it starts to burn before it gives way from the sides of the pan, reduce the heat and continue to cook. At this point, add the food coloring and remaining 1 tablespoon ghee and continue to whisk for 1 more minute. This will loosen it up.

Add the cardamom and whisk until incorporated. Continue to whisk constantly until the halwa is glossy, 14 to 17 more minutes. If the halwa begins to seize up again, add an additional 1 tablespoon ghee to loosen it. This will also help it turn its signature glossy orange color. Once the halwa is smooth, pourable, and glossy, scrape it onto the prepared sheet pan and use a silicone spatula or wooden spoon to spread it into an even layer. Top with the second sheet of parchment paper, buttered side down, pressing down gently so it adheres to the surface of the halwa. Use a rolling pin to gently roll the halwa into a thin, even layer. Carefully peel off the top sheet of parchment and sprinkle with pistachios and silver leaf (if using).

Let cool at room temperature for 15 minutes, then transfer to the refrigerator until set, 2 to 4 hours. Use the bottom sheet of parchment to lift the halwa out of the pan. Use scissors to cut the halwa (along with the bottom sheet of parchment) into 3- to 4-inch squares. Leaving the parchment on enables the halwa squares to be stored easily in an airtight container without sticking. The halwa can be refrigerated for up to 1 week.

Bombay Sandwich

MAKES 1 sandwich

PREPARATION TIME: 15 minutes, plus 20 minutes to cook the potato

The Bombay sandwich is Mumbai's most legendary street food offering, found everywhere from train stations and chaat shops to street corners and teahouses. Using white bread might seem to counter the nutritional virtue of this sandwich, but it's the traditional way to serve it and I can't imagine using anything else. When I'm trying to explain the Bombay sandwich to the uninitiated, I often equate it to India's version of a panini, but for me, whose visits to Mumbai were fueled by this wonder, it's so much more than that: It's memory, history, creativity, nostalgia, and love all pressed together between two slices of squishy white bread. I use a panini press to achieve the desired pressed sandwich result, but a skillet and a spatula pressing the sandwich as it cooks works well, too. If using the skillet method, be sure to flip the sandwich halfway through so it toasts up evenly on both sides. Since this sandwich is topped with a handful of shredded cheese before it's served, it's certainly not the tidiest sandwich to eat, but it's guaranteed to be the most fun.

1 small russet potato

Unsalted butter, at room temperature

2 slices white bread

Green Chutney (page 30)

Chaat masala

Cumin seeds, toasted

1 red beet, roasted, peeled, and cut into ⅛-inch-thick slices (see Note)

1 small cucumber, peeled and cut crosswise into 6 ⅛-inch-thick rounds

½ bell pepper (any color), sliced

1 small tomato, cut into ⅛-inch-thick slices

Generous handful of shredded white cheddar cheese

In a saucepan, combine the potato and enough water to cover by 3 inches. Bring to a boil over high heat, reduce the heat, and simmer until the potato is tender, about 15 minutes. Drain, and once the potato is cool enough to handle, peel using your hands (the skin should slip right off) and slice lengthwise into ¼-inch-thick slices.

Smear a generous amount of softened butter on both sides of each slice of bread and repeat the process with the chutney. Arrange the potato slices on one slice of bread and sprinkle with chaat masala and cumin. Top with the beet slices and sprinkle with more chaat masala and cumin. Continue the layering with the cucumber, bell pepper, and tomato, each seasoned with chaat masala and cumin before adding the next vegetable. Top with the other slice of bread and smear the outside of each piece of bread with more butter.

Preheat a panini press or a heavy skillet. Toast the sandwich in the panini press (or in the skillet, using a spatula to press it down) until it's golden brown and crispy (if toasting in a skillet, make sure to flip the sandwich so both sides get golden brown). Place the sandwich on a plate, slice into quarters, and top with the shredded Cheddar. Serve with green chutney on the side.

NOTE: *You can find vacuum-sealed roasted beets in the produce department of most grocery stores.*

Wibs
Wibs

Mumbai Faloodas

The *falooda* shops in Mumbai are a welcoming sight on a sweltering day when the temperature can easily top 115°F. A falooda is essentially an ice cream sundae with a twist (or three). It's not only the ice cream that provides a cool respite from a steamy hot Mumbai afternoon, but also the basil seeds (referred to as *takmaria* in Hindi) that are frequently added because they have a cooling effect on the body (they contribute an effect similar to adding chia seeds to a juice—the seeds become somewhat gelatinous and fun to sip; if you have trouble finding basil seeds, chia seeds are a good substitute). Falooda's origins are in Iran, where *faloodehs* have been enjoyed for centuries. The Indian falooda was introduced by the Mughal empire between the sixteenth and eighteenth centuries. The essential ingredients in a traditional falooda recipe include milk, sugar, ice cream, and a tapioca noodle frequently referred to as *sev*. It's similar to vermicelli noodles and can be found in Indian markets. There are countless falooda flavors served throughout Mumbai, including mango, dried fruit, papaya and saffron, rose and cardamom, kiwi, strawberry, mixed fruit, jackfruit, pistachio, almond, and dragon fruit—to name a few! The flavor combinations are endless, so experiment and have fun with your new go-to summertime ice cream treat.

MAKES 2 faloodas

PREPARATION TIME: 10 minutes, plus 1 hour to chill the milk

2 cups whole milk

2 tablespoons granulated sugar

1 teaspoon ground cardamom

½ cup falooda sev (tapioca noodles), broken into pieces

4 teaspoons basil seeds (takmaria)

4 scoops ice cream (flavor of choice)

Rose syrup, for serving (available at Indian markets)

Finely chopped pistachios, for garnish (optional)

In a medium saucepan, bring the milk, sugar, and cardamom to a simmer over medium-high heat, stirring occasionally until the sugar is dissolved. Remove from the heat and transfer the mixture to a heatproof container. Refrigerate the cardamom milk until well chilled.

Bring a small pot of water to a boil over high heat. Add the falooda sev and cook until tender, about 6 minutes. Drain and set aside. The noodles might get sticky as they cool, but they will break apart again once they are added to the liquid.

Meanwhile, in a small bowl, cover the basil seeds with lukewarm water and set aside until they are soft and gelatinous, 7 to 8 minutes.

To assemble the faloodas, place a scoop of ice cream in the bottom of two sundae glasses. Top with the noodles, drizzle with rose syrup, and add enough cardamom milk to cover the noodles. Sprinkle with the basil seeds, top each with another scoop of ice cream, and garnish with pistachios.

Goa

Feni Cocktail
Ros Omelette
Prawn Rissóis
Goan Beef Cutlet Pão
Fish Recheado
Potato Egg Chutney Chops

My first job after I graduated from the Culinary Institute of America in New York's Hyde Park was running my aunt and uncle Bhupinder and Vinnie Dhillon's Indian restaurant in Cherry Hill, New Jersey. The dishes we served were fairly unadulterated versions of classic Indian recipes, but there was always a part of me that dreamed of creating recipes that melded culinary traditions from different corners of the world into a single dish. This desire was why I hopped in my Mazda Miata after three years in New Jersey and drove to Chicago, where I ran a restaurant there (and eventually in New York as well) that served dishes punctuated with influences from both Mexico and India. These traditions might seem at first like unlikely bedfellows, but for me, identifying elements in one culinary repertoire that pair well with another makes perfect sense.

The seed to my thinking about recipes unhindered by geographical boundaries began when I was a child living in a building that was home to engineers from virtually every state in India. I would gobble down the meal my mother prepared for me before running to one of our neighbor's apartments, lamenting that my mother hadn't fed me again. Taking pity on me, they would share their meal, which included dishes from whatever state in India they were from. I loved identifying the elements that were similar to my mom's style of cooking while at the same time picking out those that were different. It was in the humble kitchens of my childhood neighbors where the idea of combining different culinary traditions—which I now celebrate at my Nashville-based restaurant, Chauhan Ale & Masala House—first took root. At Chauhan, I have items on my menu like hot chicken pakoras and tandoori chicken poutine that reflect my obsession with bringing culinary heritages together on a single plate.

My trips to Goa as a child and later as a college student were integral to shaping my conviction that recipes do not have to exist in geographical silos. From the sixteenth to the early twentieth century, Goa was a colony of Portugal, resulting in cuisine heavily influenced by both Indian and Portuguese culinary practices, which fused over the centuries into a cuisine that is singularly Goan. Ingredients like red beans, paprika, pork, and shrimp find their way into Indian dishes like red beans with braised pork,

ABOVE LEFT: *Goan mutton xacutti.*
ABOVE RIGHT: *Beibenca.*

curries spiked with paprika, and shrimp turnovers. A dish that might be served medium-spicy in Portugal is sweat-inducing in Goa.

One of the most powerful lessons I took from my trips to Goa, a sprawling city on the edge of the Arabian Sea on the southwestern coast of India, was at the Vasco da Gama railway station a few miles from town. It was here that I first tried a prawn *rissóis*. It looked like a Portuguese empanada (which of course is a culinary tradition borrowed from Brazil), but on the inside, its ingredients and flavor profile mirrored the repertoires of Indian and Portuguese cooking, with shrimp, chiles, nutmeg, onions, and Cheddar cheese. As with so many dishes when I travel to Goa, it was a revelation.

I took the lessons I learned in Goa with me to the United States, where I have no problem adding a black-eyed pea tikki burger to my menu. Ultimately, it's all about flavor and texture, and when I look at the delight in my guests' eyes when they bite into it, I know I've nailed it. They don't care about the narrative and purity of a dish, they're looking for something that invigorates their taste buds, perks up their senses, and encourages them to dream about new places and new flavor combinations from all corners of the world. I hope they discover that culinary traditions from different parts of the planet can share a place at the table together. In this chapter, I show off some of my favorite Goan dishes, like potato egg chutney chops and beef cutlet pão.

Feni Cocktail

This cocktail melds two unique Indian beverages, Limca and feni. Limca is a brand of effervescent lemon-lime soda that's especially welcome on blistering hot Goan days at the beach. If you can't find Limca, you can use any lemon or lime soda as a substitute. Feni (a strong brandy made from cashew fruit and produced in small batches) packs a peppery punch and is a Goan specialty. Cocktails are almost never served on board Indian trains, unless they are specialty trains that have restaurants, such as the Palace on Wheels of Rajasthan; but there is often a cocktail bar near the train station that I make a beeline for after a long journey. In addition to cashew feni, there are other feni varieties, such as those derived from palm fruit and coconut. But it's the subtle toasted notes of cashew feni that make this spirit feel truly singular, and no visit to Goa is complete without a sip or two. But tread lightly—feni sneaks up on you!

MAKES 1 cocktail

PREPARATION TIME: 5 minutes

2 ounces feni (or brandy if you have trouble finding feni)

2 teaspoons fresh lime juice

Ice

Limca or other lemon-lime soda, as needed

Lemon or lime wedge, for garnish

Add the feni and lime juice to a tall ice-filled glass. Top with the Limca and stir. Garnish with a lemon or lime wedge and serve.

Ros Omelette

(OMELET WITH TOMATO GRAVY)

SERVES 4

PREPARATION TIME: 30 minutes

Upon disembarking from the train and entering the Vasco da Gama train station, the ros omelettes prepared near the station entrance are too enticing to pass up. The aroma of the omelet begins to waft through the air from vendor stalls throughout Goa when the sun begins to set and doesn't stop until well after midnight, after tourists and locals alike have satisfied their cravings. *Ros* means "gravy" in Hindi and it's this spicy element that makes this a unique specialty of the region. The coconut gives the gravy a tropical vibe and the tomatoes and chiles add depth and heat. Goa is like the Ibiza of India, and this omelet, with its rich, comforting, fiery gravy, is enjoyed for breakfast, lunch, and dinner. Of course, you could also whip it up deep into the night, the time when most Goan partygoers looking for something to fuel their endless dancing sessions seek it out on the lively Goan streets.

ROS

- 1 tablespoon coconut oil
- 1 small yellow onion, finely chopped
- 1 medium tomato, coarsely chopped
- 1 tablespoon store-bought ginger-garlic paste
- 1 teaspoon ground turmeric
- ½ teaspoon Kashmiri or other red chile powder
- 1 tablespoon store-bought coconut paste (available in Indian markets)
- 1 teaspoon garam masala
- Kosher salt

OMELET

- 10 large eggs
- 1 teaspoon Kashmiri or other red chile powder
- Kosher salt
- 2 tablespoons vegetable oil or coconut oil
- 1 medium yellow onion, finely chopped
- 2 green chiles, finely chopped
- Lime wedges, for serving
- Finely chopped onion, for serving

Make the ros: In a medium sauté pan, heat the oil over medium-high heat until glistening, about 2 minutes. Add the onion and sauté until translucent, about 5 minutes. Add the tomato, ginger-garlic paste, turmeric, and chile powder and sauté, stirring occasionally, until the tomatoes begin to break apart, about 5 minutes longer. Stir in the coconut paste and garam masala and cook until everything is well incorporated and the smell of coconut perfumes the air, about 5 more minutes. Add a little water, if needed, to achieve a loose gravy texture. Season with salt and set aside.

Make the omelet: In a large bowl, whisk together the eggs and season with the chile powder and salt. In a sauté pan, heat the oil over medium-high heat and sauté the onion and chile peppers, stirring occasionally, until the onions are translucent, about 5 minutes. Reduce the heat to medium and pour the eggs into the pan. Rotate the pan in a circle as the omelet cooks to ensure even distribution of the eggs. Once the center of the omelet is just set, 4 to 6 minutes, flip the omelet onto itself to form a half-moon shape. Season with salt, transfer to a plate, and spoon the warm ros on top. Garnish with a lime wedge and raw onions.

Prawn Rissóis

(FRIED SHRIMP TURNOVERS)

SERVES 6

PREPARATION TIME: 45 minutes

We have the Portuguese to thank for these addictive fried turnovers stuffed with shrimp. They are essentially the Goan version of an empanada, and I would suggest doubling the batch because they go fast. They can be prepared ahead of time up to the stage of frying and refrigerated in a covered container for up to 1 day. Serve with a variety of chutneys for dipping. I love picking these up at the station and stuffing them into my bag for the long journey ahead of me. They're so portable and even taste good cold. In America, I love bringing them to potlucks, serving them at summer picnics, or piling a plate with them at birthday parties.

FILLING

1 tablespoon unsalted butter

1 small yellow onion, finely chopped

1 teaspoon minced garlic

1 pound medium to large shrimp, peeled, deveined and coarsely chopped (about 1½ cups)

¾ cup whole milk

Salt and freshly ground black pepper

1 tablespoon all-purpose flour

¼ cup shredded Cheddar cheese

¼ teaspoon freshly grated nutmeg

PASTRY

2 cups whole milk

3 tablespoons unsalted butter

2 cups all-purpose flour, plus more for kneading and shaping

Kosher salt

Vegetable oil, for the bowl

Make the filling: In a sauté pan, melt the butter over medium heat. Add the onion and garlic and sauté until the onion is translucent, about 5 minutes. Add the shrimp and sauté, stirring often, until they turn light pink, 3 to 4 minutes. Stir in the milk and season with salt and pepper to taste.

In a small bowl, stir together the flour and 1 tablespoon water to make a slurry. Add the slurry to the shrimp and cook, stirring occasionally, until the liquid is slightly thickened, 3 to 5 minutes. Remove from the heat and stir in Cheddar and nutmeg. Refrigerate until chilled.

Make the pastry: In a saucepan, combine the milk and butter and cook over medium-high heat, stirring occasionally with a wooden spoon to prevent the milk from scalding. Once the butter is melted, reduce the heat to medium, add the flour, season with salt, and, stirring constantly, cook until a smooth dough forms and it comes together in a ball and begins to pull away from the side of the pan, 5 to 8 minutes. Tend to the mixture carefully during this process to prevent it from burning; if it becomes too hot and begins to burn before coming together and clearing the sides of the pan, remove the pan from the heat for 30 seconds to cool the dough, then reduce the heat and set the pan back over the heat, stirring until a dough forms. Once a dough forms, turn it out into a bowl and set aside until it's cool enough to handle.

Once the dough has cooled enough to handle (but is still warm), dust a clean work surface with flour and knead the dough until it's smooth and springs back when poked with your finger, 4 to 6 minutes. Oil a medium bowl, add the dough, cover with a damp towel, and set aside for 30 minutes.

FOR ASSEMBLY AND SERVING

- 2 large eggs
- 1 cup dried bread crumbs
- Vegetable oil, for deep-frying
- Kosher salt
- Chutneys or dipping sauces, as desired

Assemble the rissóis: On a lightly floured work surface, roll the dough out to ⅛ inch thick. Use a 2-inch round cookie or biscuit cutter to cut 2-inch rounds out of the dough, resulting in approximately 24 2-inch rounds. Fill a small bowl with water and lightly dab water around the edges of a dough round. Spoon about 1 tablespoon filling in the center of the round and fold the dough over to form a half-moon shape. Press the edges together to close securely. Repeat with the remaining dough rounds and filling.

In a small bowl, lightly beat the eggs. Place the bread crumbs in a second bowl. Dip both sides of the turnover in the egg with one hand and shake lightly to remove excess. Using your dry hand, dredge the pastry in the bread crumbs, shaking to remove any excess. Transfer to a plate and repeat with the remaining turnovers.

Line a plate with paper towels. Pour 2 inches oil into a medium sauté pan and heat the oil over medium-high heat to 325°F on an instant-read thermometer. Working with 5 or 6 rissóis at a time (do not overcrowd the pan), use tongs to place the turnovers into the oil. Cook until the pastries are golden brown on the bottom, about 2 minutes, then flip over and cook until the filling is cooked through, an additional 2 to 3 minutes. Transfer to the paper towels to drain and season with salt.

Serve while still hot with a variety of chutneys or dipping sauces.

Goan Beef Cutlet Pão

(FRIED BEEF SANDWICH)

MAKES 12 sandwiches

PREPARATION TIME: 30 minutes, plus 4 hours to overnight to marinate the beef

Since the consumption of beef is prohibited in the Hindu religion and is virtually impossible to find in most parts of India, this is a rare recipe where beef is celebrated, topped with a vibrant salad and stuffed into a bun. Note that the beef needs to marinate for at least 4 hours before it's prepared. The beef in this sandwich is a reflection of the Portuguese Catholic-inspired cooking of Goa. It's due to the Catholic influence that beef is acceptable in Goa. In most of the other parts of India, where Hinduism is the primary religion, cows are considered sacred because Hindus believe they represent Mother Earth, and beef is strictly taboo. Cows are allowed to wander wherever they like, including train stations. I'll never forget the time Jody and I were standing on an indoor train platform waiting to board a train from Mumbai to Goa. I felt something massive push us apart and looked over to discover a cow standing between us. We looked at each other and laughed across the knotty shoulders of our new bovine friend. She stood there with us, staring straight ahead, until our train arrived several minutes later. I was sad to bid her farewell.

CUTLETS

- 2 tablespoons minced garlic
- 1-inch piece fresh ginger, peeled with a spoon and finely chopped
- 4 green chiles, finely chopped
- 10 black peppercorns
- Kosher salt
- 1 beef tenderloin (4 pounds), trimmed of excess fat and sinew and cut crosswise into 12 equal medallions
- Malt vinegar
- 1½ cups semolina
- Vegetable oil, for pan-frying

SALAD

- 2 large carrots, peeled and shredded
- 2 cups shredded green cabbage
- 1 tablespoon fresh lime juice
- ½ tablespoon distilled white vinegar
- 1 teaspoon sugar
- Kosher salt

Make the cutlets: In a blender or mini food processor, combine the garlic, ginger, chiles, and peppercorns and blend on high speed to form a paste. Season with salt.

Sandwich each beef medallion between sheets of parchment or plastic wrap and pound with a mallet or meat tenderizer to about ¼ inch thick. Season the cutlets with salt and sprinkle with malt vinegar. Spread the garlic-ginger paste all over the cutlets, transfer them to a bowl, cover, and refrigerate for 4 hours or overnight.

Line a plate with paper towels. Place the semolina in a bowl and dredge each cutlet through it, shaking to remove any excess. In a sauté pan, heat 3 tablespoons oil over medium-high heat until it glistens, about 3 minutes. Fry 3 cutlets at a time until golden brown on both sides, about 4 minutes per side. Transfer to the paper towels and season with salt. Add more oil as needed to fry the remaining cutlets.

Make the salad: In a large bowl, toss together the carrots, cabbage, lime juice, white vinegar, and sugar. Season with salt, cover the bowl with plastic wrap, and refrigerate until ready to serve.

Assemble the pão: In a small bowl, stir together the mayonnaise and ketchup. Slather both sides of the bun with it. Top each side of a bun with a beef cutlet. Spoon salad on top of one of the cutlets, close the sandwich, and serve.

FOR ASSEMBLY

¼ cup mayonnaise

¼ cup ketchup

6 pillowy white sandwich buns, split open

Fish Recheado

(FRIED FISH STUFFED WITH CHILE PASTE)

SERVES 4

PREPARATION TIME: 30 minutes, plus 2 hours 30 minutes to marinate

16 dried red chiles, broken into small pieces

8 medium garlic cloves, minced

1-inch piece fresh ginger, peeled with a spoon and finely chopped

2 tablespoons tamarind paste

1 tablespoon sugar

1½ teaspoons freshly ground black pepper

1 teaspoon cumin seeds

1 teaspoon ground turmeric

1 teaspoon ground cardamom

1 cinnamon stick, crushed using the bottom of a pan

½ teaspoon fenugreek seeds

4 whole cloves

¼ cup distilled white vinegar

Kosher salt

4 whole 12-ounce pomfret, rinsed and scored

Vegetable oil, for shallow-frying

Lime wedges, for serving

Icy cold beer

I have fond memories of the fish stands that line the beaches of Goa, the vendors selling fresh seafood straight from the sea and then frying it up on the spot. One of my favorite beaches is Colva, which is about three miles and a quick rickshaw ride away from the Madgaon Junction train station. My friends and I would inhale the chiles from the fish recheado at cheap plastic tables set up next to the lapping ocean waves, always at sunset, digging our bare feet into the sand while sipping beer between bites of freshly fried fish. Fish recheado was one of my favorites, a Goan specialty featuring the spicy-tangy flavor of tamarind and red chiles. The ingredient list might be long, but the steps are easy and it all comes together in no time. The fish is served whole, for dramatic effect. Please note that the fish should be marinated for at least 30 minutes before it's fried. It's the perfect dish to serve on a lazy summer evening. If you have trouble sourcing pomfret, a white-fleshed fish, substitute barramundi or mackerel.

In a medium bowl, combine the chiles, garlic, ginger, tamarind, sugar, pepper, cumin, turmeric, cardamom, cinnamon pieces, fenugreek, cloves, and vinegar and stir well to combine. Cover and set aside at room temperature for 2 hours for the flavors to mingle. Then transfer to a food processor and blend at high speed to form a paste. Season the paste with salt.

Place the whole fish on a sheet pan and season the exterior and the interior cavities with salt. Stuff about 1 tablespoon of the paste into the fish and then coat the fish on both sides with paste. Refrigerate for 30 minutes.

Line a second sheet pan with paper towels. Pour ½ inch oil into a large sauté pan and heat it over medium-high heat until it glistens, about 2 minutes. Using tongs, place one fish in the oil and fry until golden brown on both sides, about 3 minutes per side. Transfer to the paper towels and season with salt on both sides. Repeat with the remaining fish.

Serve while still hot with lime wedges and icy cold beer.

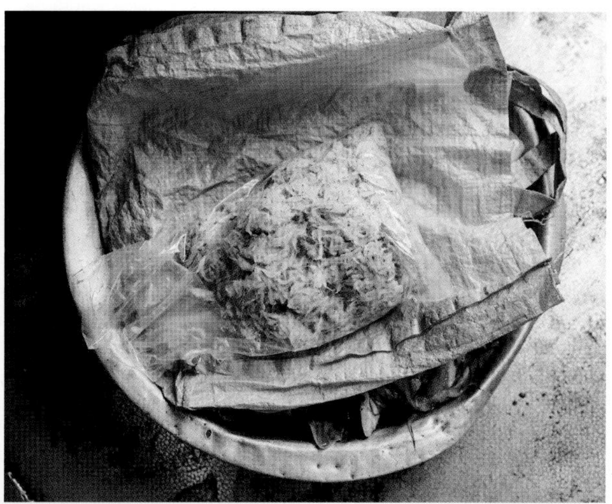

Potato Egg Chutney Chops

(GOAN SCOTCH EGGS)

I refer to these as the Goan version of Scotch eggs. The preparation is remarkably similar with the addition of spices and other aromatics. There was almost always a potato egg chutney chop vendor waiting for me upon my disembarkation at the train station in Goa. (The word *chop* is sometimes used in India to refer to an appetizer-sized snack.) I'd gobble up one (or three) the moment I exchanged my rupees for one of these delicacies. It laid the perfect foundation for soaking up all the feni (page 23) I inevitably found myself enjoying with friends during our festive nights (and early mornings) in Goa. The potato mixture should be quite dry or it will become soggy when fried and will not hold together. Serve the chops while still very hot with a dash of hot sauce.

MAKES 8 chops

PREPARATION TIME: 30 minutes, plus 20 minutes to cook the potatoes

CHUTNEY

- 1 cup unsweetened shredded coconut
- 1 cup lightly packed finely chopped fresh cilantro leaves
- 4 green chiles, finely chopped
- 2 garlic cloves, minced
- 1 teaspoon cumin seeds, toasted
- Pinch of sugar
- Fresh lemon juice
- Kosher salt

CHOPS

- 2 russet potatoes, boiled, peeled, and coarsely chopped
- 2 tablespoons all-purpose flour, plus more if needed
- 1 teaspoon cumin seeds, toasted
- 1 teaspoon freshly ground black pepper
- ½ cup finely chopped fresh cilantro leaves
- Kosher salt
- 4 hard-boiled eggs, peeled and halved lengthwise
- 3 fresh eggs
- 1½ cups dried bread crumbs
- Vegetable oil

Make the chutney: In a bowl, combine the coconut, cilantro, chiles, garlic, cumin, and sugar and stir to incorporate. Season to taste with lemon juice and salt.

Make the chops: Use a potato ricer to rice the potatoes into a bowl. Stir in the flour, cumin, black pepper, and cilantro. The texture should be on the dry side or it will turn into a gooey mess when fried. If it's too wet, add a little flour. Season with salt.

On a clean work surface, spoon about 2 tablespoons potato mixture, top with ½ teaspoon chutney, and place an egg half, yolk side down, in the center of it. Top with another ½ teaspoon chutney and 2 tablespoons potatoes and using your hands, shape the chop into an oval, making sure that the edges are sealed around the egg. Repeat with the remaining potato mixture and hard-boiled eggs.

Beat the fresh eggs in a small bowl and place the bread crumbs in a second bowl. Line a plate with paper towels. Pour 4 inches oil into a saucepan and heat the oil over medium-high heat until a drop of flour sizzles when it hits the surface of the oil. Dredge the chops first in beaten egg and then in the bread crumbs, shaking to remove excess. Working in batches of 2 (do not overcrowd the pan), fry the chops until golden brown, 6 to 8 minutes. Carefully remove with tongs, transfer to the paper towels to drain, and season with salt. Allow the oil to return to frying temperature between batches.

Pune and Ahmedabad

Kanda Bhaji
Panki
Khaman Dhokla
Khandvi
Kande Pohe
Mango Mastani

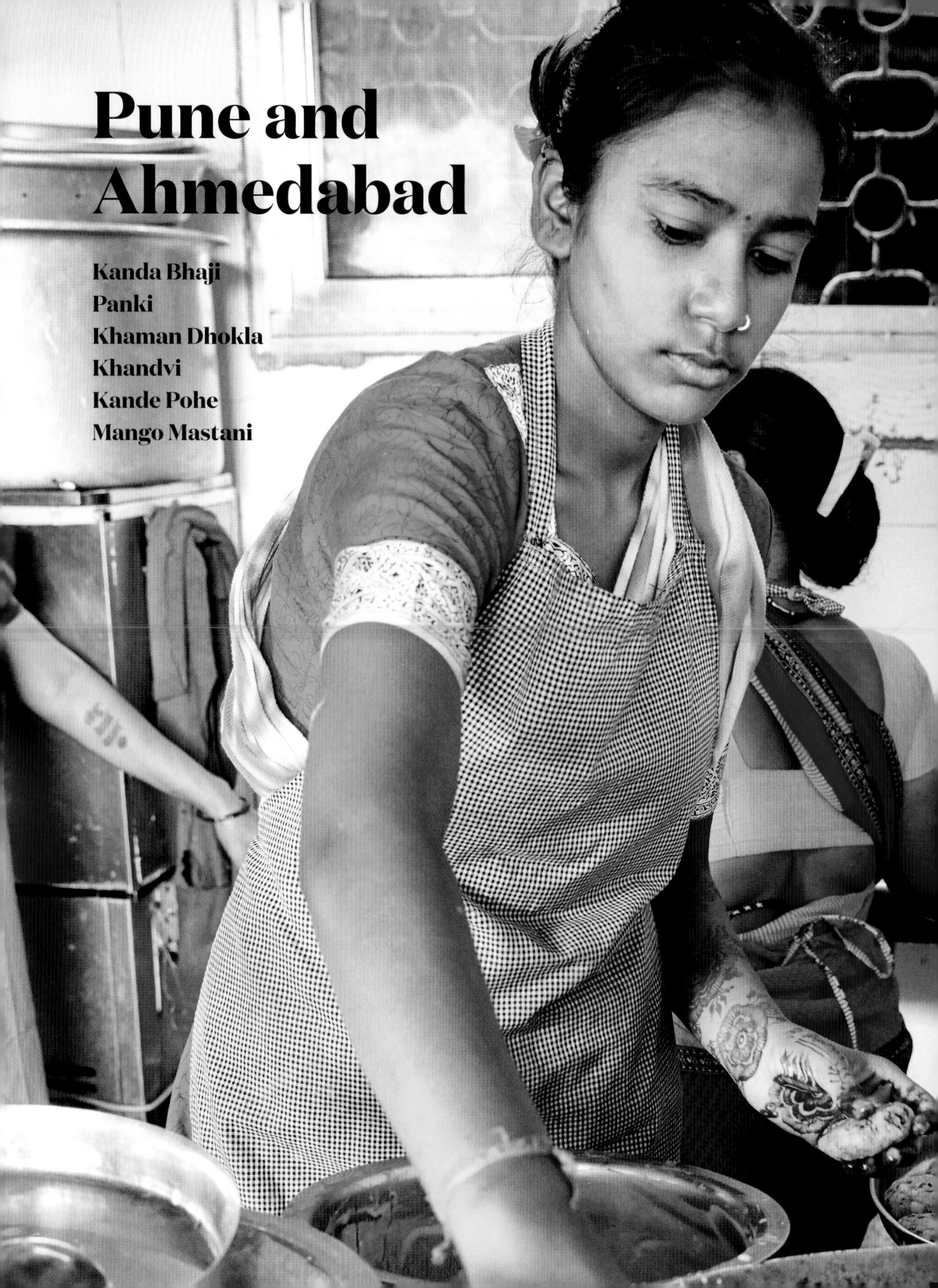

The first time I tried Gujarati cuisine was during a college break when I traveled on the train with classmates from Manali in the far north of India to the station at Chandigarh before transferring to a local train for Ahmedabad. The long journey took well over six hours to complete. I didn't mind, because it afforded me the chance to indulge in chaat I discovered at the stations along the way. I was a little apprehensive about Gujarati cuisine because I suspected it might be too simplistic for my culinary taste. I soon discovered how wrong I was when a vendor approached our train window with a platter of dhokla during one of our stops just after we entered the state of Gujarat. The bright yellow cake, neatly cut into squares, was made from rice and chickpea flour and arranged in pairs on shiny silver paper plates. Each duo was topped with fried cilantro, freshly shaved coconut, and a vibrant ribbon of green chutney. I was sold on the presentation alone until I popped one into my mouth. The fermented batter aerates the dough as it bakes, resulting in a texture akin to angel food cake; it has a perky flavor, as bright as its golden hue. I "accidentally" gobbled up my friend's dokhla, too, but thankfully it all happened so fast that the vendor was still waiting at the train window for her rupees. I greedily snatched up four more orders before the train set off again. My friend was shaking her head at me in disbelief as she reached for one of the plates that I promptly snatched away from her. "What? Didn't you get any for yourself?" I asked her (only half joking). She grinned and said, "Must you eat everything you see?" I reluctantly handed her the plate, guarding the other three like a pirate who finally discovered her treasure chest after years of searching.

I ate nonstop during that Ahmedabad visit, but it wasn't until I moved to New Jersey to help my aunt and uncle manage their restaurant that I was able to cook Gujarati cuisine for the first time. There is a large community of Gujarati expats in this region of the country, and I met one of its matriarchs when she stopped into the restaurant for a cup of chai and a chat with my aunt who she had known for years. As I often do, because I have no shame when it comes to cooking, I invited myself over to her house to learn more about Gujarati cuisine.

TOP: *Dal Dhokli.*
BOTTOM: *Handva.*

I begin popping khandvi rolls into my mouth the moment I arrive at Ahmedabad Junction and don't stop until I leave the region, so I was very excited to learn that the first recipe we'd make together was khandvi, a tangy, velvety roll made from turmeric, buttermilk, and chickpea flour and topped with fried mustard seeds, fried garlic, and coconut chutney. While she deftly smoothed the khandvi batter onto a plate, a skill that is tricky to master but that, like anything, improves with practice, I asked her if she had any tips to share about Gujarati cuisine. Without hesitation she replied, "It's easy. We Gujaratis believe in living simply because the most beautiful things are waiting to be discovered when life is lived with an uncluttered mind. The same is true for our cooking. Remove the obstacles and anything that is not absolutely necessary and you will understand the secret of Gujarati cooking."

Gujaratis believe in having the "right belief, right knowledge, and right conduct," treading lightly upon the earth until they are reincarnated (if they do not achieve enlightenment in their present state). When I bite into the simple, tangy rice flour pancake called a panki or prepare kande pohe, an airy rice dish requiring very little cooking time, I'm reminded of the Gujarati way of living and eating: Walk softly yet deliberately, without burdening yourself with heavy meals, and focus on dishes that require very little investment from the planet. Pune is home to the Aga Khan Palace, where Mahatma Gandhi's ashes are located. Gandhi, being Gujarati, was heavily influenced by the benevolence many Gujaratis try to embrace throughout their day. I usually begin my Pune culinary adventure at the train station, where the food embodies the sweet, tangy, and spicy flavor combination that I'm always on a quest to discover in my snacks and chaat.

There's something that appeals to me about the buoyancy and simplicity of Gujarati cuisine. Its character is humble yet self-assured, the flavor profile complex yet straightforward. Even the Indian prime minister, Narendra Modi, sees the appeal of Gujarati dishes: It's the style of cooking he frequently serves to visiting dignitaries. It must be his way of embracing the spirit of Gandhi, who reminded us that "Happiness is when what you think, what you say, and what you do are in harmony." I'd like to add "what you eat" to that sentiment.

Kanda Bhaji

(CRUNCHY ONION FRITTERS)

Kanda bhaji, a crunchy onion fritter, is a favorite teatime snack in Maharashtra, and my snack of choice for the train ride from Pune to Mumbai. The three-hour journey equates to at least three or four opportunities to buy a cup of chai from the chaiwalas who rush on board the train at every stop along the way. Since I need at least three fritters for a proper chai drinking experience, I typically pick up four orders from the train vendor before climbing aboard. Kanda bhaji are best served hot and fresh because they can become oily over time, but even when I space them out to last the entire journey, the extra grease doesn't bother me; in fact, I consider shiny fingers upon arrival a sure sign that I ate well along the way.

SERVES 4

PREPARATION TIME: 25 minutes

2 red onions, quartered and thinly sliced crosswise

2 serrano chiles, finely chopped

1 tablespoon store-bought ginger-garlic paste

1 tablespoon finely chopped fresh cilantro

Kosher salt

½ cup chickpea flour (besan)

2 tablespoons rice flour

2 tablespoons cornstarch

½ teaspoon Kashmiri or other red chile powder

½ teaspoon ground turmeric

½ teaspoon ajwain seeds

Vegetable oil, for shallow-frying

Chaat masala

Chutney, store-bought or homemade (pages 29–31)

Sour cream (optional), for serving

In a large bowl, toss together the onions, serranos, ginger-garlic paste, and cilantro. Season with salt and then set aside for 10 minutes to allow the flavors to mingle. Stir in the chickpea flour, rice flour, cornstarch, chile powder, turmeric, and ajwain.

Line a plate with paper towels. Pour ½ inch oil into a sauté pan and heat over medium-high heat until a pinch of flour sizzles when it hits the surface of the oil. Reduce the heat to medium, and working in batches (do not overcrowd the pan), use a tablespoon to drop fritters into the oil and fry until they're golden brown, about 2 minutes. Flip them over using tongs or a fork and brown on the second side, about 2 minutes. Transfer to the paper towels to drain, then season with chaat masala. Allow the oil to return to frying temperature between batches.

Serve hot with chutney and sour cream (if using).

Panki

(BANANA-LEAF-WRAPPED YOGURT AND RICE PANCAKES)

MAKES 4 panki

PREPARATION TIME: 10 minutes, plus 8 hours to ferment the batter

The first time I tried panki was on a train journey to Ahmedabad a few years ago. At a rural stop along the way, a woman wearing a lively orange sari trimmed in lime green ribbon approached the train window with a basket filled with banana leaf parcels. When I asked her what was inside, she told me it was panki. I asked her what it was just as the train started moving again. We both realized she wasn't going to have time to tell me and I quickly handed her ten rupees (about fifteen cents) in exchange for my panki. As the train heaved its way out of the station, she called out, "Don't worry. You'll like it!" I quickly unwrapped the leaf to discover the steamed golden pancake inside and used my fingers to scoop a bite onto my tongue. My mouth was flooded with a subtle tartness that was enhanced by ginger, a flash of heat from the green chiles and a lingering smokiness from the grill. I finished my first panki in four quick bites and regretted not buying more from the woman in the orange sari. She was right. I did like it.

Panki reflects the Gujarati philosophy of simple cooking with humble ingredients. It's easy to digest and has an appealing tangy lightness due to the yogurt and the fermented batter. It can be served hot or cold and holds together well, making it ideal for traveling. If you don't have access to a grill, fry the panki in a skillet slicked with oil—and if banana leaves aren't available, substitute foil. Note that the batter takes 8 hours to ferment.

2 serrano chiles

1 cup rice flour

½ cup whole-milk yogurt

1 teaspoon grated fresh ginger

½ cup finely chopped fresh cilantro leaves

¼ teaspoon ground turmeric

Pinch of hing (asafetida)

Kosher salt

Vegetable oil, as needed

4 banana leaves (optional)

Coconut Chutney, store-bought or homemade (page 159), for serving

In a blender, combine the chiles with 2 teaspoons water and puree on high speed until it forms a thick paste (add a little more water if needed). Transfer the chile paste to a large bowl and add the rice flour, yogurt, ginger, cilantro, turmeric, and hing and whisk to combine. Season with salt. Cover the bowl with a damp towel and set aside at room temperature for 8 hours to allow the batter to ferment.

Preheat an outdoor or indoor grill to medium heat. If not using banana leaves, cut out four 12 × 16-inch rectangles of foil. Grease the interior of the banana leaves or foil with oil. Using an offset spatula, spread about ½ cup of the batter in the center of each leaf or foil, leaving enough of the leaf edge uncovered to enable it to fold over the panki. Fold the edges over the panki to form packets and transfer them to the grill, folded side down. Grill until the batter is cooked through, about 3 minutes per side. The batter is cooked once the packet feels slightly firm. The banana leaves will develop grill marks during this step. Serve hot or cold with coconut chutney on the side.

Khaman Dhokla

(FERMENTED CHICKPEA FLOUR CAKES)

SERVES 8

PREPARATION TIME: 1 hour, plus 8 hours to ferment the dhokla batter

Dhokla is one of the most popular street snacks in the state of Gujarat, reflecting the vegetarian principles of the Jain religion. The fermented chickpea batter results in a light and airy snack that is as comforting for breakfast as it is as a midday pick-me-up. It's important to allow enough time for the batter to ferment properly in order to guarantee dhokla's signature fluffy texture and slightly pungent flavor note. This recipe calls for citric acid. If you have trouble sourcing it, substitute an equal amount of baking soda.

DHOKLA

- 1 cup chickpea flour (besan)
- 1½ tablespoons semolina
- 1 tablespoon sugar
- 1 teaspoon ground ginger
- Pinch of hing (asafetida)
- ½ teaspoon table salt
- Vegetable oil
- ½ teaspoon citric acid
- 1 teaspoon finely chopped green chiles

GARNISH

- 1 tablespoon mustard oil
- 1 teaspoon brown mustard seeds
- 1 teaspoon black mustard seeds
- 12 fresh curry leaves
- 5 green chiles, finely chopped
- 3 tablespoons finely chopped fresh cilantro, plus more for sprinkling
- 1 teaspoon ground turmeric
- Juice of 1 lemon
- 2 teaspoons sugar
- Kosher salt
- Unsweetened shredded coconut, for sprinkling

Make the dhokla batter: In a large bowl, whisk together the chickpea flour and semolina. Whisk in the sugar, ginger, hing, salt, 2½ tablespoons of oil, citric acid, and chiles. The batter should resemble a slightly fluffy sponge cake batter. If it's too thick, add water 1 tablespoon at a time until it has an airy texture. Cover the bowl with a damp cloth and set aside at room temperature for 8 hours to ferment. Preheat the oven to 350°F. Grease an 11 × 7-inch cake pan with oil.

Fill a roasting pan that is big enough for the cake pan to fit into with 1 inch of boiling water. Pour the dhokla batter into the greased pan and use a spatula to spread into an even layer. Cover with foil, carefully place in the water bath, and transfer to the oven. Oven-steam the dhokla until it has risen, the texture is light and airy, and a toothpick inserted into the center comes out clean, 15 to 20 minutes. Remove from the oven and cool for 30 minutes.

Meanwhile, make the garnish: In a sauté pan, heat the mustard oil over medium heat until it glistens, about 3 minutes. Add the brown and black mustard seeds, and once they begin to pop, after about 2 minutes, reduce the heat to low, add the curry leaves and chiles, and sauté until the chiles are tender, about 3 minutes. Stir in the cilantro, turmeric, lemon juice, sugar, and 3 tablespoons water. Remove the pan from the heat and stir until the sugar dissolves, then season to taste with salt.

Use a knife to separate the dhokla from the edges of the pan. Carefully invert it onto a clean, flat work surface. Cut into 1 × 2-inch squares and then pour the garnish on top. Sprinkle with cilantro and coconut and serve warm or cold.

Khandvi

(CHICKPEA FLOUR AND BUTTERMILK ROLLS)

MAKES 12 rolls

PREPARATION TIME: 30 minutes

Khandvi is a refreshing snack that embodies the lightness of Gujarati cuisine. The khandvi batter is made with chickpea flour and this, along with turmeric, results in a vibrant gold color. The buttermilk offers the tanginess that is a signature of Gujarati cooking. The tricky part of this recipe is to ensure that the khandvi batter does not become too thick when it's heated. If it thickens too much, it will be difficult to spread into the thin layer required to form the signature rolls. It's also important to work very quickly once the batter is ready. Otherwise it will become lumpy and difficult to spread into a thin layer. It might take a few attempts, but soon you will be on your way to khandvi heaven, because that's truly what it feels like to pop one of these velvety smooth rolls into your mouth. They can be kept refrigerated in a covered container for up to 2 days, making them an ideal make-ahead dish to bring to a party.

KHANDVI

Vegetable oil, as needed

½ cup chickpea flour (besan)

2 cups buttermilk

1 teaspoon finely chopped fresh ginger

1 teaspoon finely chopped green chiles

1 teaspoon ground turmeric

2 teaspoons fresh lemon juice

Kosher salt

MUSTARD TARKA

1 tablespoon vegetable oil

½ teaspoon black mustard seeds

1 teaspoon sesame seeds

Pinch of hing (asafetida)

10 fresh curry leaves

2 green chiles, finely chopped

Finely chopped fresh cilantro leaves, for serving

Unsweetened shredded coconut, for serving

Make the khandvi: Grease a large, clean work surface (like a cutting board) with a thin coating of oil. In a large bowl, whisk together the chickpea flour, buttermilk, ginger, green chiles, turmeric, and lemon juice. Season with salt, then strain the batter through a fine-mesh sieve and into a medium saucepan.

Set the saucepan over medium heat, and while whisking constantly, heat the buttermilk mixture until it thickens slightly but is still pourable, 8 to 10 minutes. It's important to whisk the batter constantly during this process to prevent scorching and to keep it thin (a flat paddle whisk works well).

Carefully pour half the batter onto the greased surface and, working very quickly, spread it out into a 24 × 18-inch rectangle ⅛ inch thick (it will begin to set very quickly). Cover the surface of the bowl containing the remaining batter with a damp cloth. Let the poured batter set until it becomes pliable, 2 to 4 minutes. Using a sharp paring knife, cut the sheet into 3 × 6-inch rectangles. Starting at a short end, roll each rectangle up and transfer to a plate. Oil the work surface once more and repeat the process with the remaining batter.

Make the mustard tarka: In a small skillet, heat the oil over medium-high heat until it glistens, about 3 minutes. Add the mustard seeds, and once they start to pop, after about 2 minutes, add the sesame seeds, hing, curry leaves, and green chiles and sauté until the chiles are tender, about 3 minutes.

To serve, pour the tarka over the khandvi and garnish with cilantro and coconut.

This is how Khandvi is served at a vendor stall in Old Delhi but it is even more satisfying when garnished with cilantro and coconut.

Kande Pohe

(FLATTENED RICE PILAF)

SERVES 4
PREPARATION TIME: 25 minutes

My favorite place to eat kande pohe is at the train stop in Pune. I love watching the vendor toss together the poha (flattened rice that looks a cross between rice and rolled oats—and cooks as quickly as couscous!) with peanuts, coconut, onions, spices, and a generous squeeze of lemon juice. Like in Maharashtra, where it is a comforting and quick-to-make breakfast staple, kande pohe is a favorite of my kids at home, where I usually make it for breakfast (or as a midnight snack for my husband, Vivek). Rinsing the poha and then letting it absorb the residual water before cooking allows it to become tender more quickly once it's added to the pan. You can find poha online or in Indian markets.

1½ cups poha

1 tablespoon vegetable oil

1 teaspoon black mustard seeds

1 teaspoon cumin seeds, toasted

Pinch of hing (asafetida)

2 green chiles, finely chopped

8 fresh curry leaves

½ cup roasted peanuts

1 medium red onion, finely chopped

1 teaspoon ground turmeric

½ teaspoon Kashmiri or other red chile powder

½ teaspoon sugar

Juice of ½ lemon

Kosher salt

Place the poha in a colander and rinse under cold running water for a few minutes to remove excess starch. Transfer it to a bowl, cover with plastic wrap, and set aside at room temperature for 10 minutes.

In a heavy-bottomed pot over medium-high heat, heat the oil until it glistens, about 3 minutes. Add the mustard and cumin seeds, and once the mustard seeds begin to pop, after about 2 minutes, add the hing, chiles, and curry leaves. Cook, stirring often, until the chiles are just tender, about 1 minute. Add the peanuts and cook until the surfaces of the peanuts begin to turn golden, about 1 minute more.

CHAAT MASALA

The most iconic chaat seasoning is chaat masala, of course. This spice blend gets its distinctive pungent and slightly tangy flavor from the black salt (kala namak) that's added to a combination of amchur (mango powder), ginger, black pepper, hing (asafetida), coriander, cumin, and chile powder. Its initial sour flavor gives way to a slightly funky taste and aroma derived from that sulfurous black salt, which is sourced from volcanic rock and kiln-dried. Chaat masala is available in Indian grocery stores and is an essential ingredient in the Indian chaat pantry. Train vendors often sprinkle it over their chaat as the final flourish before handing it over to their hungry customers.

Add the onion along with a bit of water if necessary to scrape up and incorporate any browned bits that have formed on the bottom of the pan. Once the onion is translucent, after about 3 minutes, stir in the turmeric and chile powder and sauté until the chile powder is aromatic, about 1 minute.

Stir in the poha, sugar, and lemon juice, and sauté until the poha is completely tender and the lemon juice has been absorbed, 2 to 3 minutes. Season with salt.

Divide among 4 plates and sprinkle with coconut and cilantro. Sprinkle with a generous handful of sev and serve with lime wedges.

GARNISH

Unsweetened shredded coconut

Finely chopped fresh cilantro

Sev

Lime wedges

Mango Mastani

(ICE CREAM FLOAT)

MAKES 4 drinks

PREPARATION TIME: 10 minutes

3½ cups coarsely chopped mango

1 quart vanilla ice cream

8 saffron threads

1 teaspoon rose water

2 cups whole milk

3 tablespoons sugar

GARNISH

Tootie Fruities cereal (optional)

Toasted nuts (select one, two, or three types): sliced almonds, finely chopped pistachios, finely chopped cashews

Maraschino cherries

Dried rose petals (optional)

I first tried a mastani at a shop just outside the entrance to the Pune railway station. It was a sweltering hot day and my skin was covered in a layer of sweat and dust from the long journey. I needed a pick-me-up and I needed it fast. I'd heard about mastanis from a college friend who grew up in Pune, but I didn't quite believe that such a riot of flavors that included rose, cherries, mangoes, and even the breakfast cereal Tootie Fruities (available at Indian markets, or substitute Kellogg's Froot Loops) would actually taste good. It sounded a bit ridiculous to me. I ordered one and waited—and laughed when the waiter handed it to me. It looked even more ludicrous than I imagined it would, but I was too hot to do anything but spoon a bite into my mouth. It was revelatory. Somehow the seemingly random flavors came together to form a cohesive and deeply pleasurable whole. I gobbled it up and moved to a booth after I ordered my second mastani. "Don't judge," I told my waiter. "This is the first time I've tried a mastani." He laughed and replied, "But certainly not your last." He was so right.

Mango mastani is the signature dessert of Pune. Legend says it was created in tribute to the Maharashtrian Queen Mastani, daughter of Maharaja Chhatrasal and wife of the eighteenth-century Peshwa Baji Rao, a renowned general of the Maratha Empire. Queen Mastani's grace and beauty were mythologized in stories passed down from one generation to the next. This is a fitting recipe to honor her: alluring in appearance, a bit mysterious in the way all of the random ingredients come together so gracefully, sure to steal your heart forever, just as Queen Mastani stole Baji Rao's heart centuries ago.

In a blender, combine 3 cups of the mango, 1½ cups of the ice cream, the saffron, rose water, milk, and sugar and puree until smooth.

Divide the puree among 4 glasses. Add 2 scoops of ice cream to each glass and sprinkle with the remaining mango chunks and the cereal (if using), toasted nuts, cherries, and rose petals (if using). Serve with a straw.

FOOD AGGREGATOR
www.ecatering.irctc.co.in
COMÉSUM
Book Food & Get It Delivered On Your Train Berth
Toll Free No.: 1323
www.ecatering.irctc.co.in
COMÉSUM

45 M
44 L

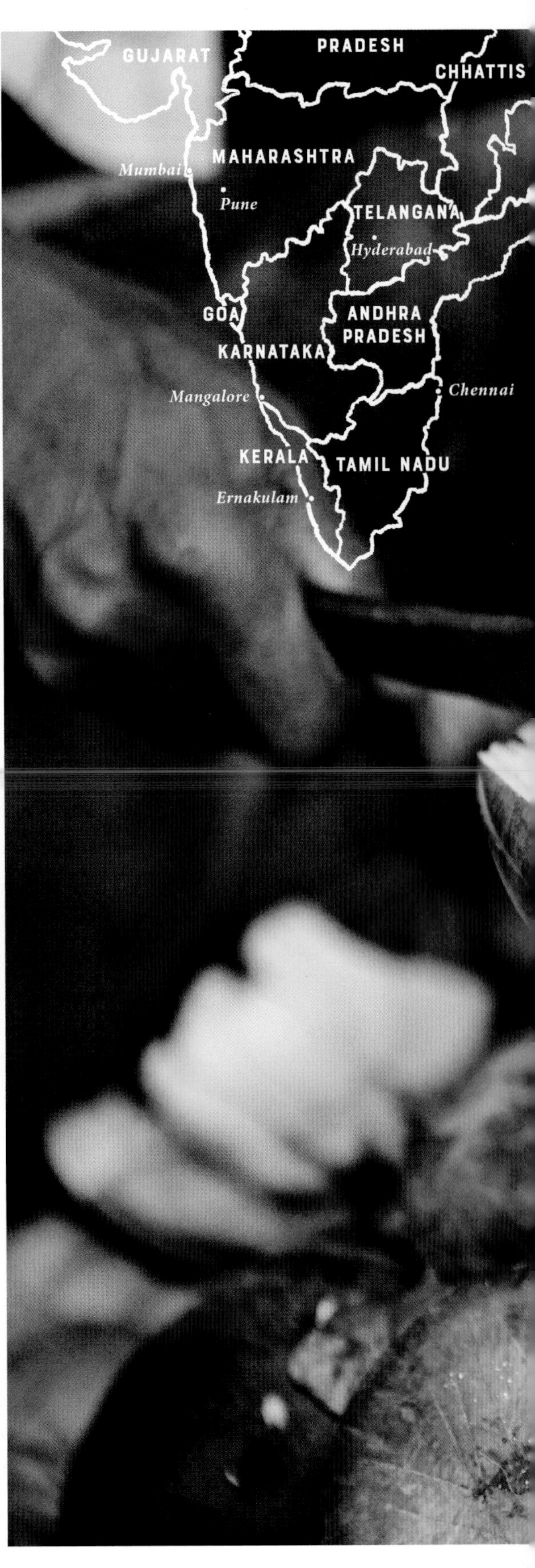
GUJARAT
PRADESH
CHHATTIS
MAHARASHTRA
Mumbai
Pune
TELANGANA
Hyderabad
GOA
ANDHRA
PRADESH
KARNATAKA
Mangalore
Chennai
KERALA
TAMIL NADU
Ernakulam

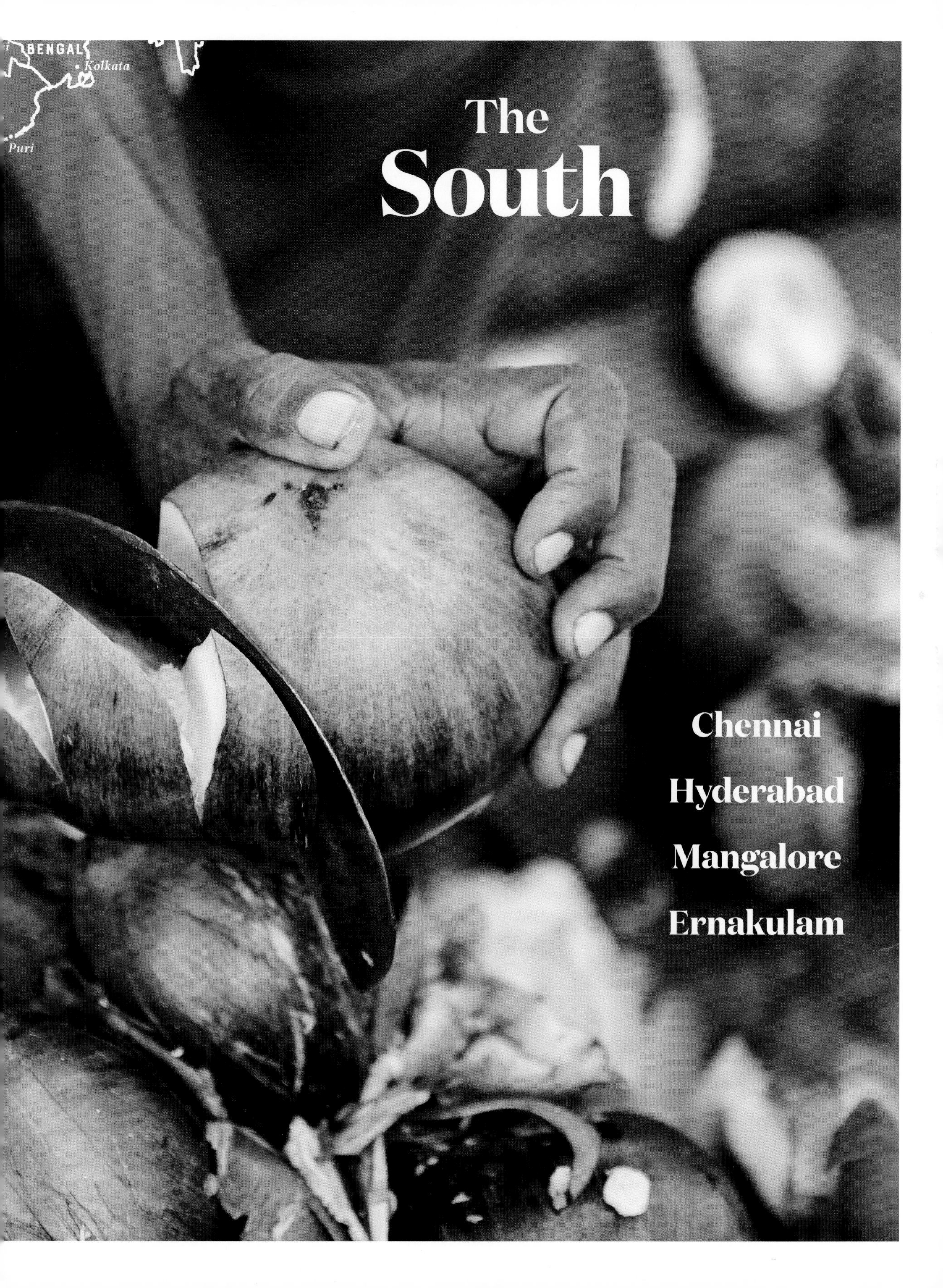

The South

Chennai

Hyderabad

Mangalore

Ernakulam

Chennai

Lemon Rice
Curd Rice
Coconut Chutney
Tomato Chutney
Idli Chaat
Tamarind Rice

There is a palpable energy buzzing within Chennai Central, South India's busiest train station, where 550,000 people rush through daily on their way to the beaches in the south, the industrial cities farther north, or the rainforest to harvest banana leaves. The leaves serve as place mats for virtually every meal served in Chennai, a city that sits on India's southeast coast. I wonder if any of the passengers stop to notice, like I always do, the details of the station, built in the Gothic Revival style in the nineteenth century. The 136-foot-high clock tower and the white minarets soaring above redbrick towers always entice me to look up for a moment—to pause and escape from the pulsating wave of humanity and from the mad dash I'm making to the exit. The station, once known as Madras Central, was built upon the remains of a seventeenth-century Portuguese merchant's garden and has been South India's most important rail station ever since.

It's inevitable that one of the six hundred station porters who work at Chennai Central will ask if I need assistance with my luggage before I reach the exit. I never say yes until I'm returning to the station after a visit to Chennai. It's only then that I need help because the empty suitcase I arrived with is now bursting with fresh tamarind, coconut chutney, and bags of Ponni rice (a Tamil short-grain rice that I use to make idli, a steamed rice pancake) that I picked up during my trip.

The people of this region, the Tamalians, adhere to the belief that preparing and sharing food with one another is a duty and obligation. It's a philosophy that I share with them, my guiding principle as a chef, mother, daughter, sister, friend, and wife. I usually try to visit the region during one of the Tamil feast days, known as virundhu, that take place in early August, because that's when the temples offer visitors dishes like tamarind rice, lemon rice, and curd rice wrapped in banana leaves. Rice is an important crop in southern India, where vibrant green rice paddies flourish. Rice is a fundamental ingredient not only in temple dishes but also in recipes like idli, round steamed cakes made of rice powder that are a breakfast staple throughout the region.

Chennai was where my family changed trains when we visited my maternal grandparents in Bangalore, which is now called Bengaluru, where we stayed for a few weeks each autumn.

Switching trains meant we had time to step outside the station to pick up banana-leaf-wrapped parcels of tamarind rice, curd rice, and lemon rice that vendors sold just beyond the station entrance. My father always tried to talk me into buying just one kind of rice, but I think he knew he'd never win the argument and usually gave in to my demand for all three varieties. I loved unwrapping the little green bundles once we were on board the train again on our way to Bangalore. Even on the steamiest southern Indian day, the rice had a cooling effect, since each flavor was tangy and refreshing in its own way.

When I was expecting my first child, Shagun, the only thing I craved was curd rice, and my poor husband, Vivek, ended up arranging it for me day after day. It brought me back to those comforting train rides when my sister and I were sitting snugly between our parents on board the train with a packet of rice in our hands on our way to see our grandparents. Rice is considered an auspicious ingredient in India and is believed to bring good fortune and wellness to those who consume it. My daughter's name, Shagun, means "auspicious blessing," and I wondered after I had her if our desire to name her Shagun had a connection to the curd rice I ate every day when I was pregnant with her.

One of the best days of my life since having Shagun was when Vivek and I took her to visit my maternal grandmother, Harjit Randhawa, in Bangalore. I spent a lot of time with my grandmother during my childhood and when I was a university student in Manipal. She's a kindred spirit, the person I believe I received the most genes from in my family because she's industrious just like me. She can't sit still even when she's not feeling well. If she told us she was feeling ill and needed to lie down in her bedroom for a few minutes, it was a virtual guarantee that we would find her two minutes later standing on a stool clearing the cobwebs from the ceiling fan. Even now, in her nineties, she stays active with an endless list of projects to accomplish each day. I internalized from her the lesson that an industrious life is a happy life, and it's a mantra I hope Shagun learns from me, too.

Another thing my grandmother taught me was how important it is to make every guest in your home (or restaurant) feel honored and cared for. I've spent a tremendous amount of time in southern India, and the hospitality that my grandmother always shows her houseguests is reflected in every dining experience I've had in this part of India. It's not only the omnipresent generosity of spirit that I connect to in southern India, it's also their way of eating. Banana leaves are traditionally spread out on the ground, serving as place mats for a traditional meal known as sappadu in Tamil. Dishes in this tropical climate tend to be lighter than in other parts of India, with a breakfast of idli and dosas served with a variety of chutneys and a vegetable broth called sambar followed by a lighter lunch that usually includes curd, similar to yogurt, to aid in digestion.

Much like the cuisine of Chennai, I feel lighter after I visit this region in India. It's a place that always teaches me something new about what hospitality means. I carry these lessons back with me to my restaurants in Nashville, where I hope my guests feel welcomed. It is truly my honor and privilege to serve them.

Lemon Rice

This rice reminds me of summer not only because of its optimistic golden hue but also because my mom used to prepare it for our family on hot summer evenings when the thought of a heavy curry made the temperature feel even more oppressive. I was always requesting it, because I love its bright flavor and also because it transported me back to the Chennai station, where I could have wandered all day eating rice and chaat if only my parents would have let me. It's easy to prepare and could be served as a main dish, as we used to enjoy it in our family, or as a base for a gravy (see Ros Omelette recipe on page 124) or dal (see pantry on page 265). There's much more to it than lemon and rice due to its combination of smooth and crunchy textures and nutty, spicy, earthy flavors. It's lovely with one of the chutney recipes (pages 29–31) in this book and with hot Chapatis (page 46), which I enjoy using as a utensil to scoop the rice up into my mouth because forks can be so boring!

SERVES 4

PREPARATION TIME: 20 minutes, plus 30 minutes to cook the rice

1 tablespoon vegetable oil

1 teaspoon black mustard

1 teaspoon cumin seeds

4 fresh curry leaves

2 teaspoons split urad dal

2 teaspoons split chana dal

2 dried red chiles, broken into small pieces

2 tablespoons finely chopped cashews

2 tablespoons finely chopped peanuts

1 teaspoon finely chopped fresh ginger

2 serrano chiles, thinly sliced

Grated zest and juice of 1 lemon

1 teaspoon sugar

1 teaspoon ground turmeric

3 cups cooked Basmati Rice, cooled (page 262)

Kosher salt

Finely chopped fresh cilantro leaves

Chutney (optional), store-bought or homemade (pages 29–31)

Chapatis (optional; page 46)

In a large sauté pan, heat the oil over medium-high heat. Add the mustard seeds, cumin seeds, curry leaves, urad dal, chana dal, and dried red chiles. Once the mustard seeds begin to pop, after about 2 minutes, reduce the heat to medium and add the cashews and peanuts. Sauté until the nuts are deep golden brown and the dals have slightly deepened in color, about 3 minutes.

Add the ginger, serrano chiles, lemon zest, and sugar and sauté until the chiles are softened, about 3 minutes. Add the turmeric and sauté for an additional 1 minute. Add the rice and remove from the heat. Gently stir in the lemon juice and season with salt.

Serve warm garnished with cilantro and, if desired, chutneys and hot chapatis.

Curd Rice

SERVES 4

PREPARATION TIME: 20 minutes, plus 30 minutes to cook the rice

When I moved to America for culinary school, the first thing I craved was curd rice, referred to as *thayir saadam* in Tamil. While I longed for its tangy flavor, what I really pined for was my family—this recipe makes me feel connected to them more than almost any other dish. I loved nothing more than unwrapping the green banana leaves and scooping up a bite of rice with my fingers—creamy, cooling, and so incredibly flavorful from the tangy yogurt, zesty ginger, and fiery chiles. Of course, it's just as good without the banana leaf (it can be wrapped in foil instead), but for a picnic or a dinner that demands a wow factor, banana leaves are a simple way to deliver it. Curd is not the same thing as whole-milk yogurt because the bacteria used to create each one is different; but because curd can be difficult to source outside of India, I've substituted yogurt here.

1½ cups whole-milk yogurt

¾ cup whole milk

1 large carrot, peeled and grated

Kosher salt

2 cups cooked Basmati Rice (page 262)

1 tablespoon vegetable oil

1½ teaspoons brown mustard seeds

12 fresh curry leaves

2 teaspoons black urad dal

2 teaspoons grated fresh ginger

2 dried red chiles, broken into pieces

4 banana leaves (optional)

Finely chopped fresh cilantro leaves

Pomegranate seeds

In a large bowl, whisk together the yogurt and milk until smooth. Stir in the carrot and season with salt. In a medium bowl, gently mash the rice with a fork or your hands until the grains just begin to break down. Stir the rice into the yogurt mixture until incorporated. Season again with salt.

In a large sauté pan, heat the oil over medium-high heat. Add the mustard seeds and curry leaves and sauté until the mustard seeds begin to pop, about 3 minutes. Add the urad dal, ginger, and chiles and sauté until the dal begins to turn brown, about 3 minutes. Remove from the heat, add the rice, and stir gently to incorporate. Refrigerate until chilled.

Spoon the rice mixture into individual serving bowls and garnish with cilantro and pomegranate seeds before serving. Or you can wrap the mixture in banana leaves or foil. If not using banana leaves, cut out four 12 × 12-inch squares of foil. To wrap it in banana leaves, arrange the a leaf dull side up on a work surface. Spoon ⅔ cup rice into the center of it. Smooth it out using a spatula until it's about ½ inch thick. Fold the left or right side of the leaf over the rice and then fold the other side over it. Next, fold the top or bottom over the rice and then fold the other side. The result should be a nice, tidy square or rectangular packet of rice. Once it's unwrapped, garnish with cilantro and pomegranate seeds before serving.

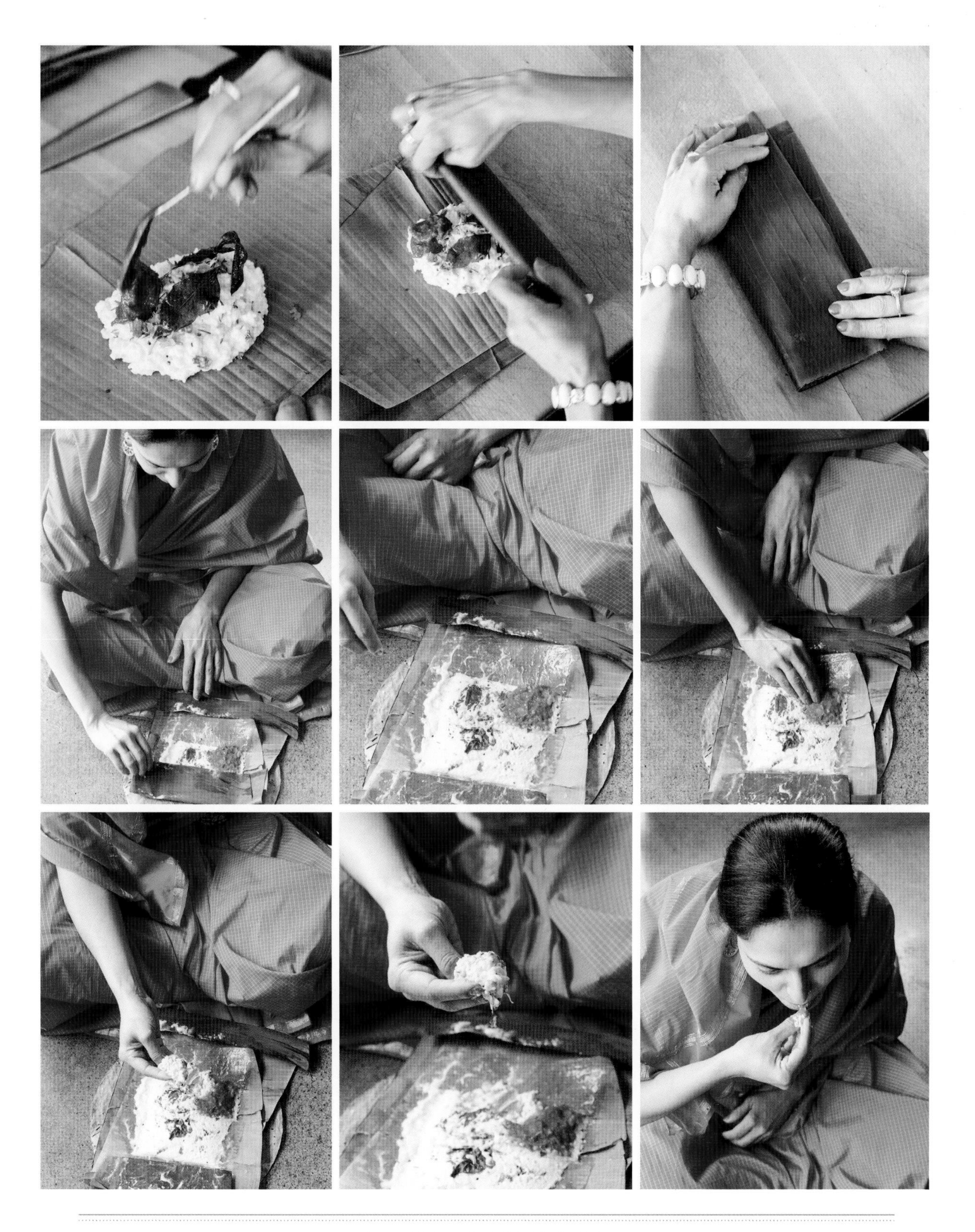

Coconut Chutney

Coconut chutney is a foundational recipe in southern India, acting as a flavor enhancer for everything from dosas (pages 186 and 189) to idli (see Idli Chaat, page 163). I always begged the rice and idli vendors at the Chennai station for an extra spoonful of coconut chutney to top my lemon rice or tamarind rice. I love it so much I could eat it like soup. I recommend that you increase the batch size and store it for up to a week in the refrigerator. No matter how much you make, it will go fast. It's perfect as a sandwich spread, potato topping, or salad dressing, or to drizzle atop your favorite chaat recipe, of course.

MAKES about 1½ cups

PREPARATION TIME: 10 minutes

1 tablespoon vegetable oil

1 teaspoon brown mustard seeds

1 teaspoon black urad dal

Pinch of hing (asafetida)

8 fresh curry leaves

1 cup unsweetened shredded coconut

2 tablespoons roasted peanuts

½ small white onion, coarsely chopped

2 green chiles, coarsely chopped

2 tablespoons tamarind paste

Kosher salt

In a medium sauté pan, heat the oil over medium-high heat. Add the mustard seeds, urad dal, hing, and curry leaves. Cook, stirring often, until the mustard seeds begin to pop, about 2 minutes. Continue to cook until it begins to turn a light brown color, about 4 minutes.

Transfer the oil and spices to a food processor and add the coconut, peanuts, onion, and chiles and process until pulverized. Add the tamarind paste and blend until incorporated. Add water, 1 tablespoon at a time, and blend after each addition, until the mixture is thick and creamy (you may need to add as little as 2 tablespoons or as much as 4 tablespoons depending upon the freshness of the dal). Season with salt. Serve or store refrigerated in a covered container for up to 1 week.

Tomato Chutney

MAKES about 3 cups
PREPARATION TIME: 30 minutes

This tomato chutney will quickly become the condiment you reach for instead of ketchup. In my family, we love slathering it on burgers and dipping our fries in it. It's also a nice dancing partner for omelets and as a chip dip. Not only does it taste good but it's packed with spices that offer health benefits such as fenugreek, one of my favorites. Known as *methi* in Hindi, fenugreek has been used in Ayurvedic medicine as an anti-inflammatory, as a hair and nail strengthener, for liver and kidney health, and as a digestive aid. The flavors of this chutney deepen over time, and it will keep in the refrigerator in a covered container for up to 2 weeks.

- 2 tablespoons vegetable oil
- 2 teaspoons fenugreek seeds
- 2 teaspoons brown mustard seeds
- 1 tablespoon chana dal
- 1 tablespoon black urad dal
- 18 fresh curry leaves
- 8 dried red chiles
- Pinch of hing (asafetida)
- 4 large beefsteak tomatoes, coarsely chopped (about 4 cups)
- 1 teaspoon ground turmeric
- 2 tablespoons tamarind paste
- 1/4 cup coarsely chopped fresh cilantro leaves
- Kosher salt

In a sauté pan, heat the oil over medium-high heat until it glistens, about 2 minutes. Add the fenugreek, mustard seeds, chana dal, and urad dal and sauté until the mustard seeds begin to pop and the dals turn a light brown color, about 4 minutes. Add the curry leaves and chiles and sauté until the chiles soften, about 2 minutes. Add the hing and tomatoes and sauté for 1 minute to incorporate.

Reduce the heat to medium-low, cover, and simmer gently, stirring occasionally, until the tomatoes have completely broken down into a pulp, 12 to 15 minutes.

Stir in the turmeric and tamarind paste and cook until incorporated, about 2 more minutes. Remove from the heat and cool for 10 minutes. Transfer the mixture to a food processor, add the cilantro, and pulse until the texture is that of a coarse chutney. Season with salt and cool completely before refrigerating in an airtight container.

OPPOSITE: *Idli with tomato and coconut chutneys, chile powder, and melted ghee.*

Specialty Times
CANTEEN CORPORATION • A MEMBER OF THE COMPASS GROUP SPECIAL EDITION
Allegations Of "Fish Stories" Par For The Course At Local Events
Top Rivals To Meet In The Potato Bowl
Record Crowds Are "Peeling Out" To Get To Potato Festival
The potato is one of only 15 food products which feed the entire world.

Idli Chaat

MAKES 12 idli (serves 4)

PREPARATION TIME: 30 minutes, plus 12 hours to soak the rice and lentils and to ferment the batter

Idli, a fermented, slightly pungent-tasting spongy steamed pancake, is as important to a classic South Indian breakfast as toast is in America. This round, fluffy, and earthy-tasting ivory-colored spongy flatbread is made from a fermented rice and lentil batter and is often served with sambar, a vegetable broth that the idli gets dipped in. If I happen to arrive in the Chennai station early in the morning, I always make a beeline for the idli vendor, who can barely keep up with the demand from the throngs of hungry passengers gathered around him. I am so inspired by idli that I created this chaat recipe for the menu at my restaurant Chaatable. I top the idli with yogurt, green and tamarind chutneys, and sev. Idli is made with Ponni rice, a strain of Tamil short-grain rice that is available in Indian markets (but any short-grain white rice will do). This recipe calls for the idli to be steamed in idli molds, which are available at Indian markets; but a poached egg mold with multiple compartments and a steaming feature is a good substitute. They won't have the traditional idli shape, but it's all about the flavor anyway.

In my version of idli chaat, I've coated the spongy cakes in a spice blend called idli podi (made from sesame seeds, dried chiles, urad dal, and chickpeas) that is available at Indian markets. The idli are fried in ghee for a crunchy exterior that gives way to a velvety interior. If you have trouble sourcing podi, simply salt the idli before frying or experiment with your own spice blend—chaat masala also works well. Of course, idli is satisfying on its own, too, without the chaat fireworks! Idli are available premade at Indian grocery stores if you would like to skip preparing them. If using store-bought, simply pick up this recipe at the point where the idlis are fried in ghee.

IDLI

1 cup white urad dal

1 teaspoon fenugreek seeds

1 cup uncooked short-grain rice

¼ cup cooked short-grain rice

Kosher salt

CHAAT

2 tablespoons idli podi, plus more for serving

2 tablespoons ghee, store-bought or homemade (page 33)

Kosher salt

18 fresh curry leaves

Whole-milk yogurt

Green Chutney (page 30)

Tamarind Chutney, store-bought or homemade (page 29)

Finely chopped fresh cilantro leaves

Fried curry leaves

Make the idli: In a large bowl, combine the urad dal and fenugreek, add enough water to cover by 3 inches, and soak for 1 hour. Drain and transfer the dal to a food processor and process until the mixture is smooth but still slightly grainy, about 3 minutes. Transfer to a medium bowl and set aside to rest for 10 minutes.

In a medium saucepan, combine the uncooked rice and water to cover by 2 inches. Bring to a boil over high heat, reduce the heat to medium, and simmer until the rice is parboiled (not fully cooked), about 10 minutes. Drain the rice and transfer it to a medium bowl. Add enough water to cover by 3 inches and soak for 4 hours.

(RECIPE CONTINUES)

Drain the parboiled rice and transfer to a food processor. Add the cooked rice and process until smooth but still slightly grainy, about 2 minutes. Add the rice mixture to the urad dal batter and stir until smooth. Season with salt. Cover the bowl with a damp cloth and set aside in a warm place for 8 hours to allow the batter to rise and ferment. After 8 hours stir to beat out as many of the fermentation bubbles as possible. The batter should be thick but still pourable, like pancake batter. If it's too thick, add a little water to thin it out.

In an idli steamer or poached egg steamer, bring water to a boil over high heat. While the water heats up, pour the idli batter into the molds, and once the water is boiling (wear oven mitts to prevent a steam burn), fit the mold into the steamer. (If you have excess batter, reserve it at room temperature and repeat the process once the first batch of idlis are steamed.) Reduce the heat to medium-low, cover, and steam the idlis until they are cooked through, 10 to 12 minutes. Remove from the heat, and once they are cool enough to handle, remove the idlis from the molds and cool to room temperature.

Make the chaat: Line a plate with paper towels. Sprinkle both sides of each idli with podi. In a large sauté pan, heat the ghee over medium heat for 3 minutes. Working in batches if necessary (do not overcrowd the pan), add the idli to the pan and fry until golden brown on both sides, 1 to 2 minutes per side. Transfer to the paper towels to drain, then season with salt.

In the same pan, sauté the curry leaves until slightly crispy, about 30 seconds, then remove from the pan and set aside. In a small bowl, whisk the yogurt with a little water to thin it to a drizzling consistency and season it with a pinch of salt.

To serve, arrange the idli on a large plate. Drizzle with green chutney, tamarind chutney, and yogurt. Sprinkle with podi and garnish with cilantro and fried curry leaves.

Tamarind Rice

Like the curd and lemon rice recipes in this chapter, tamarind rice, called *puliyogare* in Tamil, is typically served at temples on Tamil feast days, which happen several times throughout the course of a year, and is also found near the train station in Chennai. The dish is sometimes referred to as "mixed rice" since the ingredients, including mustard seeds, tamarind, jaggery, and cilantro, are mixed into the rice as opposed to being placed atop or next to it. A few teaspoons of dal are added to the rice recipes in this chapter for protein and to contribute a slightly nubby, crunchy texture to the rice. Yogurt is frequently served alongside rice throughout India because of its digestive properties and ability to enhance healthy gut bacteria.

SERVES 4

PREPARATION TIME: 25 minutes, plus 30 minutes to cook the rice

1 tablespoon vegetable oil

1 teaspoon chana dal

1 dried red chile, broken into pieces

1 teaspoon brown mustard seeds

1 teaspoon cumin seeds, toasted

8 fresh curry leaves

¼ cup finely chopped roasted peanuts

2 tablespoons tamarind paste

1 teaspoon jaggery (substitute dark brown sugar if you have trouble sourcing jaggery)

Pinch of hing (asafetida)

2 cups cooked Basmati Rice (page 262)

Kosher salt

Whole-milk yogurt

Finely chopped fresh cilantro, for garnish

Lemon wedges, for serving

In a large sauté pan, heat the oil over medium-high heat. Add the chana dal, red chile, mustard seeds, and cumin and sauté until the mustard seeds begin to pop and the chana dal turns a light golden brown, about 4 minutes. Add the curry leaves and continue to sauté until the red chiles begin to turn crispy and deep golden brown, about 2 minutes more. Add the peanuts and sauté for 1 minute.

Reduce the heat to low and add 1 cup water, the tamarind, jaggery, and hing and simmer gently, stirring occasionally to prevent scorching, until it begins to thicken and the oil begins to separate from the rest of the ingredients, 11 to 14 minutes. Stir in the rice until incorporated and season with salt.

In a small bowl, whisk the yogurt with a fork and season with a pinch of salt. Garnish the rice with cilantro and serve with lemon wedges and the seasoned yogurt on the side.

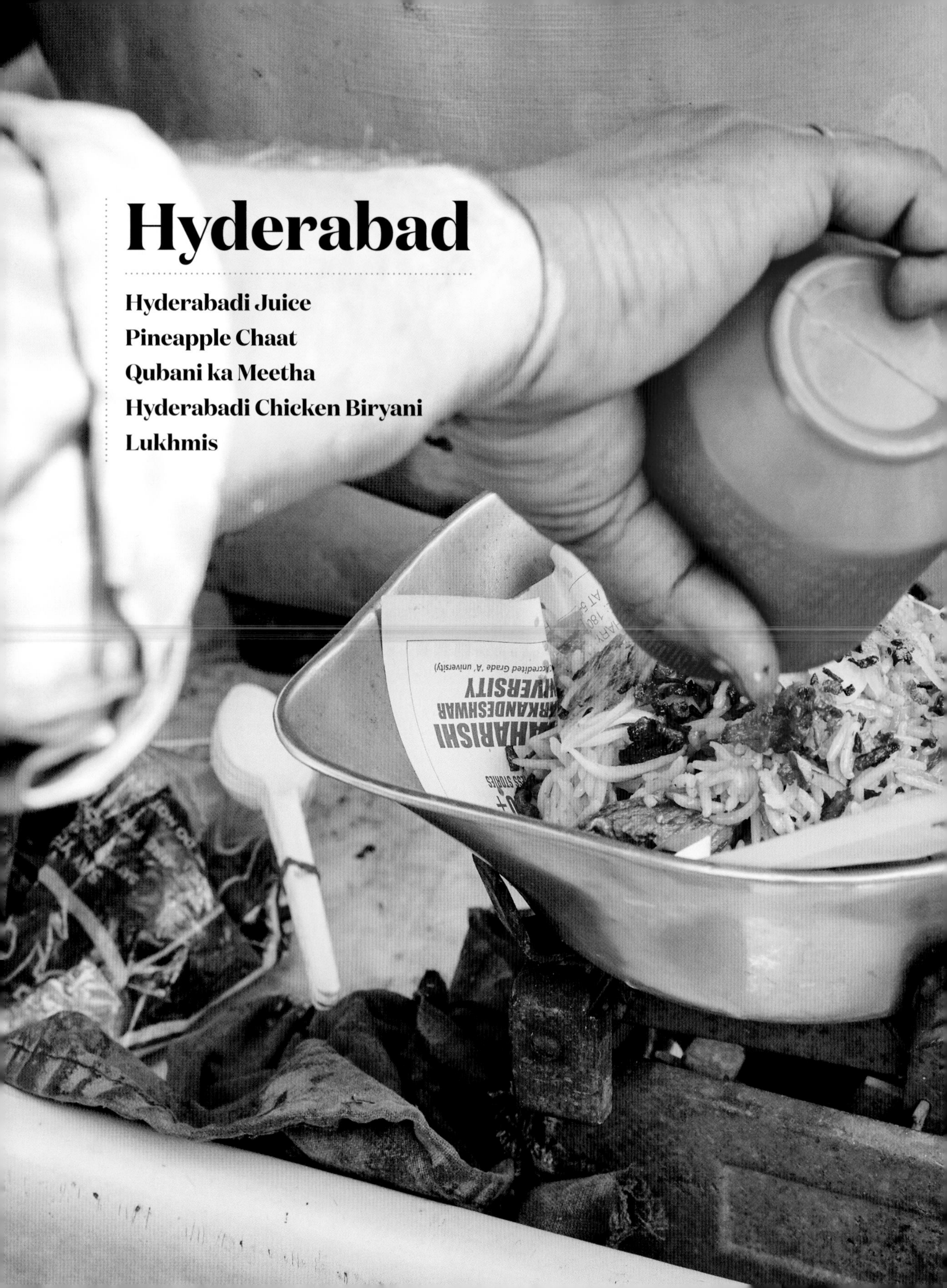

Hyderabad

Hyderabadi Juice

Pineapple Chaat

Qubani ka Meetha

Hyderabadi Chicken Biryani

Lukhmis

I always feel the tug of nostalgia when I arrive at the Hyderabad Deccan train station in Hyderabad. Referred to by locals as Nampally, this is the station I disembarked from during my university days in Manipal. I can hear the laughter of my friends who shared the train car with me as we pulled into the station. We were perpetually broke but always managed to pool together enough rupees to buy a biryani from one of the vendors awaiting our arrival. I loved the freedom I experienced as a university student when it felt like we had the world at our feet and the future held infinite possibilities. Fortunately, I haven't lost that feeling. When I think of standing with my friends at the Hyderabad station waiting for our train, shoving huge spoonfuls of biryani into our mouths between bouts of uncontrollable laughter, I can still feel that sense of invincibility that our fellowship conjured.

Though we were always hurting for funds, we also somehow always managed to find enough rupees to buy a few bags of samosas, a pineapple chaat, and a terra-cotta bowl or two of kesar phirni, an iconic saffron and pistachio rice pudding from the region. From the many juice stands surrounding the station we'd buy freshly squeezed fruit smoothies to wash it all down with. Produce such as papayas, mangoes, pomegranates, carrots, and cucumbers were stacked in towering piles that the vendor blended into hydrating smoothies enticing enough to stop even the most harried train passengers in their tracks. Our train rides from Hyderabad were riotous affairs involving music that someone was inevitably blasting from their portable radio, sweaty dancing sessions, endless gossip, heated card games, and enough chaat and snacks to fuel the party.

Hyderabadi cuisine reflects the history of this inland region of southern India. Its amalgam of Turkish, Iranian, French, and indigenous influences mirrors the rich and storied legacy of this city, established in the early sixteenth century on the Deccan Plateau. In 1724, Asif Jah I, a Mughal viceroy, claimed Hyderabad, which means "Haydar's City" or "lion city," as a sovereign region of India. He established a dynasty referred to as the Nizams of Hyderabad. The Nizams profoundly influenced Hyderabadi culture, commerce, and cuisine, infusing every

ABOVE LEFT: *A naan vendor in Hyderabad.*
ABOVE MIDDLE: *Constructing aloo chaat in Hyderabad.*
ABOVE RIGHT: *A train porter in Hyderabad.*

aspect of life with a philosophy of open-mindedness and a thirst for innovation that are still present today.

It was during this era that Hyderabad blossomed as a global cultural nerve center, attracting poets, writers, dancers, actors, intellectuals, and musicians from all corners of the world. Their influence, along with that of the Mughlai and indigenous Telugu and Marathwada people, shaped the contours of Hyderabadi cuisine. Meat and rice dishes, such as the legendary Hyderabadi biryani, are nuanced and complex, infused with Middle Eastern and Indian ingredients and techniques that tell the tale of this city, one bite at a time.

Today, Hyderabad is touted as an international nerve center of innovation and technology, enticing multinational corporations to invest heavily in a city that hasn't changed that much over the years. A few centuries ago, it might have been poets and intellectuals who were drawn to Hyderabad, while today it might be IT specialists and scientists, but the philosophy of inclusion remains the same. The way the Hyderabadi people have always embraced new cultures, ideas, and culinary traditions has resulted in a food culture as beloved for its flavor as it is for the stories it has to tell—tales that are almost as good as the stories I remember from those college train rides when it didn't matter that we were penniless. The only thing that counted was that we had one another—and samosas.

Hyderabadi Juice

Juice vendors are ubiquitous at Hyderabad train stations, where temperatures soar in the summertime months and hover just below soaring in the cooler months. A cup of cooling juice is a welcome reprieve, and the variety of fruit on offer at the fruit stands is mind-blowing. Feel free to mix this recipe up with whatever fruit or vegetables are in season. The cashews add a bit of texture and a toasty aftertaste. Popular fruit options in Hyderabad include papaya, mulberry, durian, jackfruit, and avocado.

MAKES 1 smoothie

PREPARATION TIME: 10 minutes

- 1 mango, coarsely chopped
- 1 large carrot, peeled and coarsely chopped
- 1 celery stalk, coarsely chopped
- 1 green apple, coarsely chopped
- 2 tablespoons cashews, toasted
- Juice of 1 lime
- Kosher salt

In a blender, combine the mango, carrot, celery, apple, cashews, and lime juice and pulse until everything comes together. Then blend on high speed until smooth. Season with a pinch or two of salt and serve in a tall glass.

Pineapple Chaat

SERVES 4

PREPARATION TIME: 10 minutes

There's virtually always a pineapple chaat vendor busily hacking up his pineapples with a machete near the Hyderabadi train station. The pineapples are accented with tart lime juice, sour-salty chaat masala, spicy chile powder, and cilantro and pomegranate seeds for freshness, color, and bright taste. This chaat feels so decadent with its mosaic of colors and plucky flavors, but it's such an easy recipe to execute. I love it with mango, and in the summertime it's fantastic made with watermelon. Sometimes I drizzle it with salted and water-thinned yogurt for a little more depth of flavor. I love serving it to my kids for dessert while sharing with them my tales of those Hyderabadi train rides, hoping one day they will feel as passionate and carefree and have such strong friendships as I did all those years ago.

1 pineapple, peeled, cored, and cut into bite-sized pieces

Juice of 2 limes

½ teaspoon sugar

1 teaspoon chaat masala, plus more to taste

Kashmiri or other red chile powder

Pomegranate seeds

Finely chopped fresh mint

In a large bowl, toss together the pineapple, lime juice, sugar, and chaat masala. Transfer to a plate and sprinkle with chile powder and pomegranate seeds. Adjust the chaat masala seasoning and finish with mint.

Qubani ka Meetha

(APRICOT DESSERT)

SERVES 8

PREPARATION TIME: 45 minutes, plus 12 hours to soak the apricots

Though most apricots in India are cultivated in the high elevations of the Kashmiri Himalayan mountains, Hyderabadis have adopted this fruit and completely made it their own. This beloved Hyderabadi dessert, a sweet compote made from dried apricots, is a staple of weddings in the region, but it's also found on street corners and in teahouses throughout the city, including at my favorite Hyderabadi teahouse, Blue Sea, located across the street from the train station. The compote's deep amber color is derived from dried apricots simmered in a sweet sugar syrup and infused with warming notes of cinnamon, star anise, cloves, and cardamom. In cooler regions of the world, it's a lovely dish to present during winter holidays, since the spice blend gives it that cozy factor we all crave when it's wool-socks-and-fireplace season. The only trick to ensure success in making qubani ka meetha is to have patience as it cooks to enable it to develop a thick, syrupy consistency. The freshly whipped cream suggested here is unsweetened to balance out the sweetness of the apricots, and while only almonds are suggested as a garnish, at weddings, qubani ka meetha is sometimes garnished with rose petals, saffron, and silver leaf (*varq* in Hindi) for a festive flourish.

1 pound dried apricots

3 green cardamom pods

5 whole cloves

1 cinnamon stick

2 star anise pods

1½ cups sugar

Unsweetened freshly whipped cream

Slivered almonds, toasted

In a large bowl, combine the apricots with enough water to cover them by 3 inches and let them soak at room temperature for 12 hours.

Drain the apricots and transfer them to a heavy-bottomed medium pot. Add the cardamom, cloves, cinnamon, star anise, and enough water to cover the apricots by 1 inch. Bring to a boil over high heat, reduce the heat to medium, and simmer for 15 minutes.

Stir in the sugar and continue to simmer, stirring occasionally to prevent scorching, until mushy and syrupy, 30 to 35 minutes.

Remove from the heat and discard the cardamom, cloves, cinnamon, and star anise. Serve either warm or chilled with whipped cream spooned on top and garnished with almonds. Refrigerate the compote in a covered container for up to 1 week.

RAILWAY PORTERS

The word *porter* derives from the Latin word *portare,* meaning "to carry." In India, porters have been around since the establishment of the Indian railway system in the mid-nineteenth century. Their iconic red shirts mark them as a person who can assist weary travelers with their bags to or from the train. Each porter earns 400 rupees (around $7 US) per day, and while they are not employed directly by Indian Railways, each one holds a license issued by the president of India.

In recent years, efforts have been made to modernize the system and to do away with the word *coolie*, a derogatory term for porter left over from the British colonial era. They are now referred to as *sahayaks*, a Hindi word meaning "helper." Additional luggage trolleys are also being distributed to train stations throughout India to ease the porter's physical burden of carrying overstuffed suitcases and boxes on their heads as they have traditionally done for decades. Indian citizens have supported the government's efforts to improve the conditions of train porters, but the suggestion to do away with the porter's crimson-colored shirt in favor of a more neutral color was met with uproar. This is India, after all, and we do love our vibrant colors.

Hyderabadi Chicken Biryani

(SLOW-COOKED RICE)

We have the Persians to thank for introducing so many of India's most venerated recipes during the Mughal era, which began in the sixteenth century. This includes biryani, a universally beloved recipe deriving its name from the Persian word *birian*, which essentially means "to fry before cooking." Biryani was a prized component of the royal Mughali cooking repertoire, but its unique preparation eventually found its way to the people. Variations exist in nearly every state in India, but it's the Hyderabadi version that is perhaps most famed. Biryani is typically served at a sit-down meal, but in Hyderabad it's a popular street food scooped from massive brass vats onto newspaper pages or palm frond plates. The star of a biryani is usually the meat cooked alongside the rice. The Hyderabadi version is more rice-forward, with protein such as chicken or lamb playing second fiddle to the slow-cooked rice.

SERVES 6

PREPARATION TIME: 1 hour 30 minutes, plus 12 hours to marinate the chicken

MARINATED CHICKEN

2 green chiles, finely chopped

2 tablespoons vegetable oil

2 tablespoons lemon juice

1½ tablespoons store-bought ginger-garlic paste

1 tablespoon ghee, store-bought or homemade (page 67), melted

2 teaspoons Kashmiri or other red chile powder

1 teaspoon cumin seeeds, toasted

1 teaspoon garam masala

1 teaspoon ground coriander

1 teaspoon ground turmeric

Salt

2 pounds bone-in, skin-on chicken parts (breasts, drumsticks, and thighs)

RICE

3 cups basmati rice, well rinsed under cold water

1 tablespoon store-bought ginger-garlic paste

1 teaspoon cumin seeds, toasted

2 black cardamom pods

2 green cardamom pods

½ teaspoon freshly grated nutmeg

Marinate the chicken: In a large bowl, stir together the chiles, oil, lemon juice, ginger-garlic paste, ghee, chile powder, cumin, garam masala, coriander, turmeric, and salt to taste. Add the chicken pieces and rub the chicken all over with the paste until all of the nooks and crannies are covered. Cover and refrigerate for 12 hours.

Start the rice: Place the rice in a medium bowl, cover with lukewarm water, and set aside to soak for 45 minutes.

Drain the rice and rinse again, then transfer to a large heavy-bottomed pot. Add 3 quarts (12 cups) water and the ginger-garlic paste. Fold a piece of cheesecloth over to double it and cut it into a 6-inch square. Place the cumin, cardamom pods, nutmeg, cloves, peppercorns, cinnamon, and bay leaves in the center of it, gather the corners, and use twine to tie it up in a bundle. Add the spice sachet to the rice. Bring the water to a boil over high heat, reduce the heat to medium, half cover the pot with a lid, and simmer until the rice is just tender but not fully cooked, about 20 minutes. Remove the sachet, drain the rice, and season with salt.

4 whole cloves

10 black peppercorns

1 cinnamon stick

2 bay leaves

Kosher salt

FOR THE BIRYANI

2 tablespoons ghee, store-bought or homemade, divided (page 33)

1 small yellow onion, finely chopped

1 cup whole-milk yogurt

2 tablespoons finely chopped fresh mint

2 tablespoons finely chopped fresh cilantro

½ cup whole milk

12 saffron threads, soaked in 1 tablespoon whole milk

1 tablespoon finely chopped fresh cilantro, plus more for serving

1 tablespoon finely chopped fresh mint, plus more for serving

Kosher salt

Lemon wedges

Meanwhile, for the biryani: In a small sauté pan, heat 1 tablespoon of the ghee over medium-high heat until melted, about 2 minutes. Reduce the heat to medium, add the onion, and fry, stirring occasionally to prevent scorching, until deeply golden brown, about 6 minutes. In a small bowl, whisk together the yogurt, mint, and cilantro.

Transfer the chicken to a heavy-bottomed ovenproof pot. Add the yogurt/herb mixture to the chicken, stirring well to ensure even coverage. Set the pot over medium heat, cover, and cook, stirring occasionally, until the chicken is halfway cooked through, 17 to 20 minutes. If the sauce starts to dry out, add water a few tablespoons at a time to keep it moist.

Preheat the oven to 300°F.

Remove half of the chicken from the pot and top what remains in the pot with half of the rice. Top the layer of rice with the rest of the chicken and then with the remaining rice. Drizzle all over with the milk and sprinkle with the saffron, fried onions, cilantro, and mint. Dollop with the remaining 1 tablespoon ghee, ensuring that it's evenly divided over the surface.

Cover the pot tightly with a lid and transfer to the oven. Bake until the chicken is cooked through and the rice is a deep brown color, 35 to 45 minutes. Try not to peek too often because it's the steam that circulates within the pot that results in a tender chicken and perfectly cooked rice. Season with salt.

Scoop the biryani onto a large platter and then sprinkle with mint and cilantro and serve with lemon wedges. Or serve it Hyderabadi train vendor-style and serve it scooped onto newspaper-lined plates.

KING OF KINGS
Tohfa
KING OF KINGS
Tohfa
Tohfa
का
Tohfa

Lukhmis

(LAMB SAMOSAS)

MAKES 16 lukhmis

PREPARATION TIME: 1 hour (includes 30 minutes to marinate the ground lamb)

Lukhmis are essentially the samosas of Hyderabad. They are especially popular at Muslim weddings, where they are frequently served alongside kebabs. When I was a college student I found them everywhere throughout the city, beginning at the train station. Today they are more difficult to find, having been replaced by the more standard triangular samosas found throughout the rest of India. Lukhmi, which means "bite" in Urdu, is traditionally rectangular in shape and includes ground lamb, which is what I've included in this recipe. Feel free to substitute ground chicken or beef if preferred.

STUFFING

½ pound ground lamb

1 tablespoon store-bought ginger-garlic paste

2 teaspoons Kashmiri or other red chile powder

1 teaspoon ground turmeric

Kosher salt

2 tablespoons vegetable oil

1 large white or yellow onion, finely chopped

2 green chiles, finely chopped

2 tablespoons finely chopped fresh cilantro

Juice of 1 lemon

LUKHMI

1 cup all-purpose flour, plus more for dusting

1 tablespoon whole wheat flour

3 tablespoons semolina

Kosher salt

1 tablespoon vegetable oil, plus more for deep-frying

Make the stuffing: In a large bowl, stir together the lamb, ginger-garlic paste, chile powder, and turmeric. Season with salt and refrigerate for 30 minutes.

In a sauté pan, heat the oil over medium-high heat. Add the onion and sauté, stirring occasionally, until light golden brown, about 4 minutes. Add the seasoned ground lamb mixture and sauté until the lamb just begins to turn light golden brown, about 5 more minutes. Add the chiles and sauté, stirring occasionally, until the lamb is cooked through, 8 to 10 minutes. Season with salt and stir in the cilantro and lemon juice. Cool to room temperature before stuffing the lukhmi.

Make the lukhmi: While the lamb marinates, sift together the all-purpose flour, whole wheat flour, and semolina into a large bowl. Stir in ½ teaspoon of salt and add the 1 tablespoon oil, stirring to incorporate. Add 2 tablespoons lukewarm water and knead to bring the dough together into a shaggy ball. Add additional water, 1 teaspoon at a time, if the dough does not come together. It should be a soft dough that is not sticky. Oil a bowl, place the dough inside, and cover the bowl with a damp kitchen towel. Set aside at room temperature for 30 minutes.

After the dough has rested, roll it out on a clean, lightly floured work surface into a 16-inch square about ⅛ inch thick. Using a sharp paring knife, cut the dough into sixteen 4-inch squares. Place about 1 tablespoon of the lamb stuffing on one side of a dough square.

Lightly dab the edge of half of the square with water and fold the dough over to form a rectangle. Press the edges together firmly to seal. Repeat with the remaining dough and stuffing.

Line a plate with paper towels. Pour 6 inches oil into a deep heavy-bottomed pot and heat the oil over medium-high heat to 325°F on an instant-read thermometer. Working in batches of 2 or 3 (do not overcrowd the pot), use a slotted spoon to carefully add the lukhmis to the oil and fry until golden brown on both sides, 4 to 5 minutes, turning with a slotted spoon to ensure even coloring and cooking. Drain on paper towels and season with salt. Allow the oil to return to frying temperature between batches.

Serve with small bowls of yogurt and chutneys.

FOR SERVING

Whole-milk yogurt

Chutney of choice, store-bought or homemade (pages 29–31)

Mangalore

Chukku Kappi
Brinjal Achaar
Neer Dosa
Tuppa Dosa
Goli Baje

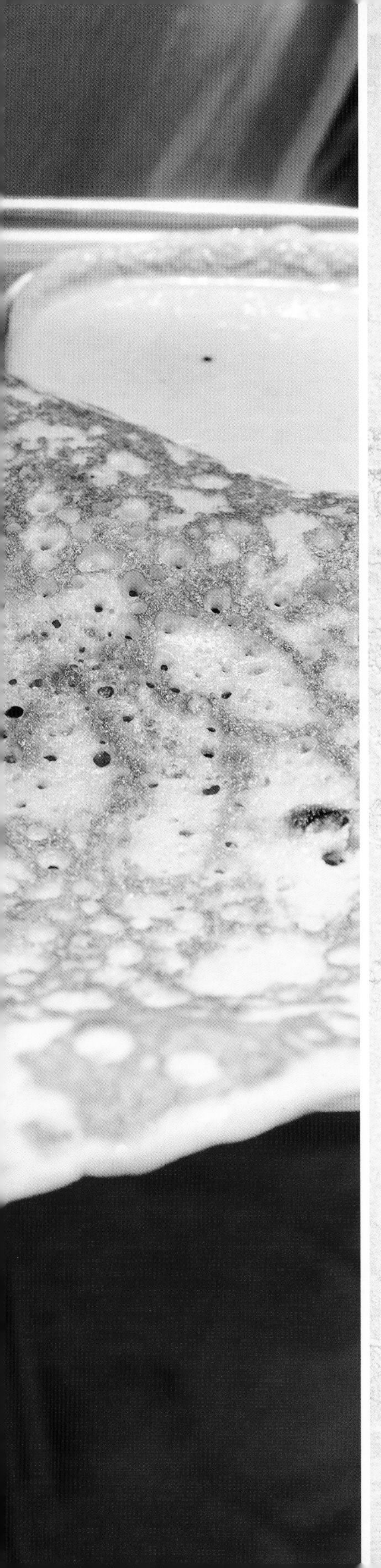

I have been to the port city of Mangalore in the state of Karnataka, with its tropical monsoon climate, many times in my life. Each visit has left an indelible mark upon who I am as a chef. It begins with my arrival at Mangalore Central, established in 1907 and the origin point of India's longest train route, where I immediately head for the dosa vendor, who expertly prepares a perfect dosa for me: edges crispy, interior slightly chewy, a sunny yellow color through and through, rolled up into a cylinder, and served with a side of coconut chutney. I am struck by how a few humble ingredients can be transformed into something so dazzling in the hands of someone who has spent a lifetime mastering their craft.

Mangalore, which is on the Arabian Sea on the Malabar Coast, has an ancient history that has enticed explorers, scholars, merchants, traders, philosophers, treasure hunters, and adventure seekers to its shores for thousands of years. The Roman historian Pliny the Elder warned sailors of the dangers of piracy in the first century, and in the sixth century, the Greek monk and explorer Cosmas Indicopleustes documented Mangalore's thriving pepper trade.

The trade of cashews, coffee, sandalwood, sugar, turmeric, ginger, cassia cinnamon, and rice has made this port city an epicenter of commerce for centuries. Known as a commercial and culinary capital, Mangalore is as admired for its proximity to the stunning Western Ghats mountain range as it is for boasting a culinary history as storied as its ancient past.

With its proximity to the sea, seafood is a critical component of Mangalorean cuisine as are coconut, curry leaves, garlic, chiles, and cashews. Then there are indigenous Upudi recipes, which are different from Mangalorean ones in that they adhere to a strict vegetarian philosophy, rejecting meat and seafood as well as onions and garlic to prevent killing the entire plant by consuming its root system. Its guiding principle is to cook with local and in-season ingredients—I admire these thoughts and try to embrace them in my cooking style.

I was virtually always in a good mood when my family and I arrived in Mangalore because it typically followed an extended stay in Bangalore, eight hours east, to visit my mother's side of

the family who lived on a tea plantation. But first things first—the dosas. With just three simple ingredients and expert skills, the neer dosa vendor reminds me yet again how it's not about complexity and expensive ingredients; it's about patiently mastering a cooking skill, investing time to properly learn a technique and then repeating it over and over again until it hovers on the brink of perfection. This lesson alone is worth the trip to Mangalore.

In the Mangalore station, my father typically bought two dosas: one for the two of us to share, and one for my mother and sister. I usually finished my half first, eating the slightly chewy neer dosa, an ivory-colored dosa made with rice batter, as quickly as I could in order to scurry off in search of the water dosa vendor.

Virtually ever since my young daughter, Shagun, learned to talk, she started pleading for dosas on Sunday mornings. I can't wait to take her to Mangalore so I can do just what my parents did when I rushed off the moment my feet alighted at the station in search of dosas: I'll let her *believe* she's free to wander wherever she needs to go to for her culinary adventures while never letting her out of my sight. As a parent I realize now how challenging it was for my parents to strike the balance they did between encouraging my culinary curiosity while quietly watching over me as I explored, one dosa discovery at a time.

Chukku Kappi

(SPICED COFFEE)

It's still rare to find coffee anywhere in India except at the international coffee chains that are popping up in major cities. But in southern India, the Tamil beverage chukku kappi, a sweetened and spiced coffee drink, is sold at train vendor stalls throughout the region. Because this is a region that appreciates Ayurvedic virtues, chukku kappi is especially popular during the winter months when its flavor is appreciated along with its health-giving properties (it's especially popular as a cold and cough reliever) that come from aromatics such as ginger and holy basil—a slightly astringent herb with hints of mint and lemon available at Asian markets. The coffee is traditionally sweetened with jaggery, but feel free to substitute brown sugar or to omit the sweetener altogether. Unlike chai, chukku kappi is not served with milk, but I have to admit that after a lifetime of drinking countless cups of milky chai, I also add it to my chukku kappi.

MAKES 2 cups

PREPARATION TIME: 10 minutes

8 holy basil leaves, coarsely chopped (or 1 tablespoon fennel fronds)

3 green cardamom pods, lightly crushed with a spoon

2-inch piece fresh ginger, peeled with a spoon and finely chopped

2 tablespoons freshly ground dark roast coffee

1 tablespoon jaggery or brown sugar (optional)

1 teaspoon black peppercorns

1 teaspoon cumin seeds

Whole milk (optional), warmed

In a small saucepan, combine 2 cups water, the holy basil, cardamom, ginger, coffee, jaggery (if using), peppercorns, and cumin seeds. Bring to a boil over high heat, then reduce the heat to medium-low and gently simmer until aromatic, 5 to 7 minutes. Strain the coffee through a fine-mesh sieve and into 2 mugs and serve very hot with milk on the side, if you like.

Brinjal Achaar

(EGGPLANT PICKLES)

MAKES 1 quart
PREPARATION TIME: 40 minutes

There's a pickle shop across the street from the Mangalore train station where I usually stock up on a variety of pickles just before catching my train. It's astonishing to stand in front of the achaar purveyor to take in the seemingly endless variety of pickles—from mango, green chile, and garlic to carrot, jackfruit, and beet—stacked to the ceiling in sealed jars. In southern India, this eggplant or brinjal pickle is a popular accompaniment for chaat and dosas. The eggplants in India are Roma-tomato-sized—much smaller than Italian or even Japanese eggplants—but because they can sometimes be tricky to source, this recipe calls for Italian eggplants. I actually prefer them because there is more flesh to work with to soak up the spices and other aromatics, resulting in a more flavorful pickle. I usually double my batch since they make wonderful host's gifts (and because my family goes through them so quickly).

- ½ cup mustard oil
- 2 teaspoons cumin seeds
- 2 teaspoons fenugreek seeds
- 1 teaspoon Kashmiri or other red chile powder
- 8 garlic cloves, minced
- 2 serrano chiles, finely chopped
- 12 fresh curry leaves
- 1 tablespoon ground turmeric
- 1 tablespoon brown mustard seeds
- 3 medium Italian eggplants, cut into bite-sized pieces
- 1 tablespoon finely chopped fresh ginger
- 1 cup distilled white vinegar
- 1 teaspoon sugar
- 1 tablespoon kosher salt

In a heavy-bottomed medium pot, combine the mustard oil, cumin, fenugreek, and chile powder. Set over medium-high heat and bring the oil to a vigorous simmer. Reduce the heat to medium-low, add the garlic and serranos, and sauté until the garlic is aromatic and the chiles have softened, about 3 minutes. Add the curry leaves, turmeric, and mustard seeds and sauté until the mustard seeds begin to pop, about 2 minutes.

Add the eggplant, ginger, vinegar, ⅓ cup water, sugar, and salt and increase the heat to medium-high. Once the liquid begins to simmer, reduce the heat to medium and gently simmer until the eggplant begins to break down and the mixture has thickened, 18 to 22 minutes. Remove from the heat and cool to room temperature before spooning it into a sterilized 1-quart jar. Cool to room temperature before sealing the jar and refrigerating until chilled. The pickles will keep for up to 1 month in the refrigerator.

INDIAN PICKLES

Achaar is the Hindi word for pickle, but make no mistake, these are not your Midwestern grandmother's sweet dill cucumber pickles! Indian pickles are often mouth-puckering affairs, typically made with a base of mustard oil in northern India and sesame oil in the south. Spices are added to achieve an alchemy of pungent, tangy sweetness and fiery heat. Achaar is served as a condiment with virtually everything, and considering how flavorful it is, the tiniest drop on a spoonful of rice is enough to transform it from timid wallflower to liveliest guest at the Bollywood party. There are countless varieties of achaar, and each state has hundreds of recipes. Indians pickle everything from eggplants, garlic, chiles, mangoes, and carrots to hibiscus, coconut, mutton, shrimp, tomatoes, and gooseberries. No chaat gathering is complete without several jars of vibrantly colored achaar on the table.

Neer Dosa

(WATER DOSA)

MAKES about 8 dosas

PREPARATION TIME: 15 minutes, plus 4 hours to soak the rice

Today, dosas are enjoyed throughout most of India, but their origins are in southern India, where they have been savored for centuries, especially for breakfast, sometimes stuffed with a wide variety of ingredients, including tomatoes, chickpea curry, or strips of fresh mango. The most familiar dosa batter is made with rice flour and lentils and fermented for 8 to 12 hours, resulting in its signature slightly crispy-yet-chewy texture. This *neer dosa*, which means "water dosa" in the Tulu language, is not fermented and doesn't contain lentils. Its texture is light and airy with a milky ivory hue as opposed to the more familiar golden dosa color. It's a low-maintenance recipe, requiring only three ingredients: rice, coconut, and water. Cooking the dosa can take a few attempts to get right (similar to making pancakes or crepes), but keep trying. Eventually you'll have the technique down. I've also added coconut to liven it up, and I usually serve it with an array of chutneys and brinjal achaar (like the Eggplant Pickles, page 184).

1 cup short- or medium-grain white rice

½ cup unsweetened shredded coconut

Table salt

Vegetable oil, as needed

Chutneys, store-bought or homemade (pages 29–31), for serving

Brinjal Achaar (optional; page 184), for serving

Rinse the rice under cold running water to remove residual starch, transfer to a bowl, and let rest at room temperature for 4 hours.

Transfer the rice to a food processor and pulse until ground, about sixteen 1-second pulses. Add the coconut and ½ cup water and process until a paste is formed, about 45 seconds—it should be very thin and runny. Add a little more water, if necessary, to achieve this consistency. Season with salt.

Lightly grease a round nonstick griddle or a large nonstick pan with oil, and then heat the griddle or pan over medium heat until it is hot enough that a drop of water flicked onto it sizzles immediately. Ladle approximately ¼ cup batter into the center of the griddle and quickly, while swirling the griddle with your other hand, use the base of the ladle to spread the batter across the griddle in a thin and even layer. Cover the griddle with a large lid for 1 minute in order to encourage steaming. The batter will not become golden brown as it cooks, but you will know when it is done when bubbles begin to form all over the surface. Use a large offset spatula to carefully fold the edges of the dosa over to form a triangle, transfer bottom side up to a plate, and serve immediately with chutneys and pickle (if desired). Repeat with the remaining batter.

Tuppa Dosa

(FERMENTED DAL AND RICE CREPE)

This is the dosa from southern India that people think of when they fall into a dosa daydream. Or does that only happen to me? The tuppa dosa batter is fermented, resulting in a punchy flavor tempered by a nutty finish from the ghee. My suggestion is to whip up the batter just before bed so it's ready for you in the morning, since dosas are typically how many in southern India begin their day.

MAKES about 8 dosas

PREPARATION TIME: 20 minutes, plus 17 hours to soak and ferment the batter

1 cup urad dal

1 teaspoon fenugreek seeds

4 cups medium-grain rice

Kosher salt

Ghee, store-bought or homemade (page 33), melted

Chutneys, store-bought or homemade (pages 29–31), for serving

Brinjal Achaar (optional; page 184), for serving

Place the urad dal and fenugreek in a bowl with enough water to cover it by 2 inches and let it soak at room temperature for 5 hours. Soak the rice in a separate bowl with enough water to cover it by 2 inches and also let it soak at room temperature for 5 hours.

Drain both the urad dal and rice and transfer them to a food processor. Process until the batter is fluffy, 3 to 4 minutes. Season with salt, transfer to a bowl, cover the bowl with a damp paper towel, and let the batter ferment at room temperature for 12 hours.

Lightly grease a round nonstick griddle or large nonstick pan with ghee and then set over medium-high heat until hot enough that a drop of water flicked onto it sizzles immediately. Ladle about ¼ cup batter onto the center of the griddle and quickly, while swirling the griddle with your other hand, use the base of the ladle to spread the batter across the griddle in a thin, even layer. Drizzle ghee over the dosa as it cooks. Cover the dosa with a lid for 1 minute and then use a large offset spatula to loosen it from the griddle and carefully turn it over. It should detach easily with a bit of practice, and you should have no trouble flipping it at this stage because it will be quite dry and pliable. Cook for about 1 more minute and then use the offset spatula to transfer to a plate. Place the spatula under one side of the dosa, roll it up into a large tube, and serve immediately with chutneys and pickle (if desired). Repeat with the remaining batter.

Goli Baje

(CRISPY FRIED FRITTERS)

MAKES about 32 goli baje

PREPARATION TIME: 20 minutes, plus 3 hours to rest the batter

Goli baje is one of the most popular teatime snacks in Mangalore. These dainty fried fritters are punctuated with coconut, chiles, ginger, and cilantro and have a humble appearance that belies their sophisticated, well-balanced flavor. They're perfect for dipping into a cup of hot chai for a midafternoon revival. At the Mangalore train station, I load up on bags of them for the long journey ahead of me.

2 tablespoons unsweetened shredded coconut

2 green chiles, finely chopped

1 tablespoon finely chopped fresh ginger

2 tablespoons finely chopped fresh cilantro

10 roughly chopped or torn fresh curry leaves

Pinch of hing (asafetida)

1 cup whole-milk yogurt

½ teaspoon baking soda

Kosher salt

2 cups all-purpose flour

Vegetable oil, for deep-frying

Coconut chutney, store-bought or homemade (page 159), for serving

Chai (page 220), for serving

In a large bowl, combine the coconut, chiles, ginger, cilantro, curry leaves, and hing. Stir in the yogurt, baking soda, and a generous pinch of salt until well blended. Add the flour and stir until a smooth batter is formed. Cover the bowl with a damp cloth and set aside at room temperature for 3 hours.

Line a plate with paper towels. Pour 5 inches oil into a heavy-bottomed pot and heat over medium-high heat to 350°F on an instant-read thermometer. Reduce the heat to medium, and working in batches (do not overcrowd the pot), use an ice cream scoop to form balls of the batter and carefully drop them into the oil. Use a slotted spoon to turn the balls as they fry until they turn a light golden brown and are cooked through, 4 to 5 minutes. Transfer to the paper towels to drain. Allow the oil to return to frying temperature between batches.

Serve hot with coconut chutney and a cup of chai on the side.

Ernakulam

Sambaram
Kerala Plantain Chips
Uzhunnu Vada
Kerala Fish Fry
Semiya Payasam

My aunt Annie Randhawa had a profound influence on my decision to become a chef. Although she lived with my uncle in Bangalore far to the east, she was from Kerala in the south, the state where Ernakulum is located, and skilled at combining culinary traditions from several Indian states into a single dish. I carried the lessons I learned from her into my own cooking style, which has always blended my favorite techniques and ingredients from every corner of the world.

There was a copy of the *Joy of Cooking* on Aunt Annie's kitchen shelf, and I loved nothing more than delving into it while she baked shortbread cookies, which perfumed the house with notes of orange and vanilla. She was also famous in our family for her peach-cashew brittle. Peaches are not indigenous to India and were a rare delicacy, but whenever she asked me what I wanted to eat, this was always my request. She usually handed me a box stuffed with the French Asterix comics that she kept just for me while she made her brittle. It was my favorite thing to read as a kid (still is), and I can't think of anything I loved more than making brittle with Aunt Annie while catching up on the antics of Asterix.

The name of Kerala, where my aunt lived, a southwestern state along the tropical Malabar coast, is from the indigenous Malayali words *kera,* which means "coconut," and *alam,* which means "land." Kerala surely is the land of coconuts, but its culinary heritage encompasses so much more than this single ingredient. Its fish curries, roasted clams, nutmeg and clove-laced chutneys, and elaborate dishes served during Hindu feast days known as *sadyas* tell the story of wave after wave of humanity who found their way to Kerala's shores. A visit to India is typically one of overstimulation: crowded markets, honking horns, cramped train cars, and an abiding exhaustion brought on by living life in perpetual motion. The energy sparked by this chaos is stitched into my DNA—it's simultaneously thrilling and exhausting—and it's what propels me forward in life. I carry it with me everywhere I go, to help fuel new projects and transform my dreams into reality.

But sometimes when I travel to India, I'm looking for more than to be swept up into the madness. I crave a sanctuary where

ABOVE LEFT: *Vermicelli payasan.*
ABOVE MIDDLE: *Mangosteen syrup with crushed ice.*
ABOVE RIGHT: *A hand-operated ice-grinding machine.*

I can escape the world for a while, a peaceful place gilded in golden light. Kerala delivers. Kerala is home to vast national parks, tranquil backwater canals, and wildlife sanctuaries providing refuge to elephants, tigers, leopards, five hundred bird species, langur monkeys, and over four thousand unique flowering plant species—nine hundred of which are used medicinally.

For over five thousand years, Kerala has bewitched waves of seekers in the same way it seduces me when I arrive at the Ernakulam Junction railway station, my gateway to culinary paradise. Some of these seekers, like the Romans who arrived in Kerala's ports two thousand years ago, came aboard ships heavy in gold to trade for black pepper. These spice adventurers sought to become wealthy from the sale of the sugar, cloves, coffee, tea, cardamom, coconut, bamboo, cashews, and nutmeg that were and are still traded here. Others, like persecuted Syrian Christians, were simply seeking a more peaceful existence.

Arabs, Chinese, Dutch, Greeks, Romans, and Portuguese have all left their mark on the cuisine of Kerala, defined by its alchemy of flavors born of seductive ingredients like vanilla, tapioca, vetiver (a fragrant wild grass similar in aroma to citronella or lemongrass), and coconut. In ancient Sumerian records, Kerala is referred to as the "spice garden of India," and that remains true today. Many were seeking riches, but I believe some of them made the long journey for the same reason I do: to find a delicious refuge from the chaos of the world.

Sambaram

(SPICED BUTTERMILK)

The Ernakulam Junction railway station is the busiest station in southern India. It's mass chaos here, but the madness is always tempered by a rejuvenating cup of sambaram sold by vendors inside the station. This chilled spiced buttermilk drink is a refreshing beverage—with notes of heat from the chiles, tanginess from the buttermilk, brightness from the lime and ginger, and earthiness from the cumin—appreciated throughout southern India for its cooling and digestive properties. It's often enjoyed on feast days, referred to as Perunnals, such as Edappally in April and Kallooppara in July (both feast days are named after villages in the region), but is also available on the streets of Kerala where it's typically served in a terra-cotta cup called a kulhar. For a less potent drink, strain it through a cheesecloth-lined fine-mesh sieve after it's blended.

MAKES 2 drinks

PREPARATION TIME: 5 minutes

1 cucumber, peeled and coarsely chopped

1 garlic clove, peeled

1 tablespoon finely chopped fresh ginger

1 celery stalk, thinly sliced

1 green chile, finely chopped

2 cups buttermilk

1 teaspoon fresh lime juice

1 teaspoon ground cumin

8 fresh curry leaves

Pinch of hing (asafetida)

6 ice cubes (abut ½ cup)

Kosher salt

In a blender or food processor, combine the cucumber, garlic, ginger, celery, chile, buttermilk, lime juice, cumin, curry leaves, hing, and ice and puree on high speed until smooth. Add 1 cup water and puree until smooth. Season with salt and serve very cold.

AYURVEDIC MEDICINE

The word *Ayurvedic* means "the science of life." It's a set of holistic principles designed to strike a balance between the body, mind, and consciousness and to encourage mental and physical wellness. Indians have incorporated Ayurvedic precepts into their culinary traditions for thousands of years. Devout adherents believe that the Hindu god of Ayurveda, Dhanvantari, passed his knowledge on to the sages who documented the health benefits of ingredients, cooking and farming techniques, exercise, and prayer. Indians have internalized these beliefs and they are integral to how many of us exist in the world. When I see a spice, I appreciate it not just for its flavor but also for the specific health benefits I know it will offer me. When I moved to the United States I was surprised by how Ayurvedic as "alternative medicine" often had negative stigma attached to it, when eating for health, strength, clarity, and balance should be an integral part of life. There is immense power in food beyond its ability to bring us together to enjoy a meal. Food empowers us, mind, body, and spirit.

Kerala Plantain Chips

(FRIED PLANTAIN CHIPS)

MAKES about 3 cups

PREPARATION TIME: 15 minutes

I remember the vendors at the train station in Kerala selling these lightly spiced plantain chips in large newspaper cones stained from the grease of the coconut oil they were fried in. Plantains are higher in starch and less sweet than their close cousin, the garden variety banana. In this recipe, the plantains are shaved directly into the oil using a vegetable peeler, resulting in a thin chip that's a bit lighter in texture than a potato chip. Once the plantains are added to the oil, a spoonful of turmeric water is added to it, which generates bubbles and infuses the chips with flavor. The residual notes of coconut oil and the plantain itself take me straight back to the tropical climate of Kerala whenever I serve up a batch in my Nashville-based restaurant Chaatable. I suggest pairing them with a chilled beer to kick-start a chaat party.

Coconut oil, melted, for deep-frying

Vegetable oil, for deep-frying

1 teaspoon ground turmeric

½ teaspoon kosher salt, plus more to taste

2 large green plantains

Ice cold beer (optional)

Line a plate with paper towels. Pour 1½ inches coconut oil into a large heavy-bottomed pot. Then pour in enough vegetable oil to reach a total depth of 6 inches. Heat over medium-high heat to 350°F on an instant-read thermometer.

In a small bowl, use a fork to whisk together ½ cup water, the turmeric, and salt and have at the ready.

Just before frying, peel the plantains. Then, using a vegetable peeler, carefully peel "chips" from the plantains lengthwise and directly into the oil. Do not overcrowd the pot, or the chips will not fry properly. Wearing an oven mitt, carefully add 2 teaspoons turmeric water to the oil. It will fizz and sputter, so be cautious during this step. Fry the chips until golden brown, about 2 minutes, using a slotted spoon or a frying spider to move the chips around as they fry to ensure even coloring and cooking. Transfer them to the paper towels and season with salt. Repeat, allowing the oil to return to frying temperature between batches.

Serve the chips hot or cold, with a chilled beer if desired.

BOTTOMS UP

Uzhunnu Vada

(SPICY CASHEW AND COCONUT FRITTERS)

MAKES about 24 fritters
PREPARATION TIME: 20 minutes, plus 2 hours to soak the dal

Uzhunnu vada is a popular breakfast and favorite teatime snack item in southern India. These spicy fritters, a staple in Tamil cuisine, are typically shaped like doughnuts, with a slightly crispy, toasty exterior that gives way to an airy interior laced with notes of cashew, coconut, chile, and ginger. My train rides north from Kerala tend to commence before sunrise, and I'm never fully alert until I find the vendor selling cups of a potent brew of spiced coffee known as kappi (page 183). After a few sips, my eyes dart around until I spot the uzhunnu vada vendor. He's usually in close proximity to the kappi stand because it's the perfect pairing. Once I see him, I buy another cup of coffee and dash over to the fritter stand as fast as the rising sun will carry me.

1 cup urad dal

¼ cup chana dal

2 tablespoons finely chopped cashews

3 tablespoons unsweetened shredded coconut

1 teaspoon ground ginger

1 tablespoon finely chopped fresh cilantro

2 green chiles, finely chopped

2 tablespoons rice flour, plus more as needed

Pinch of hing (asafetida)

Kosher salt

Vegetable oil, for deep-frying

Coconut chutney, store-bought or homemade (page 159), for serving

Chukku Kappi (page 183), for serving

Combine the dals in a colander and rinse well under cold running water to remove any residue. Transfer to a bowl and add water to cover by 2 inches. Soak at room temperature for 2 hours.

Drain the dals and transfer to a food processor. Process until a thick, smooth paste (similar to creamy peanut butter) forms, 4 to 5 minutes. Add a little water while blending to achieve this result, if necessary.

Transfer the dal paste to a medium bowl and stir in the cashews, coconut, ginger, cilantro, and chiles until incorporated. Add the rice flour and hing and stir once more until incorporated. Season with salt. The dough should not be sticky and you should be able to shape it into a ball without dough sticking to your fingers. If it's too sticky, stir in a little more flour to achieve the desired texture.

Line a plate with paper towels. Pour 6 inches oil into a heavy-bottomed medium pot and heat over medium-high heat to 350°F on an instant-read thermometer. Roll a golf-ball-sized piece of dough into a ball and punch a hole through its center with your finger (like a doughnut). Working in batches (do not overcrowd the pot), use a slotted spoon to carefully transfer fritters to the oil and fry until they rise to the surface of the oil and turn light golden brown, 4 to 6 minutes, using a slotted spoon to gently turn them over a few times as they fry. Transfer them to the paper towels to drain. Allow the oil to return to frying temperature between batches.

Serve hot or at room temperature with coconut chutney and a cup of hot chukku kappi on the side.

Kerala Fish Fry

No visit to Kerala is complete without indulging in a fish fry in this sea-kissed city. During my university days, my friends and I loved nothing better than setting up camp on the beach for an inexpensive plate of fried fish (with sand garnish at no additional cost). But even at the train station you could usually find a vendor by following the aroma of spicy fish frying in a vat of bubbling oil. Kingfish is a popular choice in Kerala, but any firm-fleshed whitefish such as halibut, cod, red snapper, or tilapia could be substituted. The coconut oil could be swapped out for vegetable oil, but you will miss out on the tropical note that the coconut imparts. Coconut oil is available as either refined or unrefined. Refined coconut oil is produced by first baking the coconuts before extracting their oil. The oil is then "bleached" by filtering it through clay. Refined coconut oil has a more neutral flavor and aroma than its more robustly flavored and scented unrefined counterpart, which does not undergo the baking or bleaching process, resulting in a more tropical flavor note.

SERVES 4

PREPARATION TIME: 1 hour

2 tablespoons store-bought ginger-garlic paste

1 small shallot, finely chopped

1 tablespoon distilled white vinegar

1 teaspoon ground turmeric

1 teaspoon Kashmiri or other red chile powder

½ teaspoon freshly ground black pepper

Kosher salt

4 kingfish fillets (8 ounces each), or halibut, cod, red snapper, or tilapia

Coconut oil, for shallow-frying

Vegetable oil, for shallow-frying

FOR SERVING

Thinly sliced red onion

Finely chopped fresh cilantro leaves

Lime wedges

In a food processor, combine the ginger-garlic paste, shallot, vinegar, turmeric, chile powder, and black pepper and process until smooth but still slightly chunky, about 45 seconds. Season with salt. Slather the marinade over the fish, ensuring that it covers all of the nooks and crannies. Place in a bowl and refrigerate for 30 minutes.

Line a plate with paper towels. Add ⅓ inch of coconut oil to a large, wide pan. Pour in enough vegetable oil to come to a total depth of 1 inch. Heat over medium-high heat to 325°F on an instant-read thermometer (or until hot enough that a pinch of flour flicked onto its surface sizzles). Reduce the heat to medium and carefully add 2 fish fillets to the oil and fry until golden brown, 2 to 3 minutes. Flip the fish over and fry until the other side is golden brown, another 2 to 3 minutes. Work carefully during this step to prevent being burned by the sputtering oil and marinade. Transfer the fish to the paper towels to drain, and season with salt. Repeat with the remaining fish, allowing the oil temperature to frying temperature before the next batch.

Serve the fish hot, garnished with onions and cilantro, with a lime wedge on the side.

Semiya Payasam

(RAISIN-CASHEW NOODLE PUDDING)

SERVES 6

PREPARATION TIME: 20 minutes

Semiya payasam is essentially the Indian version of rice pudding, made with rice noodles instead of rice grains, that is served during the Tamil New Year celebration in April. In spite of its festive connection, it's also sold by vendors throughout southern India during other times of the year. The cashews and plump raisins ratchet up the cozy factor, southern India style.

2 tablespoons ghee, store-bought or homemade (page 33)

2 tablespoons golden raisins

2 tablespoons finely chopped cashews

1 cup (1-inch) pieces rice vermicelli (break with your hands)

4 cups whole milk

½ cup packed light brown sugar

¼ teaspoon ground cardamom

Kosher salt

Line a plate with paper towels. In a saucepan, melt the ghee over medium heat. Add the raisins and sauté until plump, 4 to 5 minutes. Transfer them to the paper towels to drain. Add the cashews to the same pan and sauté until golden brown, then transfer to the plate with the raisins to drain. Add the vermicelli to the pan and sauté until golden brown while stirring constantly to prevent the noodles from burning, about 3 minutes.

Add the milk and increase the heat to medium-high. Simmer, stirring occasionally with a wooden spoon to prevent scorching, until the noodles begin to soften, 2 to 3 minutes. The milk should not boil; if the simmering becomes too vigorous, reduce the heat to bring it to a gentle simmer.

Mix in the brown sugar and cook, stirring occasionally, until the vermicelli is cooked through and the liquid slightly thickened, about 3 minutes. Remove from the heat, stir in the cardamom, cashews, and raisins and season with salt.

Serve in individual bowls while still warm or refrigerate until chilled and lightly set.

ARUNACHAL PRADESH
SIKKIM
Lucknow
ASSAM
Guwahati
BIHAR
MEGHALAYA
JHARKHAND
TRIPURA
WEST BENGAL
Ranchi
MIZORAM
Kolkata
CHHATTISGARH
ODISHA
Puri
Chennai

The East

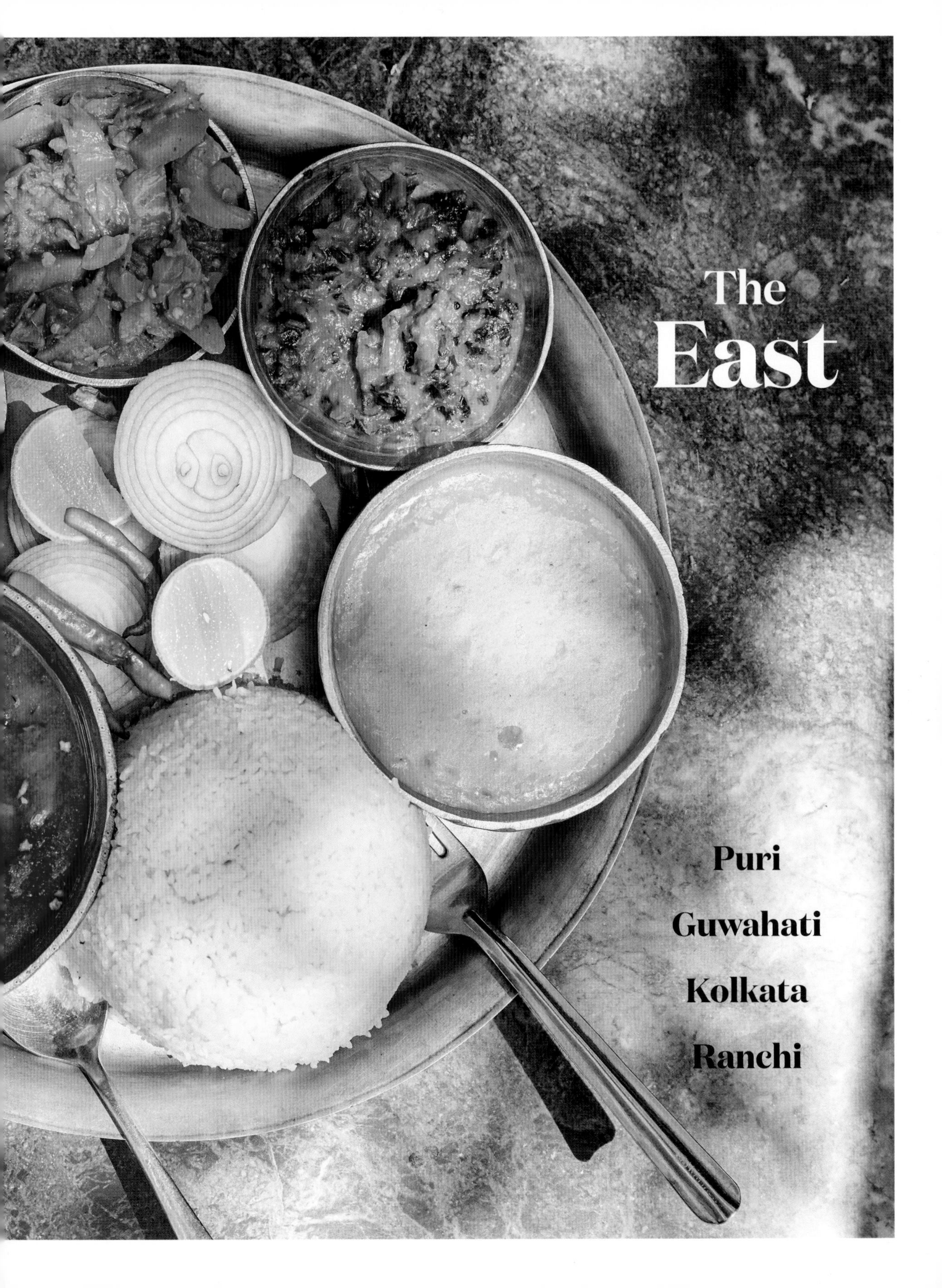

Puri

Guwahati

Kolkata

Ranchi

Puri

Tamarind Gin and Tonic
Cucumber Salad
Bhaja Masala
Ghugni Chaat
Chungdi Mulai
Chhena Poda

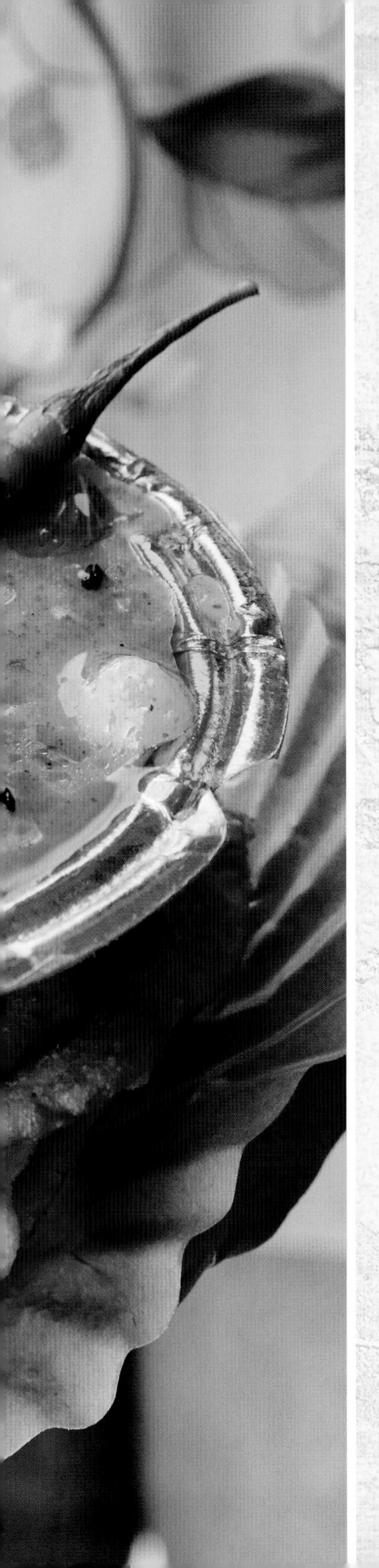

The state of Odisha in eastern India is not as familiar to visitors as states like Rajasthan or Gujarat, but the region's Oriya cuisine is one of the most esteemed in the nation. There was a time when the highly skilled, nuanced cooking of the Oriya chefs from Puri was sought out in neighboring states for important events like weddings, festivals, and to entertain visiting dignitaries. I share this admiration not only because the recipes that comprise the cuisine are sublime, but also because of the spiritual meaning it has for me and so many Hindus scattered throughout the world. I respect the value Oriya chefs place upon their ingredients and the mindful way they prepare their recipes.

Oriya cuisine often includes earthy mustard oil in its savory dishes, but in general, the recipes contain less oil than they do in other parts of the country. While the spices used are often less fiery, the flavor profile is just as nuanced and well-balanced. Green papaya, eggplant, pumpkin, plantains, chiles, potatoes, and tomatoes are all important ingredients in Oriya cuisine; it's the meaningful and deliberate way that they're prepared that distinguishes it from any other. Oriyan chefs were notable for many reasons. One was the exacting way they incorporated hundreds of ingredients into dozens of complex dishes. It is said that a master Oriyan chef would prepare over 170 dishes at the temple each day. Oriyan cuisine is revered for its deep ties to ancestral culinary traditions dating back hundreds of years, and its chefs are deeply admired for their meticulously organized kitchens.

The seashore city of Puri on India's northeastern coast was about an eleven-hour train ride from my hometown of Ranchi (not that far away by Indian train travel standards!), and I spent a great deal of time there growing up. One of my uncles was from the area and we also had good family friends who lived in the city. Our visits typically began with our arrival at the Puri railway station, opened in 1897, where I immediately started hunting for the ghugni chaat vendor. This specialty of eastern India features white peas (safed vatana), potatoes, tomatoes, tamarind, and fiery green chutney sprinkled with bhaja masala, the most notable spice blend of this region, whose main flavor notes are cardamom, cumin, fennel, and coriander.

After sating my hunger at the vendor stalls in and around the Puri station, we'd venture out into one of the most important pilgrimage sites for Hindus: Jagannath Temple, built in the twelfth century. This revered temple is an important spiritual center for Hindu and Buddhist pilgrims because of its millennium-old historical significance and because the nonsectarian god Jagannath, its namesake, is a significant deity in both religions. The temple is also responsible for generating 80 percent of Puri's revenue each year as a result of the tourists who flood the city annually. There are twenty-four important festival days revolving around the temple each year, the most important being Ratha Yatra, the festival of the chariots, which attracts millions of pilgrims to the city each summer.

Temple food is a critical component of this city's culinary repertoire. Cooks are renowned for cooking recipes from Hindu scriptures, the most revered being the feast of Maha Prasad, a meal comprising fifty-six dishes, each one representing the eight daily meals the Hindu god Krishna sacrificed for seven days because he was busy saving a rural village from a thunderstorm. I'm not sure if I would be able to make such a sacrifice, especially in Puri, where the food is so transcendent, but I am certain that I, too, would be able to eat eight meals a day if I lived here.

Tamarind Gin and Tonic

Gin and tonics are one of India's most popular cocktails. This one comes with a tamarind twist for a refreshing pucker, and orange zest for a citrusy note mellowed by the honey. You would never find alcoholic beverages within an Indian train station, due to the stigma attached to drinking in open public places such as train and bus stations, but there's a cocktail bar a few blocks from the station on Red Cross Road where I had this drink for the first time. It's not officially on the menu at my restaurants, but it's a recipe I share with the bartenders to prepare for customers who request a drink inspired by India. This is that cocktail.

MAKES 1 cocktail
PREPARATION TIME: 5 minutes

2 teaspoons tamarind paste

1 teaspoon grated orange zest

1 teaspoon honey

1 ounce gin

Ice

Tonic water, as needed

Orange slice, for garnish

In a small bowl, combine the tamarind, orange zest, and honey and use a fork to smash the mixture. Strain into a highball glass. Add the gin, fill with enough ice to reach the top, and top off with tonic. Stir, garnish with an orange slice, and serve.

Cucumber Salad

SERVES 4
PREPARATION TIME: 10 minutes

This is a refreshing salad that comes together in just a few minutes and adds a nice counterpoint to heavier dishes. For a bit more flourish, toss in cubes of paneer and a handful of roasted peanuts.

- 1 tablespoon finely chopped fresh cilantro, plus more for serving
- Juice of 1 lime
- 1 teaspoon cumin seeds, toasted
- Pinch of Kashmiri or other red chile powder
- ½ teaspoon sugar
- Kosher salt
- 1 small red onion, finely chopped
- 2 medium cucumbers, unpeeled and coarsely chopped
- 1 cup halved cherry tomatoes
- 2 radishes, thinly sliced
- 1 carrot, peeled and shredded
- 1 green chile, finely chopped
- Lime wedges

Whisk together the cilantro, lime juice, cumin, chile powder, and sugar in a medium bowl until the sugar is dissolved. Season with salt.

In a large bowl, toss together the onion, cucumbers, tomatoes, radishes, carrot, and green chile. Drizzle the dressing over the vegetables, toss to coat, and serve with additional cilantro and lime wedges.

Papaya and cucumber salad vendor.

Bhaja Masala

(CHAAT SPICE BLEND)

This toasted spice blend is popular in the Odiya cooking of Puri. Although it's a bit time-consuming, be sure to pan-toast each spice separately, because each one has its own toasting time. The spices lose their flavor over time, so this is at its freshest within a week or two, though it will keep in a dry, covered container in a dark place for up to 1 month.

MAKES about 6 tablespoons

PREPARATION TIME: 10 minutes

- 4 whole cloves
- 3 tablespoons cumin seeds
- 1 tablespoon coriander seeds
- 1 tablespoon fennel seeds
- 1 cinnamon stick, broken into small pieces
- 6 green cardamom pods
- 6 dried red chiles, broken into small pieces
- 2 bay leaves

Toast each spice separately in a very dry pan over medium heat until each one becomes aromatic, 45 to 90 seconds per spice. Combine all of the spices together in a spice grinder and blend on high speed until pulverized. Store in an airtight container in a dark place for up to 1 month.

HOW TO STORE SPICES

Spices are an integral part of countless Indian recipes. Here are a few tips for storing spices to increase their shelf life and maintain their flavor.

- Store spices in clean, dry glass containers with a tight-fitting lid.
- Store in a dark place.
- Store away from heat at a temperature below 70°F.
- Do not refrigerate spices.
- Label spice jars with the name of the spice as well as the date of purchase.
- Spices will keep for an average of 6 months.

Ghugni Chaat

(POTATO, PEA, AND TOMATO SNACK)

SERVES 4

PREPARATION TIME: 30 minutes, plus 12 hours to soak the peas

Ghugni chaat is one of East India's most popular snacks, found on street corners throughout the entire region of Odisha and West Bengal. Besides soaking the peas overnight, this chaat comes together in about 30 minutes and is a nutritious vegetarian dish to serve at a chaat party (page 214) or on a hectic weeknight when you're craving something low maintenance but with complex flavor. Bhaja masala is the spice blend typically served with ghugni chaat and is available at Indian markets, or you can create your own using the recipe on page 211.

- 1 cup dried white peas
- 1 large russet potato, peeled
- 2 tablespoons vegetable oil
- Kosher salt
- 1 teaspoon cumin seeds
- 1 medium red onion, finely chopped
- 2 teaspoons finely chopped fresh ginger
- 1 large tomato, coarsely chopped

FOR SERVING

- Green Chutney (page 30)
- Tamarind Chutney, store-bought or homemade (page 29)
- Bhaja Masala, store-bought or homemade (page 211)
- Finely chopped fresh cilantro
- Finely chopped green chiles
- Lime wedges

Rinse the peas in a colander to remove any debris or residue and place them in a large bowl. Add enough water to cover the peas by 2 inches and set aside to soak for 12 hours. Drain the peas.

In a medium saucepan, combine the potato and enough water to cover it by 3 inches. Bring the water to a boil over high heat, reduce the heat to medium, and simmer the potato until tender, about 15 minutes. Drain and, once the potato is cool enough to handle, peel it using your fingers while it is still warm so the peel easily slips away from the flesh. Coarsely chop.

In a sauté pan, heat 1 tablespoon of the oil over medium heat and fry the potatoes, stirring often, until they are golden brown, 7 to 9 minutes. Use a slotted spoon to transfer the potatoes to a medium bowl. Season with salt and set aside.

Add the remaining 1 tablespoon oil to the pan. Add the cumin seeds and sauté, stirring often, until they are aromatic, about 1 minute. Add the onion and ginger and sauté until the onion is translucent, 4 to 5 minutes. Add the tomato and sauté until it begins to break down, 3 to 5 minutes. Add the drained peas, fried potatoes, and 1½ cups water. Reduce the heat to medium-low, cover, and cook until the sauce takes on a gravy-like consistency, about 10 minutes. Season with salt.

To serve, spoon the ghugni into a small bowl, drizzle with green and tamarind chutneys, sprinkle with bhaja masala, and garnish with cilantro, green chiles, and a lime wedge.

Chungdi Malai

(COCONUT SHRIMP CURRY)

Chungdi malai is one of the most coveted dishes of Puri, showcasing the elegant flavors that are the trademark of the regional Oriya cuisine. Coconut milk and shrimp are natural dancing partners, rounded out with the earthy note of ghee laced with a tapestry of spices. The shrimp should be marinated for about 1 hour to infuse them with flavor, but otherwise this dish comes together quickly, making it an ideal family meal on a weekday that calls for something special. It was in Puri where I tried my first shrimp, which my father had bought from one of the train vendors. They were covered in a fiery red chile sauce that I didn't realize also contained large chunks of pineapple which when covered in sauce closely resembled the shape and size of the shrimp. I took a bite of what I thought was shrimp but was actually pineapple and exclaimed to my dad, "Shrimp tastes just like pineapple!" The incident still makes him laugh, and whenever he visits one of my restaurants in Nashville, I inevitably hear him tell this story at least once to a tableful of customers. Pineapple is not a traditional ingredient in chungdi malai, but sometimes I add it, especially when preparing it for my father, because it always gets a laugh out of him. If you'd like to include pineapple, add 1 cup coarsely chopped fresh or canned pineapple when you add the coconut milk.

SERVES 4

PREPARATION TIME: 25 minutes, plus 1 hour to marinate the shrimp

2 pounds (about 24) peeled and deveined medium shrimp

4 whole cloves

2 bay leaves

2 cinnamon sticks, broken up into small pieces

2 teaspoons ground turmeric

2 teaspoons garam masala

1 teaspoon ground cardamom

Kosher salt

1 tablespoon mustard oil

1 large yellow onion, finely chopped

1 tablespoon finely chopped fresh ginger

2 teaspoons ground cumin

1 teaspoon Kashmiri or other red chile powder

1 teaspoon sugar

1 cup full-fat coconut milk

2 tablespoons whole-milk yogurt

1 tablespoon ghee, store-bought or homemade (page 33)

Finely chopped fresh cilantro

Lime wedges

Basmati Rice (page 262)

In a large bowl, toss together the shrimp, cloves, bay leaves, cinnamon, turmeric, garam masala, and cardamom until the shrimp are well coated. Season with salt, cover the bowl with a damp cloth, and refrigerate for 1 hour. Remove the cloves, bay leaves, and cinnamon.

In a sauté pan, heat the mustard oil over medium-high heat. Add the onion, ginger, cumin, chile powder, and sugar and sauté until the onion is translucent, about 5 minutes Whisk in the coconut milk and yogurt until smooth, then add the ghee and shrimp and simmer until the shrimp are cooked through, 7 to 8 minutes, turning the shrimp over once during cooking. Season with salt.

Sprinkle with cilantro and serve with lime wedges and rice.

CHAAT PARTY

I tell anyone who will listen to me extol the virtues of chaat that they are essentially like a tapas party with the same small, shareable plates infused with Indian flavors. I love to throw chaat parties because it's such a lively way to eat in a communal way with old friends and new. Creativity should be the driving force when deciding what ingredients to bring to the table. Put each item in an individual bowl alongside a stack of larger bowls to enable your guests to mix up their chaat with a spoon or, more traditionally, their hands. If you are able to source banana leaves, I would spread them out over the table before arranging everything else for a bright pop of color. Remind your guests that there are no rules except to strive for that chaat alchemy of tangy, sweet, fiery, and crunchy. There is no limit except your imagination when it comes to ingredients, but here's a list to get you started:

- Coarsely chopped tomatoes, cucumbers, pineapple, mangoes, potatoes, roasted sweet potatoes, coriander, and mint
- Finely chopped onions, tomatoes, cucumbers, ginger, red and green chiles, scallions, and radishes
- Lemon and lime wedges
- Roasted corn kernels
- Star fruit slices
- Tamarind, cilantro-mint, and green chile chutneys
- Raita (whole milk yogurt whisked together with water to make it thin enough to drizzle and then seasoned with salt and freshly squeezed lemon juice)
- Roasted peanuts and cashews
- Puchkas (see page 249)
- Puffed rice
- Sev (see page 266)
- Chakri (chickpea flour crackers)
- Chekkalu (rice flour crackers)
- Thattai (spiced rice flour and sesame crackers)
- Namak para (spiced whole wheat flour crackers)
- Murruku (wheat flour crackers)
- Chaat masala (see page 265)
- Red chile powder

Chhena Poda

(SPICED CHEESE CAKE)

MAKES 1 cake that serves 8 to 10
PREPARATION TIME: 1 hour

The name *chenna poda* translates from the Odia language as "roasted cheese," and that is exactly what this unusual Oriya dessert is made of, hitting all the marks for those with a sweet tooth who also have a weakness for cheese (I am pointing at myself). In essence, this is a sweetened cake made from cheese. Paneer, which is a fresh farmhouse-style cheese popular throughout India, can be made from scratch, but it is also available at Indian markets. Unsalted ricotta could be substituted. I sometimes equate this dessert to the Indian version of Mexican flan because of its caramelized topping. It always delivers the wow factor when I serve it to guests, who can't ever quite decide if they want cheese or something sweet for their dessert course.

Ghee, for the cake pan

8 ounces paneer, store-bought or homemade (page 256)

¼ cup confectioners' sugar

½ teaspoon ground cardamom

2 tablespoons semolina

1½ tablespoons ghee, store-bought or homemade (page 33)

¼ cup whole milk

2 tablespoons roasted cashews

2 tablespoons golden raisins

3 tablespoons granulated sugar

Freshly whipped cream (optional), for serving

Preheat the oven to 350°F. Butter a 9-inch nonstick metal cake pan with some ghee.

In a large bowl, stir together the paneer, confectioners' sugar, and cardamom until incorporated but still slightly chunky. Add the semolina, ghee, and milk and whisk until smooth. Stir in the cashews and raisins and set aside.

Sprinkle the granulated sugar over the bottom of the prepared cake pan. Set the pan on the stove over medium heat and once the sugar just begins to bubble and turn pale golden brown (the sugar will continue to caramelize in the oven, so don't let it get any darker right now), after 8 to 10 minutes, remove the pan from the heat using tongs. (This step is a bit tricky and you might be tempted to move the sugar around with a spoon while it is bubbling, but don't touch it—just let it caramelize on its own.) You will know it's ready for the cake batter when it's bubbling but is still slightly grainy and just turning a pale golden color. Pour the batter into the pan, using a rubber spatula to scrape the bowl clean. It should settle into an even layer on its own, but if it doesn't, use the spatula to create a smooth surface.

Wearing oven mitts, carefully transfer the pan to the oven and bake until a toothpick inserted into the center of the cake comes out clean, 40 to 45 minutes. Transfer to a wire rack and cool in the pan to room temperature. Run a paring knife around the cake's edges and then cover with a serving platter larger than the diameter of the cake and gently flip the cake over—it should slide out, with the caramel coming out with it just like you would see in a flan (though some caramel will be left in the pan—this is fine; see Note).

Slice and serve with freshly whipped cream, if desired. The cake will keep in a covered container in the refrigerator for up to 3 days.

NOTE: *To clean the pan, add some boiling water and let sit for at least 30 minutes to loosen up the browned sugar sticking to the surface of the pan before cleaning it.*

Guwahati

Chai
Aloo Pitika
Chicken Bamboo Curry
Chicken Momos with Tomato-Garlic Dipping Sauce
Thukpa

I didn't know I needed the Himalayan chicken noodle soup thukpa in my life until I arrived at the Guwahati Junction railway station, India's first train station to be entirely powered by solar electricity, in the remote northeastern state of Assam. I was dirty and exhausted from a train journey that unfurled just south of Tibet and Bhutan and north of Bangladesh and Burma along a sliver of land squeezed between these Asian nations. The cuisine of Guwahati has been influenced by these Himalayan countries for thousands of years, and in my steaming bowl of thukpa, spooned into a tin bowl by a ruddy-cheeked vendor, I discovered the revelation that is Assamese cuisine.

Guwahati, nestled along the banks of the mighty Brahmaputra River, is one of Asia's most ancient kingdoms, the coveted tea of Assam its most revered export. The Mughals invaded this remote city situated atop the Shillong Plateau seventeen times over the centuries. The sixteenth-century Kamakhya Temple, a shrine to the Hindu gods Vishnu and Shiva, fortunately survived each invasion and still welcomes pilgrims as it has done for centuries.

Food preservation plays a critical role in Guwahati cuisine, since robust flavors from dried and fermented foods are favored in this region. Vegetables, fruit, and protein such as duck, pork, seafood, squab, and even silkworms (which are fried and enjoyed as a snack after they are preserved) are either dried or fermented to preserve them for later use. The fermentation process, made primarily through pickling, often results in a sour flavor beloved in this region of the world. Most meals begin with savory dishes known as *khar* and end on a sour note, referred to as *tenga*, due to the fermentation. Pungent mustard oil is the preferred cooking fat, and open-fire cooking is a popular way to prepare both meat and vegetables. Arguably the city's most notable dish, beloved throughout many states in India, is the stuffed and steamed dumpling called a *momo*. Guwahati cuisine is not as spice-forward as in other parts of India, since spices are not as readily available in this region as they are elsewhere.

Tibetan, Nepalese, Bhutanese, and Burmese traditions hold sway over many of the recipes from Guwahati.

Chai

(SPICED TEA)

MAKES 8 cups

PREPARATION TIME: 20 minutes

Chai translates as "spiced tea" in Hindi, and even though spices are not as prevalent in Guwahati cuisine as they are in other Indian cuisines, chai is the exception. This beverage is beloved throughout the region, and there is inevitably a chaiwala (chai vendor) selling his hot, flavorful beverage at every train station in the state. The tradition of drinking chai started during the British colonial era in India, when British employees of the East India Company paused each day for tea breaks that included black tea from Assam along with milk and sugar. Indians made the custom their own by dressing their tea up with spices like ginger, cloves, and cinnamon. Today, India is one of the largest producers and consumers of tea in the world. Even the Indian prime minister Narendra Modi, when he was a child, was a chaiwala at the Vadnagar train station in Gujarat. Though chai tea packets are readily available in most supermarkets, I recommend brewing it using fresh spices, because the result is much more flavorful and robust. Either black or green tea can be used depending upon your strength preference, but traditional Indian chai is made with black tea from Assam. Black tea results in bolder tasting notes, while green tea is milder.

- 10 whole cloves
- 8 cardamom pods
- 2 cinnamon sticks
- 1 teaspoon black peppercorns
- 1-inch piece fresh ginger, peeled with a spoon and coarsely chopped
- 6 to 8 black or green tea bags (depending on strength and tea preference)
- ½ cup sugar
- 2 cups whole milk
- Pinch of table salt

Combine the cloves, cardamom, cinnamon, and peppercorns and crush them together using the back of a wooden spoon on a clean work surface or on a plate or by using a mortar and pestle in order to release their flavors. Transfer the crushed spices to a saucepan, add the ginger and 6 cups water, and bring to a boil. Reduce the heat to low, cover the pan, and simmer gently for 8 to 10 minutes.

Add the tea bags and remove the pan from the heat. Steep for 5 to 7 minutes, depending upon how strong you like your tea. I would recommend brewing your tea a bit stronger than you usually do because the milk and sugar will dilute its potency.

Remove the tea bags and then add the sugar, milk, and salt. Return to a simmer over high heat while stirring to dissolve the sugar. Remove from the heat just after it comes to a simmer, strain into cups, and serve hot.

CHAI (SPICED TEA): THE NATIONAL DRINK OF INDIA

The sound from my childhood train journeys that left the most indelible mark is that of the chaiwala stepping on board the car at every station stop calling out, “Chai! Chai! Chai! Chai!” Chai, sometimes referred to as masala tea outside of India, is an essential part of the day. We begin our morning with it, conclude virtually every meal with it, and usually end the evening with it, too. The Hindi word *chai* is from the Chinese word *cha,* which means spiced tea.

I loved nothing more on a train ride than to watch the chaiwala fill the traditional terra-cotta cup known as a kulhar with chai, lifting his teapot high into the air as he poured for a little theater to go along with my hot cup of tea. Today, most of the chai offered at train stops is served in tiny plastic cups instead of kulhars, and in an effort to be healthier, some chai drinkers skip the sugar; but one thing will never change, and that’s my adoration of chai, the national drink of India and a surefire way to conjure nostalgia in an Indian expat like me.

Aloo Pitika

(MASHED POTATOES WITH GREEN CHILES AND ONIONS)

SERVES 4

PREPARATION TIME: 10 minutes

Several times a month I fly to New York City to tape Food Network's *Chopped*. I usually return to Nashville on a late flight, and by the time I get home, I find myself with massive hunger pangs for comfort food, but little energy to cook something complicated. This is my go-to dish for just that occasion. It takes no time at all and I usually double the batch because my kids and husband love it for breakfast, served with a side of Indian pickles and a bowl of whipped yogurt. I had this dish for the first time at the train station in Guwahati, where it was being served for breakfast. I was on a night train and awoke in my sleeper bunk with a chill. The sun had not yet risen and the windows in our third-class compartment were wide open. My teeth were chattering when I stepped off the train, and I followed the comforting aroma of potatoes, which led me to this soothing, fortifying dish. That taste memory must be why I crave mashed potatoes with chiles and onions late in the night when I need to be warmed from the inside out.

3 russet potatoes

1 large red onion, halved and thinly sliced

2 serrano chiles, finely chopped

2 tablespoons finely chopped fresh cilantro

2 tablespoons mustard oil

Kosher salt

In a medium saucepan, combine the potatoes with enough water to cover by 3 inches. Bring the water to a boil over high heat, reduce the heat to medium, and simmer the potatoes until tender, about 15 minutes. Once the potatoes are cool enough to handle, peel and add them to a large bowl.

Mash the potatoes until fairly smooth but still a little chunky, then mash in the onion, serranos, cilantro, and mustard oil. Do not overmash or the potatoes will become gummy. Season with salt and serve while still warm.

Chicken Bamboo Curry

SERVES 6

PREPARATION TIME: 30 minutes, plus 12 hours to marinate the chicken

One of the most surprising aspects of the Indian repertoire is a cuisine we refer to as *hakka*, a blend of Chinese and Indian culinary traditions inspired by the first wave of Hakka Chinese immigrants who settled in East India in the eighteenth century. Chinese restaurant owners adopted Indian spice blends such as garam masala and introduced them to Westernized versions of classic Chinese dishes like chop suey and chow mein. Indian and Chinese customers couldn't get enough of the alchemy, and hakka cuisine soon caught on in virtually every corner of India. This recipe, with its incorporation of bamboo and its quick stir-frying technique, is a nod to my love of hakka cuisine. At my Chinese restaurant Tansuo in Nashville, we use fresh bamboo shoot, which is available at Asian and Indian markets. If you have trouble sourcing it, canned bamboo shoot can be substituted. Hakka stands are located within several train stations throughout India. You can find them by following the sound of oil sizzling in a blazing hot wok.

3½ tablespoons store-bought ginger-garlic paste

1 teaspoon ground turmeric

1 teaspoon ground coriander

1 teaspoon ground cumin

6 tablespoons mustard oil

2½ pounds bone-in, skinless chicken parts (including a combination of breasts, thighs, and drumsticks)

Kosher salt

1 large red onion, three-quarters finely chopped and one-quarter thinly sliced

⅔ cup grated fresh bamboo shoot (or an 8-ounce can bamboo strips)

3 serrano chiles, finely chopped

1½ cups hot water

Basmati Rice (page 262), for serving

In a large bowl, stir together the ginger-garlic paste, turmeric, coriander, cumin, and 2 tablespoons of the mustard oil. Add the chicken to the bowl, season it all over with a liberal amount of salt, then rub the marinade into every corner and crevice. Cover the bowl with a damp towel and refrigerate for 12 hours.

In a large sauté pan, heat the remaining 4 tablespoons mustard oil over medium-high heat. Add the finely chopped onion and cook until translucent, about 4 minutes. Add the chicken and sauté until the chicken turns a light golden brown color, turning once or twice using tongs, 8 to 12 minutes.

Add the bamboo and two-thirds of the serranos and sauté until the chiles are tender, about 3 minutes. Add the hot water and bring to a vigorous simmer. Reduce the heat to medium and simmer until the sauce is thick enough to coat the back of a spoon and the chicken is cooked through, 15 to 18 minutes. Season with salt.

Transfer to a serving platter, garnish with the remaining serranos and the sliced onions, and serve with rice.

Chicken Momos with Tomato-Garlic Dipping Sauce

(STEAMED CHICKEN DUMPLINGS)

MAKES about 16 momos

PREPARATION TIME: 30 minutes, plus 1 hour to rest the dough

TOMATO-GARLIC DIPPING SAUCE

2 large tomatoes, coarsely chopped

4 dried red chiles, broken into small pieces

6 garlic cloves, coarsely chopped

2 teaspoons tamarind paste

2 teaspoons cumin seeds, toasted

½ teaspoon freshly ground black pepper

Kosher salt

MOMOS

2 cups all-purpose flour

1 teaspoon kosher salt, plus more to taste

Lukewarm water, as needed

Vegetable oil, for the bowl

8 ounces ground white-meat chicken

3 scallions, finely chopped

2 teaspoons finely chopped fresh ginger

2 medium garlic cloves, minced

2 serrano chiles, finely chopped

2 tablespoons soy sauce

Guwahati is positioned snugly below Tibet, Nepal, and Bhutan. The cuisines of these Asian nations have profoundly influenced this Indian city where momos, the local meat and vegetable dumplings, are a staple food at train stations and markets. Street cart vendors are typically surrounded by a throng of hungry patrons eagerly awaiting these steamed buns stuffed with spiced meat or vegetables. I've found over the years that there are two rules to follow when making them: The first is to be patient with yourself when shaping the momos. The perfectly pinched momo tops that the vendors sell in India are the result of years of practice. Take it slowly and, with time, your technique will improve. (Besides, no one actually cares what the momo looks like anyway!) The next thing to remember when making momos is to not overknead the dough or you will overwork the gluten, resulting in a tough skin. Once you've achieved a soft dough, stop kneading. You will need a bamboo steamer—these are inexpensive and can be picked up at most kitchen supply stores. The dipping sauce comes together quickly and is an excellent pairing for the chicken momos. It's also nice as a substitute for ketchup, and my kids love it with their French fries or on their burger buns. It makes about 1 cup and takes about 20 minutes to prepare.

Make the dipping sauce: In a saucepan, stir together the tomatoes, chiles, garlic, tamarind paste, cumin, and black pepper and bring to a boil over high heat. Reduce the heat to medium and simmer until the tomatoes have broken down and a chunky sauce is formed, 10 to 14 minutes. Season with salt. Transfer to a food processor and process until smooth. The sauce will keep refrigerated in a covered container for up to 1 week.

Make the momos: Sift the flour and salt onto a clean work surface. Create a well in the center of it and add lukewarm water, ¼ cup at a time, to form a soft dough. The dough should not be sticky, but it should not be firm either. Transfer the dough to an oiled bowl, cover the bowl with a damp towel, and let rest at room temperature for 1 hour.

While the dough rests, in a bowl, combine the chicken, scallions, ginger, garlic, serranos, soy sauce, vinegar, and black pepper. Stir until everything is well incorporated and season the filling with salt.

Divide the dough into 16 balls, and on a clean work surface, roll each ball out into a 4-inch round. Place about 1 tablespoon filling into the center of a round, put the momo in your left hand and using your right thumb and index finger, begin pinching the dough together by gathering a portion of it over the stuffing and pinching it into the next portion. Continue until a packet is formed and the momo is sealed tightly. Repeat with the remaining momos.

Spray a steamer basket with cooking spray and arrange the momos in it in a single layer. Do not let their edges touch or the skin could tear when you remove them. Fill the steamer basin halfway with water and bring it to a boil over high heat. Carefully set the steamer basket with the momos onto the basin, reduce the heat to medium, and steam until the momos are cooked through, 12 to 16 minutes.

Serve warm with the tomato-garlic dipping sauce.

1 teaspoon distilled white vinegar

½ teaspoon freshly ground black pepper

Kosher salt

Cooking spray, for the steamer

Thukpa

(CHICKEN NOODLE SOUP)

SERVES 4

PREPARATION TIME: 45 minutes

Thukpa is essentially the chicken noodle soup of Tibet, offering the same comforting aspects of chicken soup that we know and love, but with a fiery twist. The recipe originated in eastern Tibet and was brought to northeastern India by Tibetan refugees who settled in this region of the country after the Chinese occupation of their nation. The first time I tasted thukpa was after I arrived on a train in Guwahati on a cold winter's day. Seeking warmth, I followed the aroma of chicken soup to a vendor spooning golden thukpa into dented metal bowls. In that single bowl of soup I found all the reassurance I needed that the long journey had been worth it. When I lived in New York City, where the winters can be brutal, there was nothing my husband, Vivek, and I loved more than tucking into a bowl of this Guwahati comfort food.

2 large tomatoes, coarsely chopped

1-inch piece fresh ginger, peeled with a spoon

4 garlic cloves, peeled

3 serrano chiles

2 teaspoons cumin seeds

2 tablespoons vegetable oil

1 pound boneless, skinless chicken thighs

2 quarts chicken stock

1 large carrot, peeled and coarsely chopped

2 red, yellow, or orange bell peppers, coarsely chopped

1 cup coarsely chopped green beans

1 can (8 ounces) bamboo shoots, drained

1 cup shredded green cabbage

6 ounces thin rice noodles

Juice of 1 lemon

Kosher salt

Finely chopped scallions

Bean sprouts

In a food processor, combine the tomatoes, ginger, garlic, serranos, cumin, and oil and process until smooth. Transfer the paste to a heavy-bottomed pot along with the chicken and cook over medium-high heat, stirring occasionally, until aromatic, 3 to 4 minutes. Add the stock and bring to a boil.

Reduce the heat to medium and add the carrot, bell peppers, beans, bamboo shoots, and cabbage. Cover the pot halfway and simmer until the vegetables are tender and the chicken is cooked through, 20 to 25 minutes.

Add the noodles and lemon juice and simmer until the noodles are tender, 4 to 6 minutes. Season with salt.

Spoon the thukpa into bowls, garnish with scallions and bean sprouts, and serve very hot.

Kolkata

When my mom and dad married, my mother wasn't sure what she wanted to do for a living. She was tempted to become a housewife like so many of her contemporaries at the time. My dad told her he would support any decision she made, encouraging her to follow her passion. Her heart's desire was to become a high school principal, which she eventually became after years of study, because she knew what an invaluable tool education was, especially for Indian women.

I have so many fond memories of sitting at our dining room table after dinner studying with my mom and sister. My father always told all three of us that we could be anything we wanted to be in life as long as we worked tirelessly to achieve our goals. I have so much gratitude to my father for instilling in me an unwavering confidence that as long as I do my best, I can achieve anything I want to in life. I'm grateful to my mother for being a living example of this belief.

Mom was always taking new classes to advance her career as a principal, and one of my favorite memories from my childhood is when we would accompany her to the Montessori class she took on Saturdays in Kolkata, a five-hour ride from our home in Ranchi. We'd drop her off at class before heading to the legendary pastry and tea shop Flurys, open since 1927, where we indulged on cakes, pastries, chocolates, and cookies.

We stayed with family friends in Kolkata during the weekends when my mom was in school. They would light huge fire pits outside to slow-cook lamb, chicken, and goat, and the revelry lasted late into the night. My poor mom must have been exhausted when she went to class on Sunday morning, but I was never happier. I discovered my tribe in Kolkata, people who lived to eat, planning their next meal before they finished eating the one in front of them. Food was more than sustenance to our friends in Kolkata. Food was desire. It was joy. It sparked new friendships and fortified familial bonds. I owe a huge debt to those childhood experiences in Kolkata. It was there that I first realized that my lifelong obsession with food was not only acceptable but to be celebrated, and something I could build my life around.

The city of Kolkata (formerly known as Calcutta, until 2001) is a city of five million people in the state of West Bengal in north-

eastern India. Founded by the British Raj in 1686, more than almost any other city in India, Kolkata was intrinsically tied to the British during their colonization of the nation, and was the capital of the British Empire in India until 1911, when this distinction shifted to Delhi.

The origins of British Calcutta began with the establishment of a factory by the British East India Company, an entity that arrived in India as a monopolistic body trading commodities like indigo, cotton, silk, spices, opium, and tea and eventually transformed itself into the British Empire in India, leaving behind a legacy of exploitation of India's resources and its people. It was also through the East India Company that India's first train station, Kolkata's Howrah Station, was established. Howrah opened its doors in 1853 as a cutting-edge train station designed by George Turnbull, chief engineer of the East Indian Railway Company.

Howrah remains today one of India's busiest train stations, connected to a staggering 1,373 other rail stations throughout the country, with 620 passenger trains arriving at its platforms daily to service over two million passengers a day. As innovative today as it was in the mid-nineteenth century, in 2011, India's first double-decker train departed from Howrah Station to much acclaim.

Kolkata is a multicultural city due to the legacy of the British as well as other influences such as French, Dutch, Middle Eastern, and Portuguese. This is where the British tradition of pausing for afternoon tea was first adopted by Indians, and Western-style pastry and tea shops still line the colonial-era streets.

But nothing pulls at my culinary heartstrings more than the street food and chaat vendors. At Howrah Station, I always stop by the jhal muri vendor for his newspaper cone stuffed with the puffed rice chaat topped with fresh tomatoes, cilantro, and peanuts. No visit to the city is complete without a Mughlai paratha, a fried rectangle of unleavened bread stuffed with eggs, onions, and chiles. One of my favorite childhood discoveries in the train station with my family is begun bhaji, spiced eggplant slices fried in mustard oil. I eat in Kolkata by the principle I always embrace in my cooking, more is more and excess makes virtually everything taste better as long as it's conjured in a masterful way and infused with the spirit of generosity.

Kolkata Sour

(SPICED WHISKEY SOUR)

A few years ago, a friend in Kolkata picked me up at the train station and we headed straight to a bar across the street. We had years to catch up on and we did it over a drink similar to this one (okay, maybe a few of them). I lace my whiskey sours with a cardamom-and-ginger–infused simple syrup. This recipe makes more than you'll need for one cocktail, so just stash it away in your refrigerator and use it for an ice cream topping or pancake syrup (or more drinks!). Whiskey sours usually contain egg whites, but I prefer mine without. Feel free to swap out the crystallized ginger garnish for a slice of dehydrated lemon peel.

MAKES 1 cocktail

PREPARATION TIME: 5 minutes

SPICED SYRUP

¼ cup sugar

2 green cardamom pods

1-inch piece fresh ginger, peeled with a spoon and coarsely chopped

COCKTAIL

Ice

Juice of 1 lemon

2 ounces whiskey

Crystallized ginger, for garnish

Make the spiced syrup: In a saucepan, combine the sugar, ¼ cup water, the cardamom, and ginger and bring to a boil over high heat. Reduce the heat to medium and simmer until syrupy, 5 to 7 minutes. Discard the ginger and cardamom and cool to room temperature. Leftover spiced syrup will keep refrigerated in a covered container for up to 2 weeks.

For each cocktail: In an ice-filled cocktail shaker, combine 1 tablespoon of the spiced syrup, the lemon juice, and whiskey and shake vigorously until the shaker is very cold, about 30 seconds. Strain the sour into an ice-filled rocks glass. Garnish with crystallized ginger.

Corn Chaat

(CORN SNACK)

SERVES 4

PREPARATION TIME: 10 minutes

Maize (corn) is an important crop in West Bengal, where Kolkata is located. Roasted corn is a summertime favorite, and baby corn finds its way into curries and gravies. This is my celebration of corn in chaat form, with a handful of corn nuts thrown in because I like their crunchy texture and their toasty-salty flavor. They're also fun and unexpected, adding an inexpensive flourish to a chaat that comes together with little effort and in no time at all.

Vegetable oil, as needed

1½ cups fresh corn kernels

1 (14-ounce) can Chinese baby corn

½ cup corn nuts

2 tablespoons finely chopped fresh cilantro

1 finely chopped medium yellow onion

½ teaspoon Kashmiri or other red chile powder

Juice of 1 lime

Kosher salt

Green Chutney (page 30), for serving

Coat a sauté pan thinly with oil and heat over high heat until almost smoking, 4 to 5 minutes. Add the corn kernels and sauté, stirring occasionally, until golden brown and charred in spots, 4 to 6 minutes. Transfer the kernels to a bowl along with the baby corn, corn nuts, cilantro, onion, chile powder, and lime juice. Season with salt and serve with green chutney.

LIGHT-IMPACT SERVINGWARE

Since chaat are typically eaten on the go in India, a cottage industry has emerged throughout the country to accommodate the need for inexpensive, sustainable servingware. Chaat are often served on small plates or bowls made from natural products like banana leaves and areca palm leaves. Patravali is a rustic-looking plate made of leaves (from either the banyan tree, jackfruit tree, or sal tree) that are pressed together to form a plate. A kulhar is a thin, single-use terra-cotta cup used for lassi and chai. After drinking the beverage, the clay cup is recycled, making it the ultimate sustainable drinking vessel. In more recent times, newspaper has become a popular way to serve chaat: either in a simple cone that is expertly folded to seal it properly for chaat like bhel puri or jhal muri, or layered to form a plate for gol gappas and samosas.

Begun Bhaja

(FRIED EGGPLANT SLICES)

Also known as baingan bhaja, this classic Bengali recipe featuring shallow-fried slices of eggplant is served as a side dish at sit-down meals and is also a popular street snack on the perpetually humming streets of Kolkata. I first tried it at the train station there and it was a revelation to me, even at the tender age of eight.

SERVES 4
PREPARATION TIME: 20 minutes

Kosher salt

4 large Japanese eggplants, cut crosswise into ¼-inch-thick slices

¾ cup rice flour

1 teaspoon ground turmeric

½ teaspoon Kashmiri or other red chile powder

Mustard oil, for shallow-frying

Chutney, store-bought or homemade (pages 29–31), for serving

Lightly salt the eggplant slices on both sides. In a bowl, stir together the flour, turmeric, and chile powder.

Line a plate with paper towels. Pour 1 inch mustard oil into a sauté pan and heat over medium-high heat until a pinch of flour sizzles when it hits the surface.

Working in batches (do not overcrowd the pan), dredge the eggplant slices in the seasoned flour, shaking to remove excess, and use tongs to add the eggplant slices to the oil. Fry the eggplant until golden brown on both sides, about 2 minutes per side, flipping once during the frying process. Transfer to the paper towels to drain, and season with salt.

Serve hot with desired chutney.

Panch Phoron

(INDIAN 5-SPICE BLEND)

MAKES ⅔ cup

PREPARATION TIME: 10 minutes

Virtually every train station vendor keeps at their stall a tin of panch phoron, a whole-spice blend that perfumes the air with earthy cumin and lively fennel seed as they liberally sprinkle it on savory dishes like mutton curry and spicy prawn curry. Known as "Indian 5-spice," it's a traditional flavoring in Bengali cooking. Unlike many other Indian spice blends where the spices are blended into a powder, the five spices in panch phoron are left whole. If you have trouble sourcing nigella seeds, which can be found at Indian markets, substitute black sesame seeds. Store this in a covered container in a dark place for up to 6 months.

2 tablespoons cumin seeds

2 tablespoons fennel seeds

2 tablespoons fenugreek seeds

2 tablespoons black mustard seeds

2 tablespoons nigella seeds (*kalonji* in Hindi)

Heat a dry pan over medium heat until a mustard seed pops a few seconds after it hits the surface of the pan, 3 to 4 minutes. Add the cumin and toast until aromatic, swirling the pan as it toasts, about 1 minute. Transfer to a plate and repeat with the remaining spices, toasting each one separately. Cool the spices to room temperature and then transfer them to an airtight covered container and shake to combine. Store up to 6 months in a cool, dry, dark place.

Red Chili
Powder
Fennel Seeds
Cumin
Powder
Turmeric
Powder
Nigella Seeds
Chaat Masala
Sambar
Masala

Mughlai Paratha

(FLATBREAD STUFFED WITH ONIONS AND EGGS)

MAKES 6 to 8 parathas
PREPARATION TIME: 45 minutes

Parathas are stuffed, unleavened flatbreads that are beloved throughout India, each state having its own regional variations. In Kolkata, it's the Mughlai paratha that reigns supreme. Introduced by the cooks of the Mughal Empire in the seventeenth century, it's stuffed with spiced scrambled eggs and onions and has a rectangular shape that distinguishes it from the countless others found throughout the country. During our train rides from Ranchi to Kolkata when I was a young girl, I fantasized about the Mughlai parathas being fried up at Howrah Junction, India's largest and oldest train station, long before our train arrived. My kids gobble them up when I make them at home, but there is nothing like sinking into one at Howrah, where that first bite and every one thereafter felt like it was well earned, paid for in train miles and sweat equity.

2 cups all-purpose flour, plus more for dusting

1 teaspoon kosher salt, plus more to taste

3 tablespoons vegetable oil, plus more for shallow-frying

½ cup heavy cream

12 large eggs

2 tablespoons whole milk

2 teaspoons garam masala

1 medium yellow onion, finely chopped

2 serrano chiles, finely chopped

3 tablespoons finely chopped fresh cilantro

Chutney, store-bought or homemade (pages 29–31), for serving

Indian pickles (achaar), optional (see Indian Pickles sidebar on page 185), for serving

In a large bowl, sift together the flour and 1 teaspoon salt. Add 2 tablespoons of the oil, the cream, and ½ cup water. Stir until the dough starts to come together, then work it with your hands into a shaggy ball, 4 to 6 minutes. On a clean, lightly floured work surface, knead the dough until firm, 5 to 7 minutes. Shape dough into a ball. Lightly oil the bowl you used to make the dough and place the dough ball back in it. Cover the bowl with a damp towel and let the dough rest at room temperature for 30 minutes.

While the dough rests, in a large bowl, use a fork to lightly beat together the eggs, milk, garam masala, and a generous pinch of salt and set aside.

In a sauté pan, heat the remaining 1 tablespoon oil over medium heat until it glistens, about 2 minutes. Add the onion and serranos and cook, stirring occasionally, until the onion is translucent, about 4 minutes.

Add the egg mixture and cilantro to the onion and sauté, using a silicone spatula to stir often, until the eggs are scrambled. Remove from the heat and set aside.

Divide the paratha dough into 6 to 8 equal portions and shape each one into a ball. On a clean, lightly floured work surface, use a rolling

pin to roll each ball out into a 6-inch round. For each paratha, spoon about 2 tablespoons of the scrambled eggs into the center of a round and fold the dough over the eggs to form a rectangle by first folding in the right side and then the left side until the dough overlaps just slightly in the middle. Repeat the process with the top and bottom sides of the dough round and pinch the seams together to seal.

Line a plate with paper towels. Pour 1 inch oil into a sauté pan and heat it over medium-high heat until a pinch of flour flicked onto its surface sizzles. Carefully add a paratha to the hot oil and fry until golden brown, 2 to 3 minutes. Flip the paratha over and fry until golden brown on the second side, another 2 to 3 minutes. Transfer to the paper towels to drain. Repeat with the remaining parathas.

Serve the parathas very hot with chutney and achaar.

Jhal Muri

(PUFFED RICE WITH PEANUTS, CHICKPEAS, AND VEGETABLES)

SERVES 4
PREPARATION TIME: 20 minutes

This spicy puffed rice is one of Kolkata's most popular street food snacks. *Jhal* means "spicy" and *muri* means "puffed rice," but it's so much more than that, with its mouth-puckering amchur (dried mango powder), tangy tamarind paste, vibrant lime juice, and medley of chopped fresh vegetables. It's available at virtually every train station throughout eastern India and is typically served in a giant newspaper cone. The puffed rice in this recipe is the same unsweetened puffed rice found in the cereal aisle of most supermarkets. Serve the jhal muri right away to avoid soggy rice.

SPICE BLEND

- 1½ teaspoons cumin seeds, toasted
- 1 teaspoon amchur powder
- 1 teaspoon chaat masala
- ½ teaspoon Kashmiri or other red chile powder

JHAL MURI

- 2 teaspoons tamarind paste
- 1 tablespoon fresh lime juice
- ½ small cucumber, peeled and finely chopped
- 1 medium tomato, coarsely chopped
- 1 small red onion, finely chopped
- 1 serrano chile, finely chopped
- 2 tablespoons finely chopped dry-roasted peanuts
- 2 tablespoons finely chopped cooked chickpeas
- 2 cups puffed rice
- 1½ tablespoons mustard oil
- Sev, for garnish
- Finely chopped fresh cilantro, for garnish

Make the spice blend: In a bowl, combine the cumin, amchur, chaat masala, and chile powder and stir until incorporated.

Make the jhal muri: In a bowl, combine the tamarind paste, lime juice, cucumber, tomato, onion, serrano, peanuts, chickpeas, puffed rice, and mustard oil and stir until incorporated. Sprinkle in the spice blend and gently stir to combine.

Serve garnished with sev and cilantro.

Ranchi

Puchkas
Peanut Chaat
Saag Paneer
Sattu Sharbat
Paneer
Sattu ki Kachori Chaat
Basmati Rice

Ranchi is my hometown, and my first memory is from its train station. I was probably three or four at the time and was standing next to my father, who was holding my tiny hand. A steam train lurched into the station and I was terrified by its screeching wheels and massive size. (I think I crawled up my father's body into his arms and it wasn't until I saw Harry Potter waiting for the Hogwarts train at Platform 9¾ that I stopped having nightmares about that train from my childhood.) The Ranchi station was one of the most popular places for my friends and me to hang out. It was the best place to catch up on gossip—and to eat. There were rows of tables overflowing with mounds of a wheat flour pastry called *khaja* and one vendor selling roasted peanut chaat (I always managed to find him). We also indulged in puchka, a semolina puff stuffed with potatoes, tamarind and green chile chutneys, and mint-cilantro water.

Ranchi is the capital of the state of Jharkhand in northeastern India. It was here that my sister and I ran beneath the verdant canopy of trees in Deer Park. It was in Ranchi that we followed our noses to Punjab Street House for papri chaat (a snack comprised of potatoes, chickpeas, and chutneys) on the weekends. It was also where nearly every day on our way home from school, we stopped by the puchka vendor to illicitly pop a few puris into our mouths, in spite of this being the forbidden food in our house (more on that later).

My father worked as an engineer and we lived in an apartment block with other workers from his industry who hailed from virtually every state in India. It was from my neighbors that I first heard about the astonishing diversity of Indian cuisine, and it was also from them that I learned about techniques and ingredients that I still embrace in my cooking today.

Ranchi is the gateway to Betla National Park, home to elephants and tigers and to Jain and Hindu temples that delineate the horizon at sunset. The cuisine of Jharkhand is defined by Mughlai, Bengalese, Bihari, and British influences that mingle with tribal customs that place importance on understanding the health benefits of the ingredients you cook with, as a way to empower and strengthen your body, spirit, and mind. This way of cooking profoundly influenced me as a child. It's why I always turn to my pantry instead of the medicine cabinet when one of my kids is sick.

There are so many lessons I carry with me through life that I picked up as a child in Ranchi. I stitch them into the dishes I serve at my restaurants and into the meals I prepare for family and friends. Puchkas (a universally beloved snack in India with over ten names depending upon where you are in the country) are one of the favorite items at Chauhan Ale & Masala House, where they're called gol gappas on the menu because this name is more well-known than puchkas. My guests can't seem to get enough of them. When I watch someone pop gol gappas into their mouth, one after another, laughing between each massive, ridiculous bite, I can hear my sister's laughter in my ears, an echo of a past I will never fully leave behind.

We had a mango tree in our backyard and I can still envision my maternal grandmother standing beneath it during one of her visits from her home in Punjab. Being the indefatigable woman that she was, she refused our invitation for a nap after her long journey. Instead, she walked to the tree with a knife and told me to climb it to harvest the mangoes. This was something I always tried to do when she wasn't around but my mom seemed to telepathically know what I was thinking and would say to me, "Don't even think about it."

My heart leaped when I heard my grandmother's order but then I caught sight of my mom who was shaking her head from side to side in the doorway. My grandmother saw it too but then turned back to me and said, "Go ahead, Maneet. You

LEFT: *Litti chokha platter.*
CENTER: *Litti.*
RIGHT: *Sattu Kachori Ki Chaat.*
FAR RIGHT: *Dahi Pev Puri.*

can do whatever you set your mind to." My mom would not contradict her mother, and I couldn't disobey my grandmother. I dutifully (and blissfully) scrambled up the tree, plucking the ripe mangoes from its branches and dropping them down to my grandmother as I climbed. She hacked them up into bite-sized pieces on a wooden outdoor table and later on that night we turned them into pickles (page 185). When I was back on solid ground again and my mom and I were out of earshot from my grandmother she said to me, "She'll let you get away with anything." I grinned and said, "I love when she visits us." I did love it. Not because she let me get by with anything but because she made me believe I could do anything I set my mind to.

My childhood in Ranchi shaped who I am as a human being and a chef. I carry around with me the hospitable nature of my neighbors, the way they took me in and shared with me the cooking secrets of their grandmothers. I hear the message my father repeated to my sister and me over and over again that we could be anything we wanted to be in life as long as we were passionate about it and never stopped working. I hear the lesson from my mother that I would face difficulty as a woman in an industry dominated by men but that this should never stop me from achieving my goals. I even hear the message from the puchka vendor who handed us one gol gappa after another while saying, "If it's still fun, keep eating."

It's still fun. I'm going to keep eating.

Puchkas

(SEMOLINA PUFFS STUFFED WITH POTATOES, CHUTNEY, AND CILANTRO-LIME WATER)

This is the snack that had me on the verge of trouble nearly every single afternoon during my school days in Ranchi. It's made by pouring an herbal water (teekha pani) into a puri: a crispy, perfectly round, golf-ball-shaped, bite-sized semolina shell. Because the puris are filled with liquid just before the vendor hands it over, you have to pop the entire thing into your mouth at once. What follows is a flavor explosion that always ends in fits of laughter because they're so much fun to eat! My sister and I couldn't resist stopping at the puchka vendor on our way home from school even though our mother warned us repeatedly not to eat them because they included water that could potentially be sourced from a dubious place!

Also called *pani puri* or *gol gappas* in some parts of India, the crowd of people standing around the puchka vendor, popping puri after puri into their mouths, proved too big a temptation to resist for me then . . . and now, too. Even though eating them sometimes left us with stomachaches (that we could never explain to our mom), it was always worth it. I still can't resist stuffing gol gappas into my face whenever I return to India. The puris can be made ahead of time and stored in a covered container for up to 1 day, making them the perfect party food. Puris are also available at Indian markets, but here's a recipe for them if you'd like to attempt it at home.

MAKES about 32 puchkas

PREPARATION TIME: 1 hour

PURIS

2 cups semolina

2 tablespoons all-purpose flour, plus more for rolling

½ teaspoon baking soda

½ teaspoon kosher salt

Vegetable oil, for deep-frying

SPICY WATER (TEEKHA PANI)

5 green chiles, coarsely chopped

1 cup lightly packed fresh cilantro leaves

½ cup lightly packed fresh mint leaves

1 tablespoon tamarind paste

2 teaspoons ground cumin

2 tablespoons coarsely chopped jaggery (or 2 tablespoons packed, dark brown sugar)

2 teaspoons chaat masala

Make the puris: In a large bowl, sift together the semolina, all-purpose flour, baking soda, and salt. Add 3 tablespoons cold water and stir with your hands until a dough begins to come together. Add more water, 2 tablespoons at a time, until a firm but elastic dough is formed (you'll likely use about ⅔ cup water).

Lightly oil the bowl you first used to make the dough and return the dough to the bowl. Cover the bowl with a damp cloth and let it rest for 30 minutes. It's important to keep the dough from drying out or the puris will not puff up when they're fried.

Line a plate with paper towels. Pour 6 inches oil into a heavy-bottomed pot and heat over medium-high heat to 325°F on an instant-read thermometer. Add a tiny piece of test dough; it should immediately rise to the surface of the oil. Lightly flour a clean work surface. Working quickly, roll one-third of the dough into a ⅛-inch-thick

(RECIPE AND INGREDIENTS CONTINUE)

PUCHKAS

2 russet potatoes, boiled, peeled, and finely chopped (they need to be small enough to fit inside the puri)

1 cup finely chopped cooked chickpeas

3 tablespoons Tamarind Chutney, store-bought or homemade (page 29)

2 tablespoons Green Chutney (page 30)

1 tablespoon chaat masala

½ teaspoon Kashmiri or other red chile powder

Kosher salt

sheet. Keep the remaining dough covered with a damp cloth. Use a 2-inch round biscuit or pastry cutter to cut out rounds that are very close together. Slide an offset spatula beneath a round to release it from the work surface and carefully lower it into the hot oil (do not overcrowd the pot or the puris will not puff and cook properly). The puris should rise to the surface of the oil almost immediately. Using a slotted spoon, gently push them down into the oil as they fry to ensure that they puff up properly and color evenly. They should puff up after 1 to 2 minutes. Once they puff and turn a light golden brown, transfer them to the paper towels to drain. Repeat the process with the remaining dough until all the puris have been fried. Allow the oil to return to frying temperature between batches. Cool the puris to room temperature and then either store them in a single layer in a covered container at room temperature or, if using immediately or sometime soon, use your thumb to punch a small hole into the top of each puri to prepare it for the stuffing and spicy water. (I use my index finger to do this, but your thumb or the handle of a wooden spoon also works, too.)

Make the spicy water (teekha pani): In a blender, combine the chiles, cilantro, mint, tamarind, cumin, jaggery, and 4 cups water and puree at high speed until smooth. Transfer to a bowl and stir in the chaat masala. Strain into a pouring vessel that enables you to neatly pour the liquid through the hole and into the puri.

For the puchkas: In a medium bowl, stir together the potatoes, chickpeas, tamarind chutney, green chutney, chaat masala, chile powder, and salt to taste.

Spoon a small amount of the potato mixture into each puri. Pour the spicy water into the puri until it is filled by two-thirds and immediately pop it into your mouth—or someone else's!

DG-
G-88XX

Peanut Chaat

(SPICED PEANUT SNACK)

MAKES about 2½ cups
PREPARATION TIME: 15 minutes

This addictive bar snack is so easy to create, fantastic for game night or any time a quick, flavor-packed treat is needed but time is limited. Crunchy sea salt adds nice texture to the tender boiled peanuts.

- 1 teaspoon ground turmeric
- 2 cups raw (unroasted) peanuts
- 1 small red onion, finely chopped
- 2 serrano chiles, finely chopped
- 1 small tomato, finely chopped
- 1 teaspoon chaat masala
- ½ teaspoon cumin seeds, toasted
- ½ teaspoon Kashmiri or other red chile powder
- 1 tablespoon fresh lime juice, plus lime wedges for serving
- 2 tablespoons finely chopped fresh cilantro, plus more for garnish
- Flaky sea salt

In a medium saucepan, combine 4 cups water and the turmeric and bring to a boil over high heat. Reduce the heat to medium, add the peanuts, and simmer until they are tender, 5 to 7 minutes. Drain the peanuts and cool to room temperature.

In a large bowl, stir together the peanuts, onion, serranos, tomato, chaat masala, cumin, chile powder, lime juice, and cilantro until well combined.

Serve in a large communal bowl or divide into individual servings. Garnish with cilantro and sprinkle with sea salt. Serve with lime wedges.

Saag Paneer

(BRAISED GREENS WITH FARMER CHEESE)

SERVES 4

PREPARATION TIME: 25 minutes

Contrary to popular belief outside of India, *saag* means any dish made with leafy greens, not just spinach. In Jharkhand, saag dishes often include a variety of leafy greens that are indigenous to the region. In Nashville, I like to whip up this easy recipe on days when I need a reboot, packing it with a variety of greens I consume not only for their flavor but for their nutritional benefits. It feels fortifying to eat this way. Feel free to stick to the more common saag paneer recipe, swapping in spinach for the arugula and kale, but if you're feeling adventurous, pack this recipe with healthful virtue by adding in as many greens as you can get your hands on. Suggestions include collards, carrot tops, beet tops, Swiss chard, or bok choy leaves. The possibilities are endless, and it's a fantastic recipe if you cook from a desire to eliminate food waste: All those vegetable tops have a home in this saag recipe. Feel free to swap out the paneer for any salty, firm cheese such as feta.

2 tablespoons ghee, store-bought or homemade (page 33), plus more melted ghee for serving

1 teaspoon ground cardamom

1½ teaspoons ground cumin

½ teaspoon Kashmiri or other red chile powder

½ teaspoon brown mustard seeds

Pinch of hing (asafetida)

1 small yellow onion, finely chopped

2 tablespoons store-bought ginger-garlic paste

2 serrano chiles, finely chopped

2 cups packed arugula

4 cups packed baby kale

6 cups packed baby spinach

3 tablespoons finely chopped fresh cilantro, plus more for garnish

1 tablespoon lemon juice

Kosher salt

8 ounces Paneer (page 256), cut into bite-sized pieces

Basmati Rice (page 262)

Chapatis (page 46), for serving

In a sauté pan, melt the ghee over medium-high heat. Add the cardamom, cumin, chile powder, mustard seeds, and hing and sauté until the mustard seeds begin to pop, about 2 minutes. Reduce the heat to medium, add the onion and sauté until translucent and light golden brown, 5 to 7 minutes. Add the ginger-garlic paste and serranos and sauté for 2 more minutes. Add the arugula, kale, and spinach and sauté until the greens are wilted and the kale is tender, 4 to 5 minutes. Remove from the heat and cool at room temperature for 5 minutes.

Transfer the greens to a food processor. Add the cilantro and blend on medium speed until chunky but uniform. Add the lemon juice and salt to taste and return to the sauté pan. Set the pan over medium-low heat and gently stir in the paneer, being careful not to break it up. Cook until the paneer and saag are heated through, 4 to 6 minutes.

To serve, spoon the saag and paneer into serving bowls, drizzle with melted ghee, and garnish with cilantro. Serve with rice and chapatis.

Sattu Sharbat

(SPICED DAL BEVERAGE)

Sattu is roasted chickpea flour available in Indian markets. It has a nutty flavor enjoyed throughout many parts of India, including in the state of Jharkhand, where it's tucked into savory dishes, breads, and this umami-packed beverage. My train journeys nearly always began in Jharkhand, where I grew up, and nearly every single trip commenced with a glass of sattu sharbat sold by the train vendor just outside the station. The flavor brings me right back to those early Ranchi mornings filled with the excitement and anticipation of the adventure ahead. Feel free to strain the liquid before pouring it into glasses, although I prefer it a little chunky.

MAKES 2 drinks

PREPARATION TIME: 10 minutes

4 tablespoons sattu (roasted chickpea flour)

1 tablespoon fresh lemon juice

1 serrano chile, finely chopped

2 teaspoons finely chopped fresh mint leaves

2 tablespoons finely chopped fresh cilantro leaves

2 tablespoons jaggery, or packed dark brown sugar

1½ teaspoons chaat masala

½ teaspoon cumin seeds, toasted

3 cups chilled water

Ice, as needed

In a large bowl, combine all of the ingredients except the water and ice and stir until everything is well incorporated. Add the chilled water and whisk until all of the lumps disappear. Fill two glasses with ice cubes and pour the sattu sharbat over them. Serve immediately.

Paneer

YIELDS approximately 8 to 10 ounces

PREPARATION TIME: 30 minutes, plus 30 minutes to press the paneer

2 quarts whole milk

Juice of 2 lemons, plus more as needed

½ teaspoon kosher salt

Paneer is a fresh farmer-style cheese that is virtually the only cheese consumed in India. It's made from cow's milk and has a slightly tangy, subtly salty flavor with a texture similar to tofu. Premade paneer is available in Indian markets, but it's also a breeze to make at home using only three ingredients: milk, lemon juice, and salt. It works best to use whole milk because it enables the curds and whey to separate easily. The whey that results from making paneer is frequently seen as a by-product to be discarded, but I love using it as a meat tenderizer, adding it to smoothies, or drinking it just like I would a glass of milk. It's loaded with antioxidants and has an appealing tangy flavor similar to buttermilk. Paneer is best consumed right away but will keep in a covered container in the refrigerator for up to 3 days.

In a medium saucepan, heat the milk to 195°F over medium heat. Using a wooden spoon, stir frequently during the heating process to prevent the milk from scalding. Be sure to scrape the bottom of the pan when you stir because this is where the milk is most prone to sticking. The milk will become foamy and bubbles will form on its surface once it reaches the desired temperature.

Remove from the heat and stir in the lemon juice until evenly distributed, which will cause the separation of curds from the whey. The process should begin right away, but don't fret if it takes a minute or two. Cover the pan and set aside at room temperature for 10 minutes to let the acid work its magic. Check the mixture at this point: It should be slightly yellow and the curds should have completely separated from the whey. Don't panic if this hasn't happened completely yet. Simply add another teaspoon of lemon juice and set aside for a few minutes more. This should do the trick.

Line a fine-mesh sieve with cheesecloth and set the sieve over a bowl. Ladle the curds and whey into the sieve. Reserve the whey for another use. Season the curds (still in the sieve) with the salt, stirring it in using a wooden spoon, then gather up the edges of the cheesecloth into a tight bundle and squeeze the excess whey from the curds. Place the cheesecloth and curds on a large plate and

shape into a square. Wrap the cheesecloth edges around the paneer and place a second plate on top to compress it. Set aside at room temperature for 30 minutes. At this point the paneer is ready to use or it can be refrigerated in a covered container for up to 3 days.

Sattu ki Kachori Chaat

(CHILE-AND-ONION-STUFFED FRITTERS)

SERVES 8

PREPARATION TIME: 1 hour, plus 30 minutes resting time

Kachoris, spicy fried fritters, are another Indian snack enjoyed, with regional variations throughout most of the country. In Jharkhand, sattu kachori, made with roasted chickpea flour, is one of the most popular varieties. The kachori can be enjoyed on its own, without adding it to a chaat, served simply with a side of chutney, but it really finds its voice in this chaat recipe with its tangy, spicy, sweet flavor explosion. The traditional sattu kachori chaat is served with black chickpeas, but if you have trouble sourcing them, canned or home-cooked yellow chickpeas can be substituted.

KACHORI DOUGH

- **1 pound all-purpose flour**
- **½ cup sattu (roasted chickpea flour)**
- **2 teaspoons table salt**
- **2 tablespoons vegetable oil**
- **Cold water, as needed**

KACHORI STUFFING

- **1 cup sattu (roasted chickpea flour)**
- **1 medium yellow onion, finely chopped**
- **¼ cup store-bought red chile pickle (red chile achaar)**
- **2 serrano chiles, finely chopped**
- **2 tablespoons finely chopped fresh cilantro**
- **1 tablespoon store-bought ginger-garlic paste**
- **2 tablespoons mustard oil**
- **1 tablespoon fresh lemon juice**
- **½ teaspoon ajwain seeds**
- **½ teaspoon table salt**

Make the kachori dough: In a large bowl, sift together the flours and salt. Add the oil and mix it in using your fingers until it's incorporated. Add cold water, ¼ cup at a time, until a stiff dough is formed. The dough should not be sticky and should hold together well. Knead the dough on a clean, lightly floured work surface until it bounces back when poked with a finger, 4 to 6 minutes. Transfer the dough to an oiled bowl, cover the bowl with a damp cloth, and let it rest at room temperature for 30 minutes.

Make the kachori stuffing: In a bowl, combine the sattu, onion, red chile pickle, serranos, cilantro, ginger-garlic paste, mustard oil, lemon juice, ajwain, and salt and stir until incorporated.

Cook the kachoris: Divide the dough into 24 equal portions and shape each into a ball. Place the balls on a plate and cover them with a damp cloth while you work. Lightly dust a clean work surface with all-purpose flour. Use a rolling pin to roll a ball of dough into a 4-inch round. Place about 2 teaspoons of the stuffing in the center, gather the dough edges around the stuffing to form a ball, and pinch to seal it well. Gently flatten the kachori with your palm until it is about 1 inch thick. Transfer to a plate and keep covered with a damp cloth. Repeat with the remaining dough and stuffing.

Line a plate with paper towels. Pour 5 inches oil into a heavy-bottomed medium pot and heat over medium-high heat to 325°F on an instant-read thermometer. Working batches (do not overcrowd the pot), add the kachoris to the oil and fry, turning once or twice with a metal spoon, until golden brown on both sides, 4 to 5 minutes. Transfer to the paper towels to drain and season with salt.

Assemble the chaat: Add 2 tablespoons of the chickpeas to a small bowl and top with onion, tomato, and chile powder. Sprinkle with the cumin and some chaat masala and then drizzle with tamarind chutney and green chutney. Sprinkle with cilantro. Break apart 3 kachoris and arrange them on top. Repeat for the remaining bowls and serve immediately.

KACHORI COOKING

All-purpose flour, for dusting

Vegetable oil, for deep-frying

Kosher salt

CHAAT

1 cup cooked or canned chickpeas

½ cup finely chopped red onion

⅔ cup coarsely chopped tomatoes

½ teaspoon Kashmiri or other red chile powder

½ teaspoon cumin seeds, toasted

Chaat masala

Tamarind chutney, store-bought or homemade (page 29)

Green chutney (page 30)

Finely chopped fresh cilantro

A feast comprised of traditional dishes from Ranchi.

Basmati Rice

SERVES 4
PREPARATION TIME: 30 minutes

1 tablespoon unsalted butter

1 cup basmati rice

½ teaspoon table salt

Place the rice in a colander and rinse under cold running water to remove excess starch until the water runs clear, 4 to 5 minutes. Stir the rice using your hands during this step to ensure even rinsing.

In a medium saucepan, melt the butter over medium-high heat, about 1 minute. Add the rice and sauté while stirring constantly for 2 minutes. Add 1⅔ cups water and the salt and bring to a boil. Reduce the heat to low, cover, and simmer until the water is completely absorbed, 18 to 20 minutes. Remove from the heat and keep covered for an additional 5 minutes. Fluff the rice with a fork before serving.

AN INTERVIEW WITH ARJUN MISHRA, SATTU KI KACHORI, CHAAT VENDOR AT THE RANCHI JUNCTION RAILWAY STATION

How long have you been a chaat vendor?
All my life. I began working with my father, who also sold chaat, when I was seven years old. His father was also a vendor at this station and his father before him, too.

What is the most challenging part of your job?
The hours are very long. I work fourteen to sixteen hours per day, every day of the week.

What do you like most about your job?
I like to see the happiness on a hungry child's face when they are eating something that I offer them. There are many homeless children in the station, and when I can, I offer them food at no cost.

How has the system changed over the years?
Today it is more challenging because vendors are regulated by the government and there are stricter controls on us. Now most of the food sold at train stations throughout India is prepared at a central location and then delivered to the station stalls. It has become more difficult for a traditional vendor like me to sell my food to the masses. Every day I feel more and more pressure and worry that soon I will not be allowed to sell here any longer.

Where do you source your ingredients?
From the nearby market, where you can find everything you need from the dal to the vegetables. I buy my ingredients each day before the sun has risen and I sell until my ingredients run out.

How much do you charge for your chaat?
Thirty rupees.

Do you have a family, and if so, how many children do you have?
I have a wife and four children, aged six months to eight years old.

What is your advice for making the best chaat possible?
Use fresh ingredients and eat it right away.

What is your dream for the future?
My dream is to save enough money to send my children to a good school so that they might have a better life than I did. My two older children attend school, but the public schools in India are not very good. But even though I could use help throughout my day, I will not let my children work like I did at such a young age. I want them to have a better life.

टिकट घर
पूछताछ
पैदल पुल
राजकीय रेलवे पुलिस
प्लेटफार्म 2
आरक्षण कार्यालय
BOOKING OFFICE
ENQUIRY
FOOT OVER BRIDGE
G.R.P.
PLATFORM 2
RESERVATION OFFICE
रेलवे सुरक्षा बल
स्टेशन मास्टर
स्टेशन अधीक्षक
सुलभ कॉम्पलेक्स
मुसाफिर खाना
R.P.F.
STATION MASTER
STATION SUPDT.
SULABH COMPLEX
WAITING HALL
SEE ON
SEAL AREA

A Roundup of Indian Pantry Ingredients

achaar: Indian pickles that are made with spices and an oil base; there are thousands of achaar recipes featuring regional differences.

ajwain: a seed similar to caraway; also known as *carom*.

aloo: potatoes

amchur: dried mango powder, which adds a tanginess to recipes.

anardana: dried pomegranate seeds, which add vibrancy to recipes.

basmati rice: a slender, long-grained aromatic rice served with countless recipes throughout India. The Californian basmati variety is a bit fluffier than the Indian variety. Aged basmati is a variety grown in the Himalayas that is aged for two years before using in order to intensify its flavor and aroma. (See the recipe for Basmati Rice on page 262.)

besan: Flour made from ground chickpeas. When the flour is roasted, it is called sattu (see page 266).

black salt (kala namak): a kiln-fired, volcanic rock salt prized in Indian recipes for the sulfides it contains, which add distinctive pungency and a sulfurous aroma and flavor.

chaat masala: an Indian spice blend essential in many chaat recipes that contains black salt (which adds a sulfurous, hard-boiled-egg flavor and aroma) as well as other ingredients such as cumin, ajwain, coriander, tamarind powder, red chile powder, and fennel.

chole: chickpeas

churma: a powder that is made of wheat and semolina flours, spices, ghee, and a variety of nuts.

curry leaves: leaves that are sold both fresh and dried, from the curry tree, which flourishes throughout southern India. Indian recipes frequently call for fresh curry leaves. Curry powder is not simply ground curry leaves. Curry powder is typically a blend of many different spices. It became a ubiquitous name used by the British for any type of blended Indian spices during the colonial era.

dal: dried legumes including lentils, chickpeas, mung beans, and more. These are fundamental to the Indian culinary repertoire, making an appearance at virtually every meal. There is a vast variety of dals that serve different purposes—some, like urad dal and sabut urad, cook down until their original shape has vanished, while others, like kala chana and rajma, keep their shape throughout the cooking process. They are also an invaluable source of protein for the many vegetarians in India. Here's a breakdown of the dals that are most important to the Indian diet:

- Arhar: pigeon peas (page 99)
- Hare mung: whole green mung beans (see recipe for Sprouted Mung Beans on page 83)
- Chana dal: yellow hulled and split chickpeas (pages 16, 34, 78, 81, 83, 100)
- Kala chana: brown chickpeas (page 87)
- Masoor dal: split and hulled pink, orange, or red lentils (page 99)
- Mung dal: split and hulled petite yellow lentils (pages 103, 104)
- Rajma: kidney beans (page 43)
- Rongi/lobia: black-eyed peas (page 83)
- Sabut masoor: brown lentils (page 99)
- Sabut urad: black gram lentils (pages 43, 99, 156, 159, 160)
- Urad dal: split and hulled black gram lentils that become white when split (pages 155, 163, 189, 198)

garam masala: a combination of blended spices to season food. *Garam* means "hot" and *masala* means "blend of spices" and includes, among others, cumin, coriander, cloves, nutmeg, fennel, cinnamon, cardamom, dried red chiles, peppercorns, and bay leaves. It is most popular in northern India.

ghee: clarified butter with a toasty flavor, used as a fat in savory recipes (page 33).

gulab jal: rose water, which is used in both savory and sweet recipes throughout the country.

ginger-garlic paste: a paste comprising half pureed ginger and half pureed garlic that is used in many Indian recipes, both savory and sweet.

hing: also called asafetida, hing is a gum extracted from the root of a perennial herb in the celery family.

It is used in many Indian recipes to add a pungent umami flavor in the same way that tomatoes and shiitake mushrooms do. But use sparingly: A little goes a long way.

Kashmiri red chile powder: a potent and vibrantly hued powder made from ground dried red Kashmiri chiles. The powder looks similar to paprika but is much spicier. When I call for red chile powder in my recipes, it is specifically Kashmiri red chile powder that I am reaching for in my home kitchen.

jaggery: an unrefined sweetener derived from sugar cane or palm juice that is used in both sweet and savory dishes. If you don't have it or can't find it, use dark brown sugar.

jeera: cumin seeds

mustard oil: frequently used in Indian cuisine, mustard oil is an earthy, pungent oil made by pressing mustard seeds to extract their oil. It has a medium-high smoke point. Vegetable oil can be substituted should you have difficulty sourcing it.

poha: flattened parboiled long-grain rice, almost paper-like in texture, that cooks up very quickly.

puffed rice: rice that is heated until it puffs, resulting in a light and airy texture; used in many chaat recipes. This is the same as the unsweetened puffed rice cereal found in the cereal aisle of most supermarkets.

red chile paste: Indian red chile paste is typically made with Kashmiri red chiles and is available in Indian markets. If you have difficulty sourcing it, any spicy red chile paste can be substituted.

sago: tapioca pearls, made from yuca starch (cassava), that have a chewy texture and are used to both thicken and flavor recipes.

sattu: roasted chickpea flour. You can make sattu yourself by preheating an oven to 350°F, evenly scattering about 2 cups of chickpea flour on a sheet pan, and baking until it is toasted, 3 to 5 minutes. Use a silicone spatula to mix it once during the cooking process, gently shaking the sheet. Try to redistribute it evenly. Immediately transfer it to a large dry bowl or second sheet pan to prevent it from overcooking after it is removed from the oven. Cool to room temperature before using or store it once it reaches room temperature in an airtight container at room temperature for up to 3 months.

sev: an Indian snack and chaat garnish made of chickpea flour paste seasoned with turmeric, ajwain, and cayenne before being fried into a crunchy noodle.

sooji: semolina flour available in both coarsely and finely ground textures.

takmaria: basil seeds

tamarind: a pod-like fruit with a tangy flavor that is used in both savory and sweet recipes

Acknowledgments

We would like to thank our extraordinary editor, Raquel Pelzel, along with our photographer, Linda Xiao, who journeyed to India with us only six months after giving birth. We are grateful to our talented designer, Marysarah Quinn, along with our literary agent, Jonah Straus. We would also like to thank our friend Courtney Knapp, who generously provided us with her prop- and food-styling skills, along with Alex Fortney, Evan Sung, Neha Morarji, Deepa Jain, Ashish Sapat, and the Bhasin family.

Maneet would like to thank her husband, Vivek Deora, who is her rock, and children Shagun and Karma, who are constant inspirations. She would also like to thank her parents, Gur Iqbal and Hardeep Chauhan, who have always given her the wings and freedom to fly, along with her mother-in-law, Shashi Deora, who inspires her with her strength and wit. Her sister, Reeti Chauhan, who has always encouraged Maneet's crazy ventures. Her nieces and nephews who give her a constant source of hope for the next generation, and her agent, Cameron Levkoff. And a special thanks to all of her and Vivek's family members who have always been supportive and encouraging. Her teachers, friends, colleagues, team, and all those who were generous with their time and knowledge to make her a better person and chef.

Jody would like to thank her mother, Mary Eddy, who never wavered in her invincible love and encouraged her to travel as far as she needed to in pursuit of her dreams. She would also like to thank her grandparents, Evelyn and Peter Bragelman, along with Mark and Theresa Anderson, Willow, Niklas, and Henrik Anderson, Cortney Burns, Patrice Eddy, Todd Eddy, Janine Ersfeld, Colleen Foster, Gunnar Karl Gislason, Kjartan Gislason, Claire Handleman, Mary-Frances Heck, Martha Holmberg, the Honeycutt family, Erin Jurek, Jad Kossaify, the LaChapelle family, Anne McBride, Bridget and Ari McGinty, Rebecca Morris, Raychel O'Keefe, Anna Painter, the Pearson-Rosene family, Prannie Rhatigan, Jack Rice, Jeanne Stern, the Sweeny family, Kristin Teig, Marty Travis, and Claudia Woloshin.

Index

Note: Page numbers in italics include/indicate captions/photos.